Praise for Mark O'Conn...

D1568502

A THREAD OF VIOLENCE

"Mark O'Connell's exhilarating *A Thread of Violence* [is] a probing portrait of one of the most notorious murderers in recent Irish history. . . . [A] deft narrative. . . . Brilliant and rigorously honest." —*The New York Times Book Review*

"A masterpiece. . . . A gorgeously nimble stylist, [O'Connell] writes the sort of sentences that get me checking my own in agitated competitiveness. . . . [*A Thread of Violence*] is a marvel of tact, attentiveness, and unclouded moral acuity." —*The Observer*

"[A] true crime gem. . . . Swirling together dogged reporting with questions about the media's coverage of crime, O'Connell manages a gripping account that casts a skeptical eye on its own genre. Even readers put off by profiles of killers will be piqued." —*Publishers Weekly* (starred review)

"A vividly written account. . . . The resulting picture of the killer is seen as if through a proverbial dark glass—and it's as chilling, in the end, as any Hitchcock film. A superb study of real-life crime and punishment." —*Kirkus Reviews* (starred review)

"A profound meditation on violence and its roots. . . . This book is an outstanding achievement, and a worthy addition to literary attempts to understand the human propensity for evil." —*The Guardian*

"[A] queasily brilliant book. . . . Clever and thoroughly disquieting." —*Financial Times*

"Remarkable. . . . A book that tells the true story of a crime while scrutinizing our desire for such true-crime stories and the often simplistic explanations they offer for the terrible things people do." —*Slate*

"*A Thread of Violence* is nourished by a powerful moral intelligence and an enormous curiosity. Mark O'Connell circles the inner life of the murderer Malcolm Macarthur with subtlety and forensic care. . . . Intriguing and compelling."
—Colm Tóibín, author of *The Magician* and the *New York Times* bestseller *Brooklyn*

"Like all great books, *A Thread of Violence* is the document of a great writer's obsession. Mark O'Connell draws the reader into a deeply engrossing story. . . . This is a superb and unforgettable book." —Sally Rooney, *New York Times* bestselling author of *Normal People*

"In the pantheon of writers fascinated by criminals, Mark O'Connell proves himself among the most brilliant. It is one of the boundaries that cuts humanity in two: those who have killed someone, those who have not. O'Connell roams around this boundary, in this gray area, from which he has brought a fascinating narrative."
—Emmanuel Carrère, internationally bestselling author of *The Adversary*

"Mark O'Connell takes us on a deep dive into the most unfathomable depths of human nature. . . . Evil, in O'Connell's morally complex and mesmerizing tale, is revealed as both banal and mysterious."
—Fintan O'Toole, *New York Times* bestselling author of *We Don't Know Ourselves: A Personal History of Modern Ireland*

MARK O'CONNELL

A THREAD OF VIOLENCE

Mark O'Connell is the author of *Notes from an Apocalypse* and *To Be a Machine*, which was awarded the 2019 Rooney Prize for Irish Literature and the 2018 Wellcome Book Prize and shortlisted for the Baillie Gifford Prize for Non-Fiction. He is a contributor to *The New Yorker*, *The New York Review of Books*, *The New York Times Magazine*, and *The Guardian*.

ALSO BY MARK O'CONNELL

To Be a Machine
Notes from an Apocalypse

A THREAD OF VIOLENCE

A THREAD
of VIOLENCE

A STORY OF TRUTH,
INVENTION, AND MURDER

MARK O'CONNELL

Vintage Books
A Division of Penguin Random House LLC
New York

FIRST VINTAGE BOOKS EDITION 2024

Copyright © 2023 by Mark O'Connell

All rights reserved. Published in the United States by Vintage Books,
a division of Penguin Random House LLC, New York, and distributed in
Canada by Penguin Random House Canada Limited, Toronto. Originally
published in hardcover in the United States by Doubleday, a division
of Penguin Random House LLC, New York, in 2023.

Vintage and colophon are registered
trademarks of Penguin Random House LLC.

The Library of Congress has cataloged the Doubleday edition as follows:
Names: O'Connell, Mark, [date] author.
Title: A thread of violence : a story of truth, invention,
and murder / Mark O'Connell.
Description: First edition. | New York : Doubleday, 2023.
Identifiers: LCCN 2022036462 (print) | LCCN 2022036463 (ebook)
Subjects: LCSH: Macarthur, Malcolm. | Murderer—Ireland. |
Thieves—Ireland. | Violence—Ireland.
Classification: LCC HV6535.I742 O36 2023 (print) |
LCC HV6535.I742 (ebook) | DDC 364.152/309415—dc23
LC record available at https://lccn.loc.gov/2022036462
LC ebook record available at https://lccn.loc.gov/2022036463

Vintage Books Trade Paperback ISBN: 978-0-593-31420-3
eBook ISBN: 978-0-385-54765-9

Author photograph © Richard Gilligan
Book design by Maria Carella

vintagebooks.com

Printed in the United States of America
10 9 8 7 6 5 4 3 2 1

And my lawyer, rolling up one of his sleeves, said with finality, "Here we have a perfect reflection of this entire trial: everything is true and nothing is true!"

—Albert Camus, *The Stranger*

CONTENTS

PART ONE

IS THIS FOR REAL?

———————

ONE

One Sunday in early May 2022, I went for a walk with my son in Sandycove, a coastal suburb just south of Dublin. It was a bright and beautiful day, and the first fine possibility of summer was in the air; the beach was crowded with picnicking families and children flinging themselves, shrieking, at the icy sea. We made our way up the hill past the bathing area at the Forty Foot, and when we came to the squat Martello tower in which James Joyce set the opening chapter of *Ulysses,* we paused for a moment. As I dutifully informed my son of the building's significance, and as he dutifully listened, my gaze drifted along the coastline and came to rest on a cluster of three-story apartment buildings on the very edge of the rocks above the bay. I knew this apartment complex well, though I had not been there since childhood.

I pointed the place out to my son, and told him that my grandparents had lived there when I was a child, and that I remembered it very vividly. I remembered in particular, I told him, the view of the bay from the kitchen window, and my grandfather's insistence that on an especially fine day you could see clear across the Irish Sea to Wales. I was, I said, fascinated by this prospect of seeing Britain from the kitchen window. Whenever I visited them I would always head for the binoculars that hung from a hook on the wall, and I would peer east across the water; but, Ireland being what it was, the view was never clear enough.

I told my son that I wanted to show him the place, and so we walked a further ten minutes or so, past the fine Victorian terraced houses between Sandycove and Dalkey, until we reached the sea again at Bullock Harbour. The apartment complex, which was called Pilot View, was sealed off from the road by a set of large electric gates. It was the kind of place that estate agents habitually refer to as "an exclusive development," or "highly sought-after." In my grandparents' time, a lot of well-off people lived there: couples whose children had grown up and moved out, or older professionals who had never married. (As a boy I had an enthusiasm for luxury cars, and I remember being deeply impressed by all the Jaguars and Mercedes-Benzes in the parking spaces out front.)

Standing outside the entrance to the car park, I pointed out to my son the door to my grandparents' building. Like most children of his age, he liked to hear about his parents' childhoods, and so he listened contentedly as I recalled playing in the garden behind their ground-floor apartment, the lawn that sloped down toward the rocks, and the Irish Sea beyond.

As I spoke, however, my mind was elsewhere. It was not really my grandparents I was thinking of, or even my own childhood as such, but a thing that had happened in 1982, when I was three years old. A murderer had been arrested there, in the apartment building adjacent to my grandparents'. This murderer was among the most notorious in Irish history, and the story of his crimes and their aftermath was one that had haunted me, in various ways, since childhood. It was one that had haunted our country too. I knew that my son would have been interested to hear of this—more interested than he was in James Joyce, certainly, or in my own early memories—but I said nothing about it.

As I continued to tell my son about my grandparents, I was gazing up at a window of the penthouse next door, imagining the murderer gazing down in our direction, an expression of watchful abstraction on his face. This was the window, I knew, in which the detectives who arrested him had seen his face appear as they were preparing to close in. It was as though the image of this murderer—the knowledge of what he had done and of the circumstances of his arrest—had overwritten my own childhood memories of the place.

In this way, too, the murderer and his crimes had come to be superimposed over my experience of the city I lived in. I would go for a run in the Phoenix Park, and as I passed the Wellington Monument I would see him standing there, peeling and eating an orange in the moments before he attacked his first victim. Farther on, I would reach the American ambassador's residence, and as I stopped to stretch before turning back for home, I would see in my mind what had happened there almost forty years before. I would see this man bundling a young woman into the back seat of her own car. I would see the eruption of sudden savagery with the hammer; the car speeding off down the jogging track, a fine spray of blood across its windows.

«

It was from my own father that I first learned about the murderer, whose name was Malcolm Macarthur. I was about nine, the age my son is now. My father gave me only the broad outline of the events that had culminated in Pilot View, in, as I remember it, that same car park in front of my grandparents' apartment. One of my grandparents' neighbors, my father told me, a man named Patrick Connolly, had once been a very prominent political figure. He lived in an apartment on the top floor, and my grandparents knew him—though only passingly, I gathered, in a polite and neighborly sort of way.

Some years before, my father told me, this man and his apartment had been at the center of a bizarre and scandalous incident. A friend of Connolly's, Malcolm Macarthur, had murdered two people, and for two weeks there was a very public investigation and manhunt, and when the Gardaí (the Irish police) had finally tracked him down and caught him, he was staying in Connolly's home. They had arrested Macarthur right there, my father told me, in the apartment complex where my grandparents lived, where I came to stay when my parents went away on weekends, where I played in the hallway and on the lawn and on the rocks along the shore. From then on, whenever we visited my grandparents, my head would swirl with action-film scenes: SWAT teams descending from helicopters on ropes, rappelling down the side of the building. Shoot-outs in the car park. Snipers on the roof of the nursing home across the street.

None of this kind of thing happened, of course, but even now when I think about Macarthur's arrest, it is hard for me not to imagine it playing out like that, the way I'd constructed it in my mind as a child. But I will try to keep my imagination out of this, one way or another. There is more than enough reality to be getting on with.

«

The people of Dublin know this story well. But we know it only as a story. Although Macarthur was convicted of murder, there was hardly a trial at all. He pleaded guilty, and so no evidence was heard in court. What details emerged in the press about the culprit were largely leaked, or garnered by reporters from acquaintances in the days and weeks after his conviction. The case came to trial very quickly and was over as soon as it began; all of this, along with the involvement of the attorney general, led to lingering suspicions about the government intervening to mitigate embarrassing revelations.

It wasn't until years later that I came to understand these events more fully; but even then there was something opaque and elusive about the story of Macarthur, as much urban legend as historical fact. When he committed these murders, he was thirty-seven years old, and a well-known figure about the city—though much less so than now, and for very different reasons. There are Dubliners of a certain age who remember him in those days: a handsome, erudite man with a refined manner of speech, who drank in the city's more sophisticated bars, and mixed with an assemblage of bohemian and establishment familiars. They remember him as an incongruously suave proposition, sitting alone in a quiet corner, sipping a glass of wine and reading, for some reason, a copy of *Le Monde*. Emerging from the front arch of Trinity College, contentedly absorbed in his thoughts. The silk bow ties, the tasteful brogues, the Harris tweeds. And the hair—the dark, dense curls, swept back from a high, aristocratic forehead.

He came from a well-off landowning family in Co. Meath, where he had grown up on a large country estate, with a housekeeper, a gardener, and a governess. He thought of himself, and was thought of by others, as landed gentry. In his twenties, he came into a large inheritance, and he lived well on this bounty. His life was a project of refined hedonism. His days were entirely his own. He was a free man.

But the money, as is the way of money, did not last. He

had loaned too widely, and spent too deeply, and on the cusp of middle age, having never had a job in his life, he found that he was going broke. And this would not do.

He decided that the quickest and most efficient way out of this situation was to commit an armed robbery. Such heists were often in the news at the time: the IRA had lately been conducting a campaign of bank jobs in order to fund their armed struggle. He was a clever man, he reasoned, and a capable one, and so why should he not be able to pull off something along those lines?

He had, at that point, been living for some months with his partner and son in Tenerife, a Spanish island off the coast of Morocco. Explaining that he was leaving to attend to some financial affairs, he returned to Dublin. Two weeks after his return, he still had not succeeded in pulling off the planned heist, but in the effort to attain a gun and a getaway car, he had murdered two complete strangers. His first victim was the nurse Bridie Gargan, whom he beat to death with a hammer in the Phoenix Park in the process of stealing her car. His second was the farmer Donal Dunne, in Edenderry, Co. Offaly, who had agreed to sell him a shotgun, and whom he shot point-blank in the face. Both of his victims were twenty-seven years old.

Having committed these murders, Macarthur was still no closer to carrying out his plan. He was further, in fact, than he had been when he started, because the crimes had become the focus of a very public investigation, and a great deal of media interest. Deciding he needed a more suitable place to hide than the guesthouse where he'd been staying, he accepted an offer from his friend Paddy Connolly, who knew nothing of his crimes, to stay in the spare room in his penthouse apartment.

When Macarthur was finally arrested, almost three weeks later, there followed a great and enduring convulsion of captivated outrage: not just because this murderer had finally been caught, but because of where he had been caught, and whom he was staying with. Patrick Connolly was not just Macarthur's friend: he was also the attorney general. He was the most senior legal official in the country, a significant figure in an already embattled government.

«

Even now, almost forty years after the murders, the public fascination with this story has not abated, and has in certain respects intensified since Macarthur's release, after thirty years in prison, in 2012. Among Irish people old enough to remember the summer of 1982, he is as close to a household name as it is possible for a murderer to be; though his name is not surrounded by anything like the miasma of malice and depravity that arise from, say, the name Peter Sutcliffe in the UK, or Jeffrey Dahmer in the United States, it carries, in this country, a similar generational weight.

This fascination draws much of its strength from paradox: Malcolm Macarthur, the genteel brute; the savage intellectual. One of the most well-known photographs of him, taken at the time of his trial, captures this faintly surreal tension between the visual signifiers of aristocracy and those of criminality. In it, he is pictured walking out of the court after a hearing; his right wrist is cuffed to that of a Garda, and there is another uniformed officer at his back, but if you were to crop the image just so, you would never suspect that this man was any sort of criminal at all, let alone one who had, over the course of a recent dire weekend, beaten one perfect stranger to death and shot another in the face. He is wearing a stylish sport coat with a handkerchief in a breast pocket, a crisp white shirt, and a silk bow tie. He is handsome, in a prim sort of way, his expression quizzical, as though he is contemplating some mildly troubling abstraction: an eyebrow slightly cocked, the nostrils nobly flared. He seems both there and not there: handcuffed to the wrist of a cop, and yet aloof and detached from the scene of which he is the center. This is a man not of mere vulgar wealth, but of class.

Class and power—Macarthur's social class, and his proximity to the political establishment—were more than mere contexts for these crimes; they are at the center of their enduring fascination. Had the murderer been an addict from the inner city, or even a member of the professional middle class gone berserk, it is unlikely that the killings would have made anything like as deep and lasting an impression. There is, in its most simplistic telling, something of the fable about this tale of an heir who murders a nurse and a farmer. As complex and confounding as the story turns out to be, it is always tempting to read it as enigmatic allegory, its meaning hovering just out of reach.

If this man, and the murders he committed, seem still to occupy a kind of mythic register, it is largely because the story has never really been told. Or rather, it has been told, endlessly and luridly, but always in the same tone of breathless incredulity, and with a sullen and persistent silence at its center.

«

It was that silence that drew me toward Macarthur, that brought me into his life, and him into mine. I had seen endless images of him: mug shots from the time of his arrest; press photographs of frenzied scenes outside the courthouse; tabloid shots of him walking the streets in the weeks after his release from prison. I had read novels based on his life and crimes; I had once attended a play, a one-man show, whose protagonist was based on a version of Macarthur in one of those novels—an adaptation of a fictionalization of a reality that was barely known. I had read countless newspaper interviews with acquaintances and family friends about his childhood, his upbringing, his lifestyle. I had watched television documentaries about the murders, the investigation, the complex political consequences. And in the years since his release, I had even passed him in the street, many times, as he walked through the city in a state of abject freedom. But I had never heard or read so much as a word from his own mouth about the things he had done, or his reasons for having done them. Not a word about his victims, or their families, or how he lived with the weight of his deeds.

I wanted to pierce that silence, and break through to whatever lay beneath it. As naive as it sounds to me now, I wanted to know the truth of this story that had haunted me for so many years. I wanted to know who and what this man was.

I did eventually come to know him, and there were times when I felt that I had glimpsed this truth. But there were other times, far more frequent, when I understood that such knowledge was impossible, and that I had wandered into a labyrinth of endlessly ramifying fictions.

It was, I think, this uncertainty, this knowing and not knowing, that prevented me, as we stood outside the apartment complex at Pilot View, from speaking to my son about Macarthur. Had I done so, I might well have felt a compulsion to admit that I in fact knew this man, this murderer, and that I had over the course of the previous year spent a great deal of time in his company, that I had been spending my days writing a book about him and his crimes. He would have asked me what this man was like—whether I was afraid of him, whether he was evil—and I would not have known what to tell him. Even now, I am not sure what to tell myself.

TWO

Even more than my tenuous family connection with Macarthur's crimes and his subsequent arrest, it was a fictional representation of those crimes that was the real origin of my fascination. I spent my late twenties and a portion of my early thirties doing a PhD in Trinity College on the work of the Irish writer John Banville. One of Banville's most well-known books is a novel called *The Book of Evidence*. The novel's narrator-protagonist is a man named Freddie Montgomery, a patrician loafer who returns home to Dublin after getting into deep financial trouble while living abroad. In the process of attempting to solve his money problem, by stealing a painting from a wealthy acquaintance, he is interrupted by a housekeeper, whom he beats to death with a hammer. He then hides out in the home of a friend, a prominent art dealer, before being arrested and brought to trial. *The Book of Evidence* is his testimony, a slippery, stylish hybrid of self-justification and confession. Freddie is an Irish Humbert Humbert: a clever, cultured, and supremely narcissistic son of a wealthy Anglo-Irish family, whose crime is the result of a kind of moral drift. He is loosely, but very obviously, based on Malcolm Macarthur. (Two of Banville's subsequent novels, *Ghosts* and *Athena*, also feature Freddie Montgomery as protagonist, though as the trilogy progresses the character strays further and further from the biographical realm of Macarthur's life and crimes.)

Around the time I was finishing my PhD, Macarthur was in the newspapers a lot, the question of his release having lately become the focus of intense media speculation. He had by then been in a minimum-security prison for some years, and his behavior throughout the three decades of his incarceration had by all accounts been impeccable. He was being let out on temporary release on a fairly regular basis, and these occasions—trips to art galleries, museums, and so on—were frequently the subject of newspaper articles, and these articles were invariably illustrated by photos of, for instance, Macarthur standing at a train platform or walking out of a shop with a distracted look on his face.

I remember one particular headline from that time for its combination of salaciousness and banality: "Serial Killer Macarthur Bumps into McWilliams." The story was about how Macarthur had crossed paths with "celebrity economist" David McWilliams in the doorway of a shop in Dún Laoghaire. According to the source quoted in the article, Macarthur seemed to have recognized this economist, who often appeared on television, but the economist showed no sign of knowing who Macarthur was. "The pair apologised to each other and walked on after the incident," the article continued, "but murderer Macarthur did a double take when he thought he may have recognised" McWilliams.

The point of these articles was always the same: his presence in a shop, or a city street, was the occasion for pointing out that this man walked among us, though he had done these terrible things. Whenever I saw the photographs that accompanied these articles, I would always think to myself, There he is, there's Freddie Montgomery, waiting for a train, or walking out of a shop. Likewise, reading *The Book of Evidence*, whenever I tried to conjure an image of Montgomery in my mind, it was always Macarthur I pictured, with his bow tie, his air of thoughtful arrogance, and his undulating carapace of dark hair.

In September 2012, more than thirty years after the murders, Macarthur was finally released from prison. By then, I had finished my PhD, and, for want of anything more constructive to do, I was back in Trinity College doing a postdoctoral fellowship, the point of which was to edit my thesis for publication as an academic book—a book which, once published, would mount an unanswerable case for my permanent employment as a university lecturer at one of the better English departments in Britain or Ireland.

One evening that autumn, I had just emerged, from the gloom of the Berkeley library, into a warm October evening. I was drifting across the cobbled front square when I noticed, drifting toward me, a man whom I could not quite place, but whose face was immediately familiar to me. He looked to be in his mid-sixties. He had a thatch of dense hair, very white but very vigorous. His face was pale, and he was wearing a tweed jacket with a silk handkerchief in the breast pocket. At first I thought perhaps I had attended one of his lecture courses as an undergraduate, and I was about to nod blandly toward him in a gesture of noncommittal acknowledgment. Then I realized where I knew him from. It was Macarthur.

My expression, as we passed each other beneath the campanile, must have betrayed my surprised recognition, because he shot me a sidewise look of almost cartoonish wariness and culpability, swiveling his eyes toward me and then away, and then sharply back again. I could see that he knew why I was looking at him. He knew that I knew who he was. What he could not have known, though, was that mine was a reaction not just to seeing a famous murderer walking around the university campus, but to seeing a character from a novel manifested in the physical world, the realm of supposed real-

ity. I could not help but think of it as a tearing of the thin
fabric that separated fiction and nonfiction.

«

Not long after I saw him that first time, I read in a gos-
sip column in one of the Sunday papers about an event that
had taken place in the building where I had my workspace.
This was a so-called digital humanities institute, dedicated
to interdisciplinary research in the arts and humanities,
located beside the Old Library of Trinity College. I had a
little cubicle on the top floor of this building, a large, light-
filled space with floor-to-ceiling windows on all sides. My
desk overlooked an atrium on a lower floor, in which social
events were often held: academic conference sessions, panel
discussions, occasional book launches. One evening, during
my time as a postdoc, there was a discussion on the work of
the Irish essayist Hubert Butler, to mark the posthumous
publication of a collection of his work. The discussion was
between John Banville and the journalist Fintan O'Toole.
Macarthur, it turned out, had shown up at the event.

At some point during the event, as he surveyed the faces
of the audience, Banville was startled to see Macarthur gazing back at him from the far end of the room. When the
discussion ended, instead of hanging around for a glass of
wine, Banville made for the exit as quickly as he could. He
saw that Macarthur was standing by the door, presumably
intending to speak with him, but he avoided eye contact and
hurried past.

The thought of this near-meeting fascinated me, as though
reality itself had employed the slightly threadbare postmod-
ern trope of the author encountering his own character. I had
at that point recently read a book by Bret Easton Ellis called
Lunar Park, a sort of auto-metafiction in which Ellis himself

is stalked by his most famous creation, the investment banker and mass murderer Patrick Bateman. This business of Macarthur showing up at an event where Banville was speaking seemed to me to be a real-world iteration of that corny conceit (and further evidence, as such, for my long-standing belief that reality itself was a niche subgenre of fiction).

This question of truth and fiction has always been at the heart of my fascination with Macarthur and his crimes. After all, from the first moment I learned, as a child, about the raid in my grandparents' apartment complex, it was already entangled in my mind with the visual clichés of cop shows and action movies.

The confusion as to what is real and what is not entered, too, into the crimes themselves. In the statement he provided to the Gardaí after his arrest, Macarthur described the moments leading up to his murder of Bridie Gargan. He said that he saw a car parked close to the entrance of the American ambassador's residence, and a figure lying in the grass beside it. When he came within a few feet, he saw that it was a woman sunbathing, and he pointed the gun at her and told her to get into the car. "She was very calm," he told them, "and she said: 'Is this for real?,' and I said: 'Yes it is.'"

This question, *Is this for real?*, is one that seems to me to echo throughout these events and their long aftermath. She must have asked this question because what was happening to her seemed not to be real, to be somehow a performance, or a joke, or a game.

«

Years later, I met a man named Trevor White, a writer and former magazine publisher who had attended the event in Trinity, and who remembered noticing Macarthur without at first realizing who he was. He'd written about the event in his journal, and he gave me a copy of the notes he'd taken. He was struck, he wrote, by this older man's bearing and dress. There was "something literary," he said, about this "stiff, over-formal figure." He thought at first that this man seemed "like a character in a Wes Anderson film" but then decided that he looked like a famous author. After the event, over by the wine table, he started a conversation with him.

"Do you mind me saying," he said, "you look a lot like John Banville. Are you related?"

"No," said Macarthur. "But I do have a connection *with* Mr. Banville."

Macarthur paused for a moment, as though relishing the suspense.

"I feature as a character in three of his novels."

It was at that point that a middle-aged woman removed herself from a nearby cluster of wine drinkers and asked the man whether he was Malcolm Macarthur, and his meaning became clear.

«

Macarthur became somewhat notorious, in the years after his release, for attending such events around the city. One evening, he showed up at the launch of a memoir by the retired politician Alan Shatter. It was Shatter who, during his term as minister for justice, had finally signed off on Macarthur's release.

The launch was attended by journalists and press photographers, and the following day there were newspaper articles, of varying degrees of breathlessness, about this bizarre encounter. A story in the *Irish Independent* ran with a photograph of Macarthur getting his copy of the memoir signed by Shatter, and reported that he "appeared at home among the gathering," dressed "casually in white linen jacket and slacks." After he had finished getting his book signed, the journalist approached Macarthur and asked him what he thought of Shatter.

"I have an absolute regard for him," said Macarthur. "He knows the law."

He also said that he had introduced himself to Shatter as he was signing the book. He seemed, in Macarthur's telling, not to have known who he was.

«

In the years that followed Macarthur's release, I saw him from time to time around the city. It wasn't that I ever quite got used to seeing him, because it was always an unnerving experience when I did, but it happened frequently enough that I came to half expect it.

One evening, I remember, I stopped to browse for books in Hodges Figgis, and I saw him as I was coming out the door onto Dawson Street. It had been a while since I had seen him last, six months or maybe a year. He saw me looking at him as we approached one another, and he returned my gaze, and held it for what seemed an uncomfortably long time. And then we passed, and he was gone, head down, his stride slow and methodical, in the direction of Stephen's Green.

As always after such encounters, I felt oddly giddy, both disturbed and exhilarated, like how I imagined it would be to see, and to be seen by, a ghost. It felt as though he should not have been there, that there was something wrong about his presence.

I continued on toward home, and as I reached the river it began to rain. I pulled up the hood of my coat and wondered whether he was also caught in the rain. Did he live nearby? Did he live alone? He must have, I thought; it was impossible to imagine him sharing a home with someone else. Perhaps he was sheltering in the bookshop I had just left, lingering by the true crime section, aware that he was being watched by other eyes, knowing that he was known. And not for the first time, I wondered what it would be like to know that people recognized you, that they knew who you were, the evil you had done. I thought what a rare and strange form of abjection that must be.

And with this thought came a realization: that I was going to write about Macarthur. And not only was I going to write about him, but I was going to talk to him, too. It would have been possible to tell this story, or a version of it, without speaking directly to him. By interviewing people who were involved—detectives, politicians, journalists, people close to the murderer and his victims—and by sifting through newspaper archives, I had no doubt that I could have pieced together a reasonably vivid account of the murders and the events surrounding them. But I found that I had little interest in such a story, because it could only ever affirm and embellish what everyone already knew, or believed we knew, about Macarthur.

I wanted to learn things I did not already know, things I could barely imagine. Macarthur's own account of his motive for the murders, given in a statement after his arrest, was blankly rationalistic: he had mismanaged his finances, he said, and he intended to commit an armed robbery to remedy the situation. "The object," as he put it, "was to get money." But there was so much about these crimes that did not make sense. Surely, there were easier ways for a man like Macarthur—educated, privileged, exceptionally well connected—to improve his finances. Even within the criminal logic by which he was operating, the murders themselves were entirely superfluous, and in fact counterproductive to his ends. (There was, in other words, no need for either Bri-

die Gargan or Donal Dunne to die for Macarthur to take
what he wanted from them.) Beneath the cold rationale of
the crimes was something frenzied and nonsensical, reducible to neither financial nor psychological expediency. It was
the force of this paradox, this rational madness, that drew
me toward Macarthur. And only by speaking to him could
I get a sense of what was going on in his mind before the
murders, and in the days from then until his arrest. Was he
crushed by the dull weight of his deeds? Did the memory of
his victims' faces, and the thought of the suffering of their
families, torment his days and haunt his dreams? How could
he live, how could he walk about the city, knowing that we
knew who he was and what he had done?

When I ask myself now what it was about Macarthur
that made me want to write about him, my tendency is to
invert the question and to ask instead what it was about *me*
that made me want to write about him. It may be frivolous,
but it is nonetheless true, to say that I am a writer, and that
his was an extraordinary story, rich in violent absurdity and
political intrigue, and that I was therefore drawn to it like
a prospector to an unexploited oil reserve. He was nearing
eighty, and he would likely not be around for many more
years, and if I didn't try to speak to him now, his story, this
valuable narrative resource, would die with him.

But there was another level to my fascination that had
less to do with pure extractive opportunism, and more to
do with proximity of various kinds. Macarthur was there,
in my childhood, a flickering presence on the far margins
of my life, this murderer who had hidden out in my grandparents' apartment complex. He was there, years later, as a
fictional character in a sequence of novels I read and reread
with forensic interest and gained a PhD in writing about.
And he was there, an uncannily physical presence on the
streets, an old man in a tweed jacket, strolling abroad in the

city whose memory he had stained with blood. Something about these different levels of proximity, the various ways in which he felt close enough to reach out and touch, unsettled and compelled me like a haunting.

And I was drawn, too, by what I knew of him—his privilege, his apparent refinement of manner, his reputation as an intellectual loafer—not because I was interested in these qualities in themselves, but because they seemed to me to make him more approachable. (I knew people like this; I was perhaps one of them.) And what I wanted to approach was, for want of a better term, evil. The sheer awfulness of what he had done seemed unfathomable, and yet I felt strongly that we might share a language in which he could speak to me of it. I became determined to try.

THREE

Not long after I decided I was going to write about Macarthur, he disappeared. It wasn't just he who disappeared; everyone did. It was the spring of 2020, and the pandemic had sent the whole country into hiding. Absence was general all over Ireland. It had been my complacent assumption that sooner or later I would encounter him on the street, and that I would buttonhole him and convince him to speak to me. But just like everyone else, everywhere, he was nowhere to be found.

That is not quite true. I did see him once. One day, toward the end of May, about two and a half months into Ireland's long and comprehensive first lockdown, I was cycling down Dame Street, on my way to meet a friend across town. I was close to the front gate of Trinity College when I saw, rounding a corner on the far side of the street, the masked but unmistakable figure of Macarthur. I crossed the street and stopped on the footpath, a short distance from where he was waiting to cross, and began to work up the courage to speak to him, wondering what I might say, how I might introduce myself. (Looking back on this now, two years later, I see myself hesitating on the threshold of a fiction, looking for a way to introduce myself as a character in a narrative that had nothing whatsoever to do with me.)

Right then, a guard appeared at my side and started rebuking me, in what seemed to me an unnecessarily surly fashion, for being on my bike on the footpath. I pointed out that I wasn't actually cycling, but he was having none of it, and by the time I had dismounted and concluded my encounter with the surly guard, Macarthur had disappeared. I considered for a moment that I might try to find him—he could not, I reasoned, have gone that far, because the whole exchange had taken less than a minute—but I was already shaping up to be late for my friend, and so I got back on my bike and kept going.

My reasoning, in the moment, had been that I would surely encounter Macarthur again before long, and that when I did it would be better to have some kind of opening gambit prepared, a pitch that he might find compelling. But during that long, strict lockdown, I rarely had cause to leave my own neighborhood. And so eventually it became apparent that the only way I was likely to encounter him was if I went out of my way to do so.

«

There commenced a period of many months in which it was my custom to spend two or three afternoons a week walking around the abandoned city, hoping to bump into Macarthur on his daily constitutional. On those afternoons I would cycle to the city center, lock my bike, and wander the empty streets for an hour or two. I stuck mainly to the part of town where I'd always encountered him in the past, an area of perhaps a square mile in the south inner city between Trinity College and Stephen's Green. I would walk around the city, conscious—sometimes acutely, though more often vaguely—of the ridiculousness of my project. I seemed to myself an obviously pathetic figure, walking the drizzle-slicked streets like a jilted lover hoping to accidentally cross paths with the object of his thwarted affections.

The summer passed, and then the autumn. I remember one afternoon in late November, walking the length of Grafton Street in the dwindling light and hearing music blaring from the entrance to the Brown Thomas department store onto the street. It was an upbeat, brassy swing rendition of "Santa Claus Is Coming to Town." It had just started to rain, and that whole stretch of the street was almost entirely deserted, save for three homeless men having a bitter argument, the hoods of their anoraks pulled tightly about their faces against the rain. I saw that an elaborate Christmas display had been installed in the window of Brown Thomas, for the benefit of whoever might be passing, and I felt a pang of absurd loss.

As I rounded the corner onto Wicklow Street, I saw a man walking in my direction. He was holding a black umbrella, and he had on a greenish tweed hat and a beige macintosh. His hair was very white, and quite long, and I felt my heart quicken as I scrutinized him in the middle distance, but as we neared one another, I saw that it was not Macarthur but merely a man of roughly his age and roughly his manner of dress.

This was not the first time something like this had happened. It happened pretty much every time I went on one of these walks. I would see a figure in the distance and be convinced, briefly but absolutely, that this was Malcolm Macarthur, and I would accelerate my pace to a near trot, only to see that it was just a random man of roughly his age and manner of dress. I developed a hypersensitivity to men with white hair in their seventies. My wife seemed to have caught it too. She would call me over to our bedroom window, to look at some old guy on the street below, standing in the socially distanced queue for the café across from our

house, and ask me whether that was Macarthur. Or we'd
be driving our son to school and she would point to a man
walking along the quays, and ask whether it was him. It
never was.

I was experiencing the city in a new and unfamiliar way;
every street corner, every intersection, seemed charged with
the possibility of his presence. As I wandered the streets
in a more or less random and instinctual manner, I would
sometimes become convinced, for no good reason, that he
was physically very near but somehow obscured from my
vision. I would imagine that he was inside a shop I had just
passed, or that he was walking down a narrow side street
parallel to a narrow side street I myself was walking down.
Turning a corner, I would have a sudden cinematic vision,
an aerial drone shot of myself walking. I would imagine the
shot getting wider and higher, the drone rising up above the
streets, to reveal the figure of Macarthur walking around
the same corner I had just walked around, coming in the
opposite direction. This was how I visualized my own frustrated obsession with his proximity. I knew he was close, I
knew it absolutely and unequivocally, and yet he was nowhere
to be found.

My frustrated search for Macarthur became conflated,
in my mind, with the experience of walking the streets of
Dublin during the lockdown, which was among the strictest
and longest of any place in the world. Everything was shut.
Dublin seemed to me to be a labyrinth composed entirely of
dead ends. The whole city felt like a vast Potemkin village, as
though its former vitality and noise and humor had been an
illusion, and the streets and the buildings were now revealed
as an elaborate facade. It was somehow hard to believe any of
it had ever been real.

«

I started making a point of telling people, whenever it was even remotely appropriate, that I was hoping to write about Macarthur, on the principle that the more people I spoke to about it, the more likely it would be that someone would tell me that they knew where I could find him. Dublin is a small city, after all, and I felt sure that I was bound to know someone who knew him, or at least to know someone who knew someone who knew him.

At one point, during an email exchange with a writer of my acquaintance, in response to what was surely no more than a polite expression of hope that my work was going well, I blurted out that I was planning to write about Macarthur. She responded by saying she'd seen him a couple of months previously, on a bike. ("I thought to myself," she wrote, "why is John Banville cycling down the seafront?") I replied with unseemly haste and enthusiasm, requesting further details. It turned out she saw him in roughly the same spot not infrequently, that it was "one of his routes." She tried to avoid him, she said, presumably because she found the sight of him disturbing.

Not long after that, someone else I'd been talking to about the case sent me an email pointing out that the phone book contained a listing for an "E MacArthur." Macarthur's middle name, he pointed out, was Edward; it was not inconceivable, given that he was one of the most notorious criminals in the country, that he might be using his middle name. It had seemed extremely unlikely that Macarthur would be listed in the phone book at all, but the address happened to be in a place that was linked by a cycle route to the same coastal suburb the writer had told me she kept seeing him in.

So it was that I spent a drizzly morning that autumn lurking in the vicinity of a small house overlooking the sea, hoping to see Macarthur emerge for his daily constitutional. I spent perhaps an hour walking up and down the road, try-

ing to look inconspicuous while endlessly doubling back on
the same stretch of the seafront, all the while glancing over
at the house. At one point, a woman who looked to be in her
mid-thirties emerged from a side door, holding a bag, which
she then put in a bin.

That was that; there was no way this could be Macarthur's house. What would a woman in her mid-thirties be
doing in his house in the middle of a pandemic? I knew for
a fact that he had only one child, a son in his mid-forties. It
seemed barely conceivable that he would have any kind of
romantic partner, let alone one so much younger than him.
(Brenda Little, his son's mother, had been Macarthur's partner at the time of the murders, and I knew that she had been
a regular visitor throughout the years of his imprisonment. It
was entirely possible, I supposed, that she was still in his life,
but she would have been well into her sixties by that point.)

Then it occurred to me that this woman might have been
a nurse. The more I thought of it, the more likely it seemed
to me that this was the case, and the more certain I became
that she was in the house because Macarthur was sick, very
sick, in fact almost certainly dying, and that I had found him
at the precise moment it was too late.

After the woman went inside again, I continued lurking
on the road, emboldened by my growing conviction that she
was a nurse, and specifically Macarthur's nurse. Then, about
a half hour later, I caught sight of a figure in an upstairs
window. It was an older woman this time, in her seventies or
perhaps her eighties. She was standing, framed by the window, holding some papers in her hands. She was wearing blue
plastic gloves. Although she was much too far away for me
to get any sense of what the pages were, I immediately suc-
cumbed to a preemptive despair, concluding that this woman
was likely a relative, or perhaps an old friend, of Macarthur's,
and that she was going through his papers because he had

recently died. How else to explain the blue gloves? In fact, the gloves suggested that he had died of Covid-19. Yes, this woman was a relative of some sort, perhaps a cousin, who had come to look through his personal effects, and sort out his affairs, such as they were. He must have died that very day, in fact, because it would certainly have already been a major news story if he'd died any earlier. This was just my luck. Precisely the thing I most feared had now come to pass. Macarthur had died of Covid before I'd had a chance to speak with him; he was already en route to hell, and he was taking his story with him.

At some point the possibility occurred to me that this woman might herself have been the resident of the house. I took out my phone and googled the name "Elizabeth Macarthur," which seemed like the most likely woman's name to be listed under "E Macarthur," along with the address of the house. Among the first results was an old, archived listing of an application, under that name, for planning permission for some kind of extension to the property. I had spent the morning stalking an elderly woman who likely had no connection whatsoever with Malcolm Macarthur other than sharing his last name.

«

A couple of weeks later, I was walking through the door of my local Tesco when I met a former English professor of mine. Although we lived in the same part of town, I had seen her only very occasionally since leaving academia, seven years previously. After the usual pandemic small talk—working from home; teaching online; being at once grateful to live close to, and thoroughly sick of visiting, the Phoenix Park— she asked me what I was working on these days. I said I had made something of a "hard left turn," that I was at work on what might most easily be described as a true crime book. She seemed at first a little surprised to hear this, but when I told her that the book was about Malcolm Macarthur, she nodded shrewdly and said that it was interesting to see me returning to my roots. It took me a moment to realize that she was referring to my former life as an academic, and specifically my work on Banville.

Speaking of Macarthur, she said, she supposed I was aware of his history with the department? I was not, I said. Not long after his release, she said, Macarthur started showing up at the departmental administrator's office, and inquiring about the prospect of enrolling, as a mature student, in an undergraduate English degree. This, she said, would have been around the time that I myself was doing a postdoctoral fellowship, and teaching a course in contemporary fiction, so it was somewhat surprising that I had not heard about it. The administrator had at first taken this dapper and erudite older man for a recently retired professional of some sort, perhaps a senior counsel or a doctor, who fancied spending the years of his early dotage attending lectures on Middle English poetry and Jacobean revenge tragedies. He had already dropped by the departmental office two or three times, said my former professor, picking up leaflets and application forms and lingering on each occasion for an affable if stilted chat, when one of the older lecturers asked the administrator, who was then in her early thirties, if she knew that this man who kept dropping by to talk about enrolling as a mature student happened to be the most notorious murderer in recent Irish history.

He came by on a couple of occasions after that. Although he was very polite, she said, the departmental administrator was quite shaken by this man who had murdered two people, and who kept dropping by to make inquiries about enrolling for a degree in English literature. Somehow or other, said my

former professor, it was imparted to him that it would not
be possible for him to enroll. She wasn't sure exactly what
had happened, but she thought that some of the students
may have become aware who he was, and someone had had a
word with him. Eventually, he stopped dropping by.

«

Scrolling through my Twitter feed one afternoon, I
encountered a link to an article about Macarthur in one of
the daily tabloids. "MASKING A MURDERER," blared
the headline. "Double killer Malcolm Macarthur backs
Covid lockdown restrictions—labelling them 'necessary precaution.'" It featured a photograph of a masked Macarthur,
striding along a city center street in a beige overcoat, and
leveling a wary, sidelong gaze in the direction of the camera.
The lapels of the overcoat were of such startling width that it
seemed likely he had owned it before going to prison.

The article began with the announcement that the "notorious murderer believes the current health rules are based
on 'scientific facts' and is confident they are working." Then,
after providing a brief recap of the murders and the ensu-
ing political scandal, it veered back into Macarthur's stolidly
sensible view of the current lockdown.

Since his release, it read, the killer had "spent most of his
time as a free man out of the limelight. But speaking to *The
Irish Sun* this week, Macarthur backed the current level 6
lockdown restrictions, expressing confidence in the government's pandemic strategy. He insisted: 'I believe in the scientific facts. I also believe in the lockdown restrictions and
that they are a necessary precaution. I also think, in terms
of the vaccine, that there will be necessary boosters required
down the line.'"

Toward the end of the article, the reporter asked him

what he did with his days. "I'm retired, old boy!" Macarthur replied. "I walk around town a lot, I am an avid radio listener, and I read the newspapers."

I found the reporter's contact details and called him, telling him that I was hoping to write about Macarthur's case. I asked him about what he was like, and how he had reacted to being approached. The reporter was friendly and talkative. We spoke for perhaps ten minutes; at one point he mentioned the supermarket outside which he'd approached Macarthur. As we spoke, it struck me that he had likely not encountered Macarthur there by chance, that he had probably been waiting there for him, and that Macarthur must therefore have lived close to this place, or in any case have frequented it regularly.

FOUR

I was about to give up and go home for the afternoon. I had been strolling up and down a short stretch of the street all morning, alternating between different sides in each direction out of some likely misguided notion that it would make me look less suspicious if I crossed the street before doubling back and retracing my steps. It was lunchtime, and I was getting hungry, and I had no desire to stand on a corner eating a sandwich, and so I was about to begin the walk home across the city when I saw, rounding an intersection on the far side of the street, a masked figure I immediately recognized as Macarthur. Despite all those times in the past year I'd seen a well-dressed, white-haired man walking alone in the city and wondered whether it was him, there was now no doubt in my mind. In my days of waiting, of drifting through the quiet streets in idle pursuit, I had often asked myself how I would react when I did eventually see him. I sometimes worried that some immovable inhibition, some complex combination of shyness and fear and shame, would prevent me from speaking to him, and that instead of approaching him I would just follow him at a short distance, observing him on his ramble through the city as I attempted to work up the courage to approach him. But that's not what happened. What happened was that, as he waited at a pedestrian crossing a little way down the street, I walked toward the other side of the crossing so that I would be there when he made it over. It was as though I were not in control of my movements, as though something stronger than mere volition had caused me to walk toward him.

I approached him very tentatively and politely asked him if he was Malcolm Macarthur. He seemed a little startled; he stopped, and stood aside to let people pass. Up close, his skin was strangely smooth and lucid for a man of his age. He asked me whether I had known he would be here, whether I had been following him. His voice sounded strange to my ears. It had a slightly strangulated quality, as though pushing firmly against some restriction. He spoke with a drawling precision, and in a manner that seemed an imperfect imitation of the pronunciation and cadences of the English upper class. I told him I had not, but that I had been hoping for some time to bump into him. I told him that I was very interested in his case, that I had been fascinated by it for many years.

He asked me then whether I was a journalist. I had known that this question would be coming, and felt it was important to frame myself as someone who was not a journalist, to intimate as strongly as possible that my interest in him was less puerile than that of the crime writers and tabloid reporters whom I knew to have approached him over the years. And so what I said was that I did not think of myself as a journalist, that I thought of myself as more an essayist than anything else. Even as I was saying this, I felt a heat rise in my face, and I was viscerally aware of my own absurdity. It happened to be true, but was no less embarrassing for being so.

I took my bag off my back and reached inside, and as I did so I noticed that my hands were trembling a little. I was surprised at how nervous I was, and hoped it wasn't too obvious. I took out the copy of one of my books that I had been carrying around with me. It was a paperback edition of my first book, a work of reportage about transhumanism, a social movement advocating for the technological enhancement of humanity. I knew that Macarthur was interested in science. I also had in my bag a recent issue of *The New York Review of Books*, which contained a piece I had written. This I also gave to him, hoping that it would help to establish me in his mind as a serious proposition. I will admit that my strategy here was to appeal to his intellectual vanity, and to present myself as the kind of figure with whom he might be glad to associate. Inside the front cover of the paperback I had handed him was a letter I had written in expectation of our meeting, explaining my intention to write a book about him, and my hope that he would assist me with it, and in which I was careful to mention my association with Trinity College and the number of languages my work had been translated into.

He told me immediately that he was reluctant to talk. He had been given a life sentence, he said, and the nature of his release was that he could be recalled to prison on a moment's notice if he broke any of the conditions of his license. One of those conditions was that he not speak to any members of the media about his crimes.

It would have been absurd to ask if his release license contained any stipulations about speaking with essayists. I told him that I understood, but that if it helped matters I would be happy to confine our conversations to matters other than his crimes and his imprisonment. I would be glad, I said, to hear about his childhood, and the years leading up to the events of 1982, and about his life since he had been released from prison.

"That may be possible," he said. "We shall have to see."

Despite his show of reticence, Macarthur was surprisingly voluble. This, clearly, was a man who liked to talk, and who did not often have the opportunity to do so. He seemed to want to give me a brief history of his entire life, right there on the street. He spoke about his childhood, the estate he had grown up on in Co. Meath, the various histories of his mother's and father's families. He spoke about his love for libraries, of how before the pandemic he would spend hours every day sitting in a local library reading various newspapers, books, and periodicals.

As he spoke, his medical mask repeatedly slipped down the bridge of his nose, coming to rest on his upper lip, and with a delicate movement of his hand he would lift it up again. His pale eyes peered out over the mask with a watchful intensity. I wondered why he was telling me all of this; I wondered why he was speaking to me at all.

«

I was curious about whether Macarthur was often recognized when he was out and about. He told me that although people knew who he was, he was almost never approached by strangers; it was rarer still, he said, that any kind of unpleasant situation arose. Only once or twice since his release from prison, he told me, had he gotten into unpleasant situations in public.

There had, he said, been an odd incident some years previously. Not long after his release from prison, he was sitting quietly at a desk in the reading area of his local library when he felt a firm jab between his shoulder blades. When he turned around, a man of about his own age was looming over him, calling him a bastard and telling him he should be ashamed to show his face in public. Macarthur stood up and, as politely as he could, asked the man to please avoid making a scene. The man became angrier still. *You brought this country to its knees,* he said. *You single-handedly destroyed the entire economy.* Macarthur was taken aback, he told me, by the economic content of this accusation. He had murdered people, yes, but it could not fairly be said that he had destroyed Ireland's economy in the process. It soon emerged that the man had in fact mistaken him for Seán FitzPatrick, the former chair of Anglo Irish Bank, who was arrested in 2011 for a hidden loans fraud that had bankrupted the company, after which the Irish government had stepped in to nationalize it.

"I eventually convinced this man that I was not Seán FitzPatrick, and went back to my reading," Macarthur said. "I didn't dare tell him who I actually was."

The point of this anecdote seemed to be that if I imagined that Macarthur had to deal with people angrily taking him to task for murdering two innocent people whenever he left the house, I was wrong. Not only was it a very rare occurrence, but when it had happened it was a case of mistaken identity.

Forty minutes later we were still standing at the same spot, Macarthur's autobiographical torrent showing no sign of abating, when this view of things was seriously and violently undermined. As he was speaking, Macarthur broke off midsentence and redirected his gaze sharply at something over my shoulder. When I turned around, a tall man in a raincoat was standing in the street looking at us, holding a compact Panasonic camera. He had a thick beard and appeared to be in his late fifties. At first, I stood aside, out of the absurd and short-lived belief that he was taking photographs of the unremarkable building we happened to be standing outside. When he raised the camera, Macarthur asked him, with elaborate politeness, whether he was taking

photographs of us. The man said that he was, and Macarthur
asked him whether he would mind not doing so.

"You didn't give that poor girl much of a chance, did
you?" said the man.

Macarthur seemed taken aback, but not especially
rattled.

"Thank you, all right," he said, with brusque civility, as
though the man had asked him whether he'd like to see a
wine list.

"You didn't give her any chance at all," said the man, in a
low and treacherous drawl. "You cunt."

"I must tell you," said Macarthur, "that you are at risk of
causing a public order breach."

I am not at my best in situations of conflict, but the complexity of this scenario was especially acute. I felt that some
kind of violence was imminent. It was not so much the man's
fury I found disturbing as the extent to which he seemed to
be enjoying it, relishing this unexpected encounter with a
person to whom anything could be said, and perhaps even
done.

My own reaction to this scene was itself hardly honor-
able; it was, in fact, both cowardly and opportunistic. I felt
that I needed to extricate myself from this situation, but to
do so without jeopardizing my connection with Macarthur.
I needed him to feel, consciously or otherwise, that I could
be trusted—even that I had his back. Even as I felt this to be
necessary, I understood it to be craven.

I turned to him and said that perhaps we should move
on, and gestured down the street in the direction of Temple
Bar. Macarthur and I began to walk, but when we stopped
at a crossing, I looked around and saw that the man was
following us, slowly but with purpose. He had clearly not
finished saying what he wanted to say. Macarthur suggested

then that we continue our conversation in the safety and seclusion of his apartment building, which was very close. We could stand in the foyer, he said. I agreed that this was a good idea, and we turned and walked back up the street. We had to walk past the man again to get there, and some further words were exchanged—angry and threatening on his part, tersely legalistic on Macarthur's—but we made it to Macarthur's building without incident.

Macarthur told me that he had not objected to anything the man on the street had said. Many people held such feelings, he said, and this man was just one of the very few who would express them.

We stood in the foyer of his building talking for perhaps a further hour, but I was distracted and only barely following the thread of Macarthur's monologue. I had been rattled by the incident on the street, and found myself obsessively returning to it in my mind. The intensity of the encounter had arisen not merely out of the confrontation itself, and the possibility of violence that seemed to hover in the air as it unfolded, but the complexity of my own role within it. For the better part of two hours, as we stood on the street speaking, I had been able to maintain a sense of myself as an observer-narrator figure, taking in the spectacle of Macarthur and his self-justifications. Although for the most part I was merely listening, I felt myself to be in control, receiving the raw material which I would later, at my leisure, shape into the form of my own narrative.

But as soon as the tall man appeared on the scene, with his compact camera and his obscenely truthful language, I was no longer in control. I was no longer the one composing the scene; I had, instead, been forced into this man's narrative. I have no idea whether he did manage to take a photograph of Macarthur and me in the end. But if such an image does exist, it is one in which I appear not as a writer

finally making contact with a subject he has been pursuing
for months, committing to memory as much as he can so
that he can later sit at his laptop and create his own scene
from it, his own meaning, but as a random guy who happens
to be chatting to Malcolm Macarthur—even worse, perhaps,
a friend. Whether I liked it or not, I was implicated.

FIVE

That Sunday, as I was eating breakfast, my phone buzzed in my pocket. The word "Macarthur" appeared on the screen, a sudden and bizarre intrusion into the peaceful domesticity of my morning. I had not been expecting to hear from him. When I had left him in the foyer of his apartment building earlier that week, it was with an agreement to give him some time to think about my proposition, to decide whether he wished to speak to me for the book I intended to write. We had exchanged numbers, and I told him I would call him in perhaps a week or so. Staring at his name on my phone screen, I went outside onto the street, leaving the children on the sofa watching cartoons. I answered the phone.

"Macarthur here," he said.

His voice sounded thick and a little croaky, and I wondered whether he had spoken aloud since we had parted ways earlier that week. He had read my book, he said. He had known a small amount about transhumanism, from his general reading, and he had found the book very interesting, and well executed. He would be amenable to speaking further, he said. If I was going to write this book with or without his cooperation, as I had told him I would, I might as well do so with the correct facts in hand, he said, facts with which only he could supply me. He wanted to clarify certain things about his past, he said, which had been misreported after his arrest and had calcified over the years into an accepted version of his life, and of what he called his "criminal episode."

I told him that I was interested, first of all, in his childhood, but that I hoped that, when we sat down to speak, we would be able to go through his life more or less sequentially.

"Well," he said, wasting no time in making his case, "the first thing to be said is that I lived a blameless life until 1982. Entirely blameless. If you were to plot my life along a graph, morally speaking, you would see a very flat line for the first thirty-seven years, then one very sharp spike in the middle, followed by another completely flat line right up until the present day."

"Given," I said, "that that seems to be the case—"

"Oh, it is the case," he said.

"Well, I thought we might try to talk about why it happened."

"Fine," he said. "But you must remember that this was a financial situation. It wasn't what you might call irrationality, or lack of control. There was a problem to be solved. And you might well ask, well, why solve it using this particular *technique*? And that's a legitimate question. But it wasn't an act of madness."

After the call ended, I remained sitting on the bench, thinking about what Macarthur had said. I stared at the phrases and words I had scribbled in my notebook as we spoke. With my pen, I slowly circled the word "problem," and then the word "technique." I knew that by this last term he meant the robbery he had planned, rather than the murders he had actually committed, but nonetheless felt that his use of these words revealed a certain remoteness from his own deeds and their consequences.

We arranged to meet the following Thursday. That morning, I dropped my son off at his primary school and

walked the twenty minutes or so across the city to Macarthur's building. Although we had already met in person, and
spoken at length on the phone, I was apprehensive about the
encounter. If it went as I hoped, it would be the beginning of
an extended series of conversations. This was what I wanted,
and what was required if I was going to answer the question
I set out with, but the consequences of spending time with
this man were a source of concern to me.

As I approached Macarthur's building, I saw him standing in the doorway, peering up and down the street, awaiting
my approach. He was wearing a mask again, and the same
beige jacket he'd had on the last time we'd met. When he let
me in, he told me to take the lift up to his floor, saying that he
would take the stairs. He had only had his first vaccination,
he said, and it was better to be cautious about these things.

When I got out of the lift, he was there to meet me, and
ever so slightly out of breath. Though he'd avoided the lift
primarily for reasons of social distancing, he said, he relied
quite heavily on the stairs for exercise. He did thirty minutes
every day, walking up and down. He tended to do this in
midmorning, he said, because at this time he would encounter fewer of his neighbors heading out to work.

It was a small apartment, with one bedroom and a little
living room–cum–kitchenette. When we entered the living
area, he directed me toward a small frosted glass dining table
with a couple of wooden chairs, while he sat across from me
on a dark brown couch. There was not much natural light
in the place, and the only window faced across a side street
toward another apartment building. On the couch was a
single green cushion shaped like a gigantic flower. I tried to
conceal the extent of my curiosity about the place, but while
putting my jacket on the back of my chair I took a quick
glance at the kitchenette behind me. It was through an arch,
from which hung an opaque peach-colored curtain, tied back

so that the way was open. The kitchenette's work surfaces were bare, save for a blender and a large tray piled with a truly prodigious quantity of oranges and lemons.

I sat down at the table. I rummaged in my backpack for a few moments and took out my notebook and pen, and my MP3 voice recorder, and placed them neatly on the table in front of me. I told him I would be recording the conversation, purely for my own personal records, and that I would also be taking notes as we spoke. I was aware that I was behaving more formally than I normally did in such situations. My manner was polite but serious, at times even officious. (At one point, I heard myself ask him whether he found the apartment building a "convivial" place to live.) I find it hard to say whether this pose was deliberate or instinctive, but either way it was a pose, whose function was to impose a barrier of professionalism between myself and Macarthur.

My attention was soon diverted toward a more remarkable aspect of the room. In the corner by the window was a low console table on which sat an object that appeared to be a television, and which was entirely covered in black plastic bin liners, tightly wrapped and sealed with tape. Between the table I was seated at, and the couch on which Macarthur was now sitting, was another item of furniture, long and low to the floor. This, too, was completely sealed with plastic bin liners.

I pointed to the television in the corner and asked why it was covered with bin liners. He said that the apartment tended to be very dusty, and that this was the most efficient way of keeping the dust off the television set. He pointed to the item of furniture that lay between us and said that this was the shelf where he kept all his books and other written materials. When he wanted a book, he said, he removed the plastic covering and selected one, and then replaced the covering. That way he could keep the dust off his books. The same with the television. If he wanted to watch the news or some other program, he simply took the plastic off the television, and would not have to wipe dust off the screen.

I was having trouble concealing my bafflement.

"Would it not be more straightforward just to dust the place?" I said.

"I hadn't realized your line of questioning would be so forensic," he said, a little sharply. I detected no irony in his tone, and his face mask made his expression largely illegible.

Attempting to steer the conversation back toward safer ground, I remarked that he presumably did not watch a lot of television, and asked what he did with what must have been a considerable quantity of spare time. He read, he said, and also listened to the radio a great deal. Here he gestured toward a small AM/FM radio that lay on the far side of the frosted glass table I was seated at. It was the old-fashioned kind, with an aerial and a manual dial. Every Saturday, he said, he bought *The Irish Times* and went through the radio listings for the following week, making note of the programs he planned to listen to. Here he removed from an inner pocket of his jacket some small pieces of paper, which he had cut down to pocket size with scissors, and on which he had jotted the names and times of various shows he intended to listen to. These programs, he said, tended to be on the BBC. Radio Four was a particular favorite. He shuffled through these little pieces of paper, fingering them tenderly, and pausing momentarily to look at the names and times of these radio programs, perhaps to remind himself of entertainments that lay ahead, or to reflect on those that had already passed.

«

When I told Macarthur that I had done my PhD on the novels of John Banville, and that writing about *The Book of Evidence* had deepened my fascination with his case, he said that he was not as a rule especially interested in fiction. His interest was in facts, he said; he was very much a *fact person*. But he had made an exception for *The Book of Evidence*, he said, because it was based, however loosely, on the facts of his own life. He seemed primarily to be interested, and even amused, by the ways in which Banville had altered these facts to create the fictional character of Freddie Montgomery. Even the name Montgomery, he said, was an obvious play on his own; the names Macarthur and Montgomery were, after all, primarily associated with famous generals of the Second World War—one American, the other British.

But what interested him about the book especially, he said, were those places in which Banville had unwittingly written the truth. Among the more widely reported details in the days after his arrest, for instance, was that just as the police were about to pounce, a taxi had pulled up outside the attorney general's apartment building, carrying certain items that Macarthur had requested to be delivered, including hacksaw blades, a copy of *Town & Country* magazine, and several bottles of Perrier spring water. The business about the Perrier was repeated endlessly in the media, presumably because the brand was at the time so associated with expensive taste and, along with the copy of *Town & Country*, reinforced the popular characterization of Macarthur as a bow-tied toff.

In *The Book of Evidence*, Macarthur reminded me, there is a scene in which his fictional doppelgänger drinks a bottle of carbonated spring water in the home of his friend the prominent art dealer Charlie French, where he is hiding out after committing a murder.

But the interesting thing, he said, was that Banville changed the brand from Perrier to Apollinaris, which was at the time another quite expensive brand of bottled water.

He presumably changed it, said Macarthur, as a means of distancing his story from the supposed facts of his own case. But in reality the press had gotten it wrong about the Perrier. It was in fact Apollinaris he had ordered to be delivered to Paddy Connolly's apartment. Connolly was very fond of the stuff, he said, because it was very lightly *fizzed*. While he was staying there he had drunk quite a lot of it and diminished Connolly's supply, so he wanted to replace what he had drunk. But in attempting to turn fact into fiction, said Macarthur, Banville had inadvertently converted this small fiction back into fact.

«

Later, when I thought about the business with the plastic bin liners, I wondered whether it had to do with Macarthur's upbringing. Macarthur had grown up in a large country house, after all, with full-time staff, who would have attended to his family's every domestic requirement. As a child, he was unlikely to have seen either of his parents dusting, and less likely still to have done any dusting himself. And in such large country homes, where entire wings of the house might be unused for long stretches, and perhaps left unheated in the winter months, it was customary to cover the furniture with sheeting, against the thick settling of dust. A person who had spent his early years in such a place, and his middle years in prison, might well take this kind of eccentric approach to what he referred to as "the problem of dust." When I got to know Macarthur a little better, this technique of his seemed to me to be evidence of his peculiar approach to the solving of problems, which was often so logical as to be almost entirely irrational.

When I spoke to friends about Macarthur, they were often curious about how he lived, and what his home was like, and I sometimes mentioned the bin liners. Invariably, these friends would find this detail unsettling. What was he hiding? Why bin liners? And had it not occurred to me that he might be covering his furniture with plastic because he wanted to minimize the mess it would make when he decided to bludgeon me to death right there in his living room? Had I not seen the film *American Psycho,* in which the investment banker–turned–serial killer Patrick Bateman lures a colleague to his apartment, where he has covered his living room furniture with sheets, before murdering him with an axe?

But what troubled me about the bin liners was not that Macarthur might be planning to murder me, which seemed in any case a vanishingly remote prospect, but the way in which they signaled a deeper concealment. Whenever I visit someone's house, I am always drawn toward their bookshelves. And my curiosity about their books is a curiosity about their curiosities. When you look at a person's books, you are seeing what that person is interested in. A bookshelf is a self-portrait, a kind of haphazard autobiography. Like the medical mask over the lower half of Macarthur's face, the plastic covering his books concealed something crucial, something real.

«

It was in one of my first conversations with Macarthur that the complexity—perhaps the impossibility—of the project I had undertaken revealed itself to me. It stemmed from our discussion of certain handwritten notes that detectives had found when they searched Connolly's apartment after Macarthur's arrest, tucked inside a medical textbook that had been in his possession. Hidden inside this book was a collection of loose notebook pages, on which Macarthur had written out what seemed to be a meticulous plan, complete with a diagram, to electrocute a female relative by rewiring an electric heater. In the aftermath of Macarthur's conviction, these pages were presented in the media as evidence of Macarthur's plan to murder his own mother in order to secure what remained of his sizable inheritance.

In that early conversation, Macarthur raised this matter himself, as an example of the many absurd things that people believed about him. He did not deny the existence of these notes, or the fact that he was their author. But the idea that they had anything to do with a planned murder, least of all of his own mother, was a misunderstanding of farcical proportions.

He was something of a film buff, he explained. He enjoyed high-quality cinema: French film, the work of Luis Buñuel and John Cassavetes. Some of his friends, he told me, shared these enthusiasms. One evening, he was at dinner with a small group of these friends, and one of them mentioned having recently seen and enjoyed the 1949 British comedy *Kind Hearts and Coronets*. It was about a chap, he said, whose mother was from an aristocratic family, but who married down and was disinherited. When the mother died, he told me, this chap decided to murder several members of his estranged family who were ahead of him in line to inherit the dukedom.

A good-natured dispute over this film had arisen at this dinner, Macarthur told me. One friend in particular, whom Macarthur referred to as a "serious cineaste," felt that the plot was unsatisfactory and began to come up with ways in which the murders could have been more effectively carried out. Somehow or other, he said, it was agreed that, as a sort of parlor game, they would each come up with a more plausible version of a murder committed by the protagonist. And so these notes that were found by the detectives, he insisted, these notes that were supposedly about some kind of plan to kill his mother, were in fact notes he had jotted as part of this parlor game.

The evening after Macarthur told me this, I sat down to watch *Kind Hearts and Coronets*. I enjoyed its vicious frivolity but was struck by its essential quality of naïvety. It was like an elegantly constructed children's film about murder. Although the narrative is structured around eight murders, most of which occur on-screen, the killings themselves are entirely lacking in even the mood and texture of violence. All eight victims, each of whom is played by Alec Guinness, are dispatched in a cartoonish manner (one relative is bumped off by an arrow shot from an apartment window at a hot air balloon, another by means of an explosive jar of caviar) so that the murderer at the center of it—Louis D'Ascoyne Mazzini, the tenth Duke of Chalfont—seems closer to Wile E. Coyote than to the serial killer he would actually be if portrayed in any kind of realistic manner. Whatever else might be said about Macarthur's claim that he was sketching ideas for a rewrite of the film, it seemed strange to take issue with the unrealistic nature of the murders. The ludicrousness seemed practically the whole point of the film.

Later, I consulted a copy of the handwritten notes. If coming up with a more plausible murder as part of a parlor game about remaking the film had in fact been Macarthur's intention in writing them, he had immersed himself very deeply in the psychology of the murderer character. They were written, for one thing, in the first person, and in a style of grim determination: "Electric fire with faulty plug attached. Adapter left in walls perhaps fused. Adapter plug pulled out. None of my fingerprints. Make sure hers on handle. Take away one of her fuses if it appears there are too many."

The notes included a list of necessary items: a phase tester, pliers, a screwdriver, a gag, a blindfold, and "additional rope for tying up, across chest." There was significant detail, too, on what should be done in the immediate aftermath of the murder. "Wait for a while to ensure that death is final," he wrote. "During this time take a few key important items, certain small photos into my possession. Make an inventory of other important items, a list, and can check on their presence when I arrive for the funeral."

I felt sure that these jottings had nothing to do with any kind of parlor game. The "I" referred to did not seem like the "I" of an imagined character. None of it seemed like notes toward a frivolous fiction. It seemed like something stranger, and more troubling, than that.

Some months later, Macarthur attempted to explain away these discrepancies. He told me that the reason these notes were written in the first person was that *Kind Hearts and Coronets* was itself structured around a framing narrative in which Mazzini sits in a cell on the eve of his execution, writing his confession. He also told me that there were several other pages of these notes, in which it was much clearer that Macarthur's intention was purely fictional, and which somehow seem to have gone missing when the detectives were gathering evidence.

Though this did not seem credible to me, I felt that he himself believed what he was telling me, and that I was, in a strange and destabilizing sense, therefore not being lied to at all. It was my first real glimpse of the doubtful territory I had set out to explore.

PART TWO

A THREAD OF VIOLENCE

SIX

Macarthur and I would eventually meet many times, and speak frequently on the phone, over close to a year. But after that first conversation, we agreed only to a small number of meetings, in which Macarthur would tell me about his early life and about the period leading up to the murders. He told me that he had not decided whether he would speak of the crimes themselves, or of his motivations or his mental state at the time. He would have to make that call when the time came, he said. He had to think of how it would be received by the authorities. He felt that he should certainly not speak on the record about his time in prison, because of the risk that tabloid journalists would focus on these details to portray the government as being too soft on criminals. He felt, too, even more strongly, that he should not be seen to sensationalize his crimes. He was also, he said, wary of upsetting the families of the people he had murdered. (He never put it in these terms himself; he spoke only of "the bereaved," and of "the deceased"—even, on one occasion, of "the deceased *persons*.") For the time being, though, we could start where his own story began. Over the course of our earliest meetings, a picture of Macarthur's childhood in Co. Meath began to emerge.

Macarthur's early life was characterized by a precarious privilege. His family owned an estate of about 180 acres called Breemount. The house itself, built in the early eighteenth century, was architecturally undistinguished but very large: sixteen rooms, or eighteen if you included the two little servants' rooms in the attic. When he spoke to me of the house, he described it as a world unto itself. There were extensive gardens, woodland areas, lawn tennis courts, stables. On its periphery was a large hill, which when Malcolm was seven his father began quarrying for its limestone. He was an only child, and he spent long afternoons alone there, playing among the broken rocks. Sometimes he found fossilized sea creatures, spiraled shells and trilobites and other extinct creatures, preserved in the eviscerated belly of the hill. His curiosity about how these marine animals came to be there, some thirty miles from the coast, led him to the house's large library, where he read all he could find about geology and evolutionary biology.

The library was exceptionally well stocked, with books his grandfather had bought on his frequent trips to England, many of them unavailable at the time in Ireland, where the church maintained a stranglehold on the imaginations and intellects of its subjects. Malcolm spent a good deal of his time in there, reading. He was especially interested in science and history, but there were novels, too; he remembered, later, as a teenager, reading Joyce's *Portrait*—a book which, although it was never officially banned in Ireland, was all but impossible to buy. It was the first time he had read a novel in which he recognized places from his own life.

Malcolm did sometimes play with the local children, and the children of his parents' employees, but he grew up knowing that he and his family were different, that they belonged to a distinct world. The radio in the house was always tuned to the World Service. Only on rare occasions would the dial be turned to RTE or some other Irish radio station, and afterwards it would always find its way back to the BBC. Breemount was situated a couple of fields away from the ruins of Dangan Castle—the childhood home of Arthur Wellesley, the first Duke of Wellington, who defeated Napoleon at the Battle of Waterloo, and who went on to become British prime minister. The Macarthurs were very proud of the neoclassical fireplace in their drawing room, which had been taken from Dangan after it burnt down in the early eighteenth century. The fireplace was a symbol of their connection to that world, that imperial history. His parents thought of themselves as Irish; they liked the country and its people, but felt at all times a distinct and abiding connection to Britain.

His parents, he told me, read *The Times of London,* and *The Guardian.* They had no Irish party-political allegiance but saw themselves as belonging to a tradition of British political liberalism. There were lawn tennis parties at Breemount, and hunting, and horses. When I imagine the place where Macarthur spent his childhood, I see it as a half-forgotten outpost of a dying empire.

«

One common misconception about Macarthur, reported in the newspapers at the time of his arrest and conviction and frequently repeated in the forty years since, was that his family were Anglo-Irish. The Macarthurs were not descendants of the English Protestants who had "settled" Irish land and, from the seventeenth century onward, established themselves as a colonial ruling class. They were in fact Catholics, and they had come not from England but from Scotland. They were relatively recent transplants, too, having arrived in Co. Meath from Lanarkshire in 1907.

Though the Macarthurs did not satisfy Brendan Behan's famous definition of the Anglo-Irish as "Protestants on horses," they identified far more with this leisure class than they did with the rural Catholics they were surrounded by in Co. Meath. They thought of themselves as members of the landed gentry, whose Catholicism distinguished (but by no means excluded) them from the social world of the Protestant ascendancy.

When Macarthur's grandfather Daniel Macarthur, a man with considerable inherited wealth, bought the place in 1907, he brought with him from Lanarkshire in Scotland a small staff. (Among them was the family nanny, Lizzy, who eventually married the gardener, Jack, who had come attached to the estate.) They also brought with them two cars, which in the Ireland of the time immediately established them as a family of wealth and distinction.

Despite this wealth and distinction, Daniel Macarthur, known to the locals as "Old Dan," was seen as an aloof and mercurial figure. He was known for his intense religious fervor, which was extreme even by the zealous standards of Ireland in the early twentieth century. His religiosity was accounted for by a local legend. When the Macarthurs bought Breemount, people said, one of the rooms had been boarded up, because it was haunted. "Old Macarthur let the ghost out around the place," one local told a journalist, "and they had to get a Redemptorist to exorcise the place after that." The priest had imposed on him a penance for the sin of releasing the ghost: he was to attend Mass every morning, and Devotion every evening, for the rest of his days.

Breemount was among the first large houses in the area to be fully modernized. The entire place was wired for electricity and powered by a large petrol generator. (Nearby Dunsany Castle, the home of Daniel Macarthur's friend Lord Dunsany—an Anglo-Irish fantasy writer who was a major influence on the work of H. P. Lovecraft—did not even have flush toilets at the time.) Aside from the nanny, there was a small staff of servants who lived at Breemount. The five children, three boys and two girls, were all sent away to school. The boys went to boarding school in Scotland; the girls, to Switzerland.

Mostly, Old Dan was driven to church by the butler, who went to the services with him. But on First Fridays, he would attend evening prayer, and because the butler tended to be off work, he would go alone, on his bicycle. One Friday evening in early February 1936, Old Dan was on his way to Mass, freewheeling downhill from Breemount. It was a steep hill, and it was dark, and at the bottom of the hill was a woman, a former employee at Breemount, who was herself walking in the direction of the church. She was swinging a walking stick as she went, and as Dan whizzed by, she swung her stick with absentminded jauntiness right into the spokes of his front wheel, and he was thrown some distance over the handlebars, cracking his skull open on the road to the church.

Jack, the eldest son, was technically the heir and would have inherited Breemount had he not emigrated to America in his twenties. Instead, the estate was inherited by the youngest, also called Daniel, who was the only child to have remained in Ireland. In his mid-thirties, Daniel married a woman named Irene Murray, who was eleven years his junior, and whom he met at a hunt ball.

The Murrays were another family of Catholic landowners from Co. Meath, though they were wealthier and more established than the Macarthurs, having come from Britain in the 1630s. They were one of the largest landowning families in the county, until the Land Commission of the Irish Free State had forced the breakup of their eight-hundred-acre estate in the early 1930s.

»

Daniel and Irene left their young son, Malcolm, mostly to his own devices. Neither of them really worked for a living. Irene had trained as a nurse before she met Daniel, though she had never practiced. (She was, as Macarthur put it to me, the *châtelaine* of a large estate and would not have been expected to work.) Daniel did some farm management and drove a tractor once in a while, but he had a small staff of local men who labored on the farm, and some seasonal workers when the occasion called for it, which allowed him to devote most of his time to recreation. He did a great deal of fishing on the Kingsbrook, the river that ran through the estate, and on the Boyne nearby. He also read a lot. He was a man of leisure, which was the whole point of being landed gentry. You didn't work, as such, at least not for money. Money came from the land, which you owned, and from other people's work on it.

Irene, too, was dedicated to the cultivation of her own leisure pursuits. Horses, in particular, were her thing. (His father, Macarthur told me, did not share this enthusiasm; he regarded the Anglo-Irish equestrian obsession as tantamount to philistinism.) When Irene wasn't on or around a horse, she could otherwise be found tending to Breemount's gardens, or on one of the lawn tennis courts. These interests were the outward manifestations of her class, and through them she pursued her social life. She herself would later admit that, even after she had Malcolm, children didn't especially figure in her interests. "I was never a great person with children," she said in a radio interview she gave shortly after his conviction. "I carried on the tradition I had been brought up in, that children are seen and not heard."

Not once, she claimed, did she ever change a nappy. We

can assume, without hard evidence, that the same was true of her husband. They had a housekeeper who handled all that—a woman named Kate McCann, who was the widowed second wife of the estate's gardener, Jack, and who lived in a cottage near the house. Malcolm spent a lot of his time with Kate while his parents pursued their own interests. Often enough, he would spend the night at her house.

Malcolm's mother did teach him to ride a horse, a skill she felt was necessary for people of their social class, but he was never an especially enthusiastic rider. This may have had to do with an injury he suffered as a very young child. According to Irene, Malcolm had gotten behind one of his mother's hunting horses and spooked it, and it kicked out a rear leg and struck him hard in the head, splitting the skin wide open. In that same radio interview, Irene mentioned that her son still bore the scar.

A former farmhand, too, told a journalist of this accident: "He got a belt of a horse. A kick from the hind leg, right in the forehead. I thought he was a goner, but he came through it alright. But poor Malcolm, he was like his father, he had too much intelligence. And that's a very bad thing. He was too bright altogether."

«

I asked Macarthur one day about this injury, and he said that, despite what his mother and the former farmhand had independently claimed, he had never been kicked by a horse. It was true that he had suffered an injury, and that it had involved a horse, but only indirectly. He was only five when it happened, but he remembered it very clearly. As he related the event to me, he paced up and down the length of the living room; from time to time he paused and rubbed his hands together in a gesture of uncertain vigor, and it made a dry, whispering sound, like the slight shifting of fallen leaves in a breeze.

"This was early 1950," he said. "My mother had a hunter called Scarlet, in a paddock in Breemount. And in this paddock also was one of my pets, a cream-colored bantam cock with feathers down to its feet. I had all sorts of pets—dogs, cats, even a pet pheasant. This bantam cock was a present from a family my parents knew, farmers in Waynestown. And I had gone to the paddock to put out some food for it. And this horse, my mother's hunter, went to eat the food. And I ran over to it, to stop it. And there was a slight incline, and as I ran up, my feet slipped. And I can remember this very clearly. There was a small rock sticking out of the ground. My head bounced onto that. No horse kick. But a man named Joe Cox, who worked for us and who lived in our gate lodge at the time, was milking his cow in a shed, and he heard me crying. He rushed out, and when he saw the horse, he assumed I had been kicked by it. Hence the story, which my parents believed. I don't know why the story took hold; it just did. But no, I was never kicked by a horse."

Occasionally, he told me, people had looked to this head injury as a possible explanation for the murders he committed later in life. Some scientists believed that traumatic head injuries, especially in childhood, might be the cause of impaired social and moral decision-making. Macarthur himself discounted this idea, however. There had been no cognitive impairment as a result of the fall, he insisted.

His mother was right, though: he still bore the scar. It wasn't prominent, but if you were looking for it you could not but see it—a perfectly straight, perfectly white line over his right eye.

«

When Malcolm was old enough for school, he was taught at home by a governess, as both his father and his mother were as children. Ms. Mangan came to Breemount every morning to teach him and in the afternoon would set off on her bike to another country house nearby, to teach another boy from a landed gentry family. Malcolm liked Ms. Mangan and enjoyed their classes. She was quite upset when it was decided that he would be sent to the local school.

According to his mother, in that same radio interview, his father ("and after all," she said, "his father decided everything") had planned to send him to a private school in the UK, but the family came into some financial trouble, and the local national school became the only viable option. While he was at the Christian Brothers School in the nearby town of Trim, he got on pretty well with the children from the town, but there was always an awareness of social difference. He didn't go to their houses to play, and they certainly never came to his. When tennis parties were held at Breemount, they were attended by large landowning families in the area. The boys in his class were never invited.

His being sent to the local CBS sounds an incongruous note in the story of Macarthur's childhood. The fact is patently at odds with the overall narrative of his wealth and privilege. Something seems to have gone wrong for the family, and in no small way. The school his father had planned to send him to, Bedales, was an exclusive private school in Hampshire. It was fairly typical of the Anglo-Irish to send their children to school in England, and for Macarthur to have gone to Bedales would have cemented his position (and that of his family) within the social world of that class. But the money wasn't there, and so he had to go to the Christian Brothers School with the local boys.

When I asked Macarthur about why it was that the plan to send him to Bedales was never borne out, he was vague and noncommittal. It was simply decided, he said, that it would be better to have him attend school closer to home. It wasn't a big deal either way. Plus, he said, going to the local CBS meant that he would finish school earlier than he would have had he gone to Bedales.

But the difference between Bedales and the local CBS was, in terms of class triangulation, so significant that the decision cannot have been taken lightly. The Irish landed gentry did not typically send their children to be educated by the local Christian Brothers, any more than they would have sent them out to learn a construction trade at the age of fifteen.

And here a fault line begins to reveal itself in the structure of class distinction the Macarthurs built around themselves. The financial strain that led to Malcolm having to attend the local CBS may also have revealed, to him and to his parents, something uncomfortable, and perhaps unspeakable: that his family was not quite as comfortably upper class as it believed itself to be.

«

For reasons that were bound up with these financial difficulties, the Macarthurs' marriage was not a happy one. Daniel and Irene argued often about finances, and these arguments on occasion turned violent. When Malcolm was in his mid-teens, Irene had had enough. She went to live alone in a house a few miles away, and Malcolm stayed behind at Breemount with his father.

Though they were no longer living together, they maintained a relationship, and Irene visited Breemount frequently. One day, the three of them had come back from a trip late in the afternoon, and there was an argument over whether it was too late to have the cook make Sunday lunch. In her radio interview, Irene described the incident. The argument turned desperate, she claimed. There was a tussle on the lawn, during which Daniel bit Malcolm's hand. The boy had to be taken to the hospital, where he was given five stitches.

Daniel had, she said, "inherited his own father's strange ways"; he had a "sadistic streak," though it manifested mostly against her. "Malcolm," she said, "saw violence at an early age."

》

When Irene attained legal separation from her husband, Malcolm himself gave evidence to a solicitor of "things he had seen." In this statement, she said, he mentioned in particular an incident in which her husband had upended a jug of milk over her head. "There were various little incidents like that," as she put it in the radio interview. She spoke with a kind of brittle airiness that made me wonder what kind of other little incidents she was speaking of, and what sort of pain her stoic manner might be concealing.

"No doubt at all about it," she said; "he probably absorbed more than I would have thought at the time."

》

In the archive of the *Sunday Independent*, I found an article from 2010 entitled "No One Guessed the Boy in the Cravat Would Go On to Kill." After the usual rehashing of the murders, the author went on to say that when he was a teenager his family had been friendly with the Macarthurs. Irene frequently attended "lawn tennis parties" at their house, and from time to time Malcolm would be with her. "Irene," he writes, "was old school landed gentry who had no maternal instinct whatsoever. Malcolm was an inconvenience who interrupted her hunting, gardening, and tennis." Malcolm did not participate in the tennis, the article continued, and kept mostly to himself, though he would join the players after the games for cucumber sandwiches and tea. Even on the hottest summer days, he would walk around the grounds of the house wearing very heavy tweed suits, with bow ties or cravats. The article ends with a peculiar image: the author's memory of sitting on the roof of the house to gain a bird's-eye view of the tennis, and seeing the young Macarthur walking the gardens in his heavy tweed suit "topped off with his trademark cravat," carefully examining and smelling in turn each of the different kinds of flowers.

I find it very striking, this image of young Macarthur. With it he emerges from the blank screen of childhood. Not as a murderer, not yet, but as a teenager, affected and strange and apart. He feels alive to me, for the first time, awkwardly bending to examine and identify the flowers. He feels vivid and real.

Perhaps the reason it feels so real, so evocative, is because it's fiction. According to Macarthur, at least, it's entirely fabricated. The author of this article, he says, was someone who barely knew him at all and who had him mixed up with someone else entirely, a foster child of one of the neighboring families. The author of the article, he says, never saw him smelling flowers at the periphery of a tennis party, and neither, more important, was he ever "an inconvenience" to his mother.

This is the problem with Macarthur. As soon as I begin to see him, as soon as I believe I have grasped him as a subject, he slips away into darkness, and I know no more, and perhaps even less, than I did to begin with.

«

After his conviction, when Macarthur became a figure of intense public interest, other recollections of him as a child appeared in the media. A picture emerged of a boy who was neglected, perhaps abused. An unnamed former employee of the family said that they "took the young lad in" on many occasions, when he "might have been alone in the big house." "At first," said this former employee, "he could not, or would not speak, and if you addressed him, he would run and hide his head behind his hands. The poor little lad was scared stiff of everyone. Eventually he came out of his shell and began playing with our youngsters. He was even then a quiet lad, but you'd know he was very, very bright."

Another unnamed local, a former farmhand at Breemount, said: "Sure the poor lad had a dreadful childhood, never knowing whether his own wanted him or not. When he went to St. Michael's school in Trim, he took to the books in earnest, but his parents would pass him on the road in hail, rain or snow without even giving him a lift."

In the second volume of his memoirs, the Anglo-Irish art historian Homan Potterton writes about learning of the arrest of a suspected murderer in the home of the attorney general, and realizing that he knew the suspect. His father had been an auctioneer and land agent in Trim. Daniel Macarthur had been both a client and a friend. "On some occasions in the school holidays," he writes, "my father would take my brother Alan and me with him as he visited clients and we would wait in the car, or get up to some mischief, while father discussed business. At Breemount, it was different, as there was a small boy of our own age there—Mr Macarthur's son—with whom we could play about the farmyard. He was called Malcolm and was an only child: he was also a lonely one. His parents' marriage was not a happy one—in fact it was a disaster—and his mother, Irene, was rarely at Breemount.

Malcolm was very much neglected. This was sometimes discussed by my mother and father within the family's hearing and, as small children do, I took it in. I never knew Malcolm as an adult but I have happy memories of playing with him as a child in the sunny farmyard at Breemount. In light of what happened later, it is obvious that demons lurked there."

«

This lurking demons version of Macarthur's childhood— advanced by both the police and the media in the aftermath of his conviction, and detailed by his own mother in interviews she gave at the time—was one that Macarthur himself claimed not to recognize. In the weeks and months that followed my first visit to his apartment, it was a frequent subject of our conversations. He was hurt and angered by claims that his mother and father were not good parents. He was, he told me, not "regularly beaten" by his father, as one newspaper article claimed, and neither was he neglected by his mother. Far from it: his parents were gentle and thoughtful people, not given to excesses of any kind, emotional or otherwise.

The fact that he was an only child, he insisted, and that neither of his parents worked, meant that they had a lot of time for him. His mother taught him to ride a horse. He fished on the Boyne with his father in the summer, and in the winter they would play billiards in the games room at Breemount. He had a little box that he would stand on to allow him to reach the billiards table. The three of them would go for long drives together on Sundays, visiting sites of historical and natural interest, or the large country estates of their friends, often returning home to Breemount late at night.

He told me that he did spend a good deal of time alone as a child, but it was hardly the case that he was antisocial. He liked to explore the extensive grounds of Breemount, to wander the woods and climb the trees. As for the violence alluded to by people who had known the family, he said, who could really tell where these stories had come from? It was frequently the case with those in his position, as he put it, that people were desperate to find so-called *red flags* in the details of one's early life. The Irish, he put it to me one day, could often be somewhat loose in their fidelity to the truth. (It was his custom, I noted, to refer to "the Irish" as though they were a foreign people among whom he had lately found himself, and of whose peculiarities he had become acutely aware.) "To put it bluntly," he said, "you have plain people who are fabulators."

And such plain people, he believed, were always looking for some version of his story that made sense, so that one thing followed logically from another, and the sad experiences of the child could explain the terrible actions of the man. But there was, he believed, no such easy logic to his life. Despite what his mother had said in that interview—about how Malcolm had "seen violence at an early age," about his father's "sadistic streak"—he recalled no disturbing incidents at all from that time. There must certainly have been some discord between his parents, because of course they parted ways when he was still a child, but if it ever turned "physical," as he put it, such incidents never unfolded in his presence.

«

One afternoon, not long after we first met, I went to see Macarthur at his apartment. It was late spring, and my wife and I had just that afternoon gone together to pick up my daughter, who had just turned three, from her first day in kindergarten. My wife and daughter went to the car to drive home, and I set out on foot for Macarthur's apartment, and as I walked through the inner city, I felt my mood change from one of pride and contentment to one of vague foreboding. It felt strange, and perhaps wrong, to spend a warm spring afternoon engaged in activities so violently at odds with one another.

A masked Macarthur greeted me stiffly at the front door once again, and we went up to his apartment just as we had before, he taking the stairs, I going up in the lift. Once the initial pleasantries were out of the way, he removed from an inner pocket of his jacket a piece of paper, folded concertina-style, and announced that he wanted to clear up certain ambiguities about his early life. (He often commenced our meetings in this manner, making point-by-point clarifications of matters he felt were still outstanding from a previous meeting.)

Assuming an oratorical stance, and glancing down at the notes he had jotted on this piece of paper, he made the following statement:

"Excluding 1982," he said, "which is a rather large exclusion, I've had no experience, ever in my life, of violence. I have neither perpetrated it nor been the victim of it. Nor can I remember observing it, or witnessing it, to any significant degree at all. There may have been a couple of schoolyard fights, but nothing more. Certainly my parents never laid a finger on me. That would not have been their philosophy. Nor did I witness any violence between my parents, other than what might be called *a pushing match at the greenhouse door*. This was when I was sixteen. There was an argument over something or other, and for some reason my father would not let my mother enter the greenhouse. I witnessed this from some distance, across the garden. But nobody ever

saw anybody strike a blow. People try to find explanations in
the past by distorting the past. But there was never what you
would call a thread of violence leading up to 1982. That was
simply not the case."

When I asked Macarthur about the hand-biting incident his mother had described, he told me that that, too,
had been a misunderstanding. His father had never been
deliberately violent toward him in any fashion. The so-called
biting incident, he said, had occurred one evening when he
and his father were arriving back at Breemount from a visit
to another landowning family. His father was getting out
the driver-side door when he suddenly collapsed and began
writhing there in the courtyard, seemingly in the throes of
some kind of fit. Fearing that he might bite his tongue, or
worse still swallow it, Macarthur had placed his hand inside
his father's mouth.

It was true that his father had bitten him on the hand, he
said, and that he had needed five stitches as a result, but the
context for the biting had been entirely lost in the reporting
of the incident. It was, he said, this incessant search for red
flags that was once again at the root of this false narrative.
He showed me the scar: a thin, slightly raised white line cir-
cling the pad of his index finger.

Sometime after I spoke to Macarthur about his childhood, and the supposed misunderstanding around the hand-
biting incident, I sourced from the RTE archives an original,
unedited recording of the radio interview with his mother. It
is an extraordinary document, about forty minutes in length,
in which Irene Macarthur speaks plainly and at length about
her son's childhood and his crimes, and his relationship with
herself and her husband. The interviewer David Hanley's
style is calm, skillful, and subtly dogged. At one point, near
the end of the interview, he asks her about her son's relationship with the truth:

DAVID HANLEY: Did he fantasize, as a child? And was this, do you think, an inherited trait?

IRENE MACARTHUR: I think all children sort of make up stories and dreams as children, and then after a while possibly they believe them themselves. But when he grew up I think he probably inherited this trait from his father. And that was that they got something into their mind, and when they thought about it long enough, they literally believed it themselves.

DAVID HANLEY: His father invented stories which he eventually believed?

IRENE MACARTHUR: Oh yes, always! And of course how you catch these people out is that they forget, you see, what they've told you, and the next time they tell you something different. And so that being so, where Malcolm was concerned, and very often I'm sure I was quite unjust. I quite believe I was. But when he was telling me the truth I probably didn't believe it. Because you get to a stage where you don't bother.

DAVID HANLEY: You say that his father invented or fabricated stories, and that he probably inherited this trait from his father.

IRENE MACARTHUR: Oh yes, his father fabricated stories to everybody. That was quite standard . . . But you see when you're dealing with that sort of a person, it is very difficult, because when they tell you the truth, you just don't know what to believe. In Malcolm's case I would say that he might have been a dreamer.

In another interview, Irene described her son as "another Macarthur, a chip off the old block in some ways. I recognized this in him, not as a child, but as he grew into adulthood. And I realized on a few occasions that I was actually in fear of him. His late father was always referred to in the household as 'the Governor.' Malcolm also became known by this title in his turn."

Once, I suggested to Macarthur that people might more easily empathize with him, and be less likely to see him as a monster, if they believed that he had had a strange and difficult childhood, and that he had, as his mother had put it, seen violence at an early age. He acknowledged that this might be the case, but the fact was he did have a happy childhood, and that he had neither witnessed nor suffered violence. It would not be true to say otherwise, and furthermore it would be an injustice to his mother and father, who had been excellent parents.

Why, despite the weight of evidence against it, was he so doggedly committed to this story of his childhood? Perhaps he was committed to it simply because it was true. Or perhaps it was that it removed the standard psychological explanation for his crimes. Murderers tended, after all, to be people who had suffered in childhood. Violent men learned violence at an early age, and usually at the hands of their fathers. If Macarthur killed because of things he had witnessed and suffered as a child, then it stood to reason that he had not been entirely in control of his actions.

As odd as it sounds, it was important to Macarthur not to be seen as a violent man. For him, the events of 1982 were an aberration, a dark and bloody stain on the otherwise pristine surface of his life. His "episode," as he called it. Although he understood that, in the eyes of the public, he would always be defined by the murders of Bridie Gargan and Donal Dunne, he himself did not believe these murders to have proceeded from a dark wellspring of violence within him. He did not want this violence to be the expression of his true self. And if his childhood had been a happy one—if his mother had been neither cold nor neglectful, his father neither drunken nor abusive—then it could not be said that his life had followed an inexorable psychological course, a "thread of violence," as he called it.

He said that the media's approach to people like him, by which I understood him to mean murderers, was as "both villain and damaged victim." His implication was that he was neither.

His parents' breakup had, he insisted, been an amicable one. He spoke of injured pride, of feelings hurt on both sides, of standing on principle. But not hostility. He had a way of making it sound as though personal nobility, on the part of both of his parents, was somehow at the root of the marriage coming to grief, rather than any sort of antipathy. Their differences may have been known and spoken of in their social circle, but he himself was exposed to very little, and then only to very mild manifestations of the marital discord. There was, as he put it, no philandering. No excessive drinking.

"No violence at all really," he said, "apart from shoving, and maybe once or twice there were slaps. But I saw none of that."

«

Eventually, many months after I first broached the subject with him, his posture toward his childhood shifted. He admitted to, yes, having witnessed domestic violence as a child—although "admit" is probably not the right word, given that what he told me was offered by way of a defense of his father. His father, he said, was a perfect gentleman. His mother, too, was more or less unfailingly decorous and refined. But she herself was known to have had a "sharp tongue." When they did argue, it always had to do with money, and his mother could sometimes be harsh with his father on his management of the farm and the family finances.

On such occasions, he said, he had seen his father strike his mother. He had slapped her across the face, he said, but only ever with an open palm, never a closed fist.

I said that whether he hit her with a fist or a palm, it was still domestic violence, and that furthermore, in characterizing such acts of violence as provoked by his mother's sharp tongue, he was reproducing the logic of the abuser. He did not disagree, but said that the standards of what could be considered truly violent had shifted since his father's generation.

I pointed out that the violence he witnessed as a child, mild though he may have believed it to be, always resulted from tensions over his father's supposed financial mismanagement, and that financial stress was the reason to which he himself attributed the murders he had committed.

"Oh, well," he said, "that's interesting. You make a good point!"

He sounded surprised, and perhaps even a little pleased, as though I had offered a clever interpretation of a novel or film, rather than two brutal and inexplicable murders he himself had committed forty years ago. I do not mention this exchange in order to portray Macarthur as cold and abstract toward his crimes, but to underline the strange spirit of open-mindedness he often evinced with respect to his own motivations and complexities. This almost scientific curiosity existed in a strange and irresolvable tension with what seemed to me an unwillingness to speak frankly about the darker aspects of his family life.

Especially remarkable to me was the incident in which his father was said to have dumped a jug of milk over his mother, an event that Macarthur had attested to during his parents' separation. He never spoke of it with me, perhaps because it would have been harder to downplay the implications of the incident. Though it was not an act of violence in the way of a slap, it is hard to miss the cruelty and humiliation of it. A son looking on as his father lifts a jug full of milk from the table and upends it over his mother's head. It would be hard to forget that, the milk running down your mother's face, mingling with her tears. Or perhaps there were no tears. Perhaps she was not the type to cry, even in such situations. These "little incidents," as she called them.

SEVEN

In 1963, when he was seventeen, Macarthur went to California to study. He lived at first with his father's older brother, Jack Macarthur, and his wife, Hilda. Jack, as the eldest son, had been the heir to Breemount but had as a young man relinquished his claim in order to move to the United States, where he studied at Stanford. While at Stanford, he took a job working with horses for a wealthy family of German origin named Gehringer. In 1930, he married the boss's daughter. After Stanford, Jack took a job in industrial relations at U.S. Steel. He and his wife lived in the small city of Concord, in the East Bay. They had no children, and they were well off.

Macarthur was struck, in general, by the wealth disparity between California and Ireland. When he left Co. Meath, pretty much everyone got around by bicycle; California was all convertibles and gas-guzzling Cadillacs. He had never in his life seen anything like his uncle Jack's car, a 1961 Lincoln Continental sedan. ("Beautiful motorcar," Macarthur told me. "Very low slung. The same model, in fact, that President Kennedy was shot in.")

Jack's house was large, and luxurious. Every week, a group of Japanese men came to tend to the gardens, which extended over two acres. Later, Macarthur did some work in the gardens himself, cutting grass and collecting leaves and so on. He socialized with the children of his uncle's work colleagues, and sometimes went to drive-in movies with them. There were weekend trips to Lake Tahoe. He became an associate member of Contra Costa Country Club, where he used the swimming pool, and took up golf.

After doing a year at Diablo Valley, a local junior college, Macarthur went up to Oregon State for another year and then completed his junior and senior year at UC Davis. There he took advantage of the University of California's credit-transfer scheme and attended seminars at Berkeley. Berkeley's libraries were far superior to those at Davis, and so Macarthur was drawn to spending as much time there as he could. The institution had, at that time, its own internal television network, which enabled students at one campus to attend live broadcasts of lectures from another. This system allowed Macarthur to attend lectures given by the Marxist philosopher Herbert Marcuse, whose book *One-Dimensional Man* had recently been published, and whose ideas were a major influence on the American radical left.

Although Berkeley was at the center of that counterculture, Macarthur's involvement with it never got much more intimate than those remote-viewed lectures. When he arrived in 1963, it had been crew cuts as far as the eye could see; by the time he returned to Ireland in '67, it was all long hair and free love. He never took drugs; he had no desire to break the law and did not like the idea of relinquishing control of himself. For the same reason, he did not drink much. The legal drinking age in the United States was twenty-one. Very occasionally, he would have a glass of wine in the company of his uncle and aunt, but partook of neither the boozy bacchanalia of the university frat culture nor the antiestablishment hedonism of the Bay Area hippie scene.

He avoided the frequent antiwar protests on the Berkeley campus. Although he was opposed to America's presence in Vietnam, he felt that it would have been fundamentally poor manners to go around raising his fist in defiance of the foreign policy decisions of a country in which he was a guest.

He dismissed the hippies as irrational and atavistic. The whole movement was, he felt, a bit unrealistic, and some of it—the commune trend, for instance—even verged on the pathological. He felt himself to be detached from the spectacle of the counterculture, though from time to time he found it amusing.

One evening, while walking in the Haight-Ashbury neighborhood of San Francisco, he encountered a mime troupe staging a performance on the street corner. He had no idea who these people were, but found their antics entertaining enough to spend an hour or so of his time watching them. Later, he learned that they were an anarchist street theater group known as the Diggers; they staged elaborate avant-garde happenings in and around Haight-Ashbury, and were seen as an animating cultural force of the entire hippie movement. Like the seventeenth-century English proto-anarchists from whom they borrowed their name, the Diggers aimed to establish a community entirely free of laws, and without money.

«

I find it difficult to picture all this: Macarthur as even a peripheral presence at Herbert Marcuse lectures, Berkeley free-speech protests, hippie theater troupes cavorting on the streets of San Francisco in nothing but animal masks. I imagine him hovering irresolutely between superiority and bafflement, unsure whether to see himself as an aloof observer or an awkward bystander. I think of that article about Macarthur as a young man—an article which he himself dismissed as complete fabrication—in which he was depicted drifting on the periphery of a tennis party at the author's house, examining and smelling in turn the various kinds of flowers in the garden.

Something else that comes to mind here is *The Book of Evidence*, in which Freddie Montgomery also spends a period studying at Berkeley in the 1960s. There's a moment in that stretch of the novel that has remained with me since I read it, long before I ever met the real-life inspiration for the character, where Freddie steps out of an art gallery into a sunlit Shattuck Avenue in downtown Berkeley and notes "a smell of cypresses and car exhaust, a faint whiff of tear-gas from the direction of the campus." The detail struck me at the time, and strikes me still, as a delicate illumination of Freddie's narcissistic self-enclosure. History, in all its thrilling immediacy and violence, is unfolding in real time no more than a few hundred yards away, and it registers on his consciousness as only a "faint whiff," no more than the smell of cypresses or car exhaust. There is no further mention of the tear gas, or the reason for its deployment.

In that same gallery in Berkeley, Freddie encounters a woman named Anna he knows slightly from childhood, the daughter of an aristocratic family of his parents' acquaintance. When she introduces Freddie to her housemate, another upper-class Anglo-Irish woman named Daphne, the three become involved in a *ménage à trois*. Their relationship is sustained as much by their mutual sense of superiority to their cultural surroundings as by erotic energies: "We had a lot of fun together laughing at the Americans, who were just then entering that stage of doomed hedonistic gaiety through which we, the gilded children of poor old raddled

Europe, had already passed, or so we believed. How innocent they seemed to us, with their flowers and their joss-sticks and their muddled religiosity."

Macarthur seems not to have had anything like the sexual adventures of his fictional avatar—a character who in any case always seemed to me to contain at least as much of his creator as his real-life model. (Banville himself spent some time in the Bay Area as a young man in the late sixties, and a fictionalized version of his experiences there may be grafted onto Freddie's story in *The Book of Evidence*.)

Macarthur described himself to me as "an observer, rather than a participant" in the countercultural scene, with its political and sexual radicalism. When I asked him whether he had girlfriends during his time in California, he hesitated, and expressed surprise, and perhaps a little irritation, at the level of detail I was going into. He had friends who were girls, he said. He was keen to move on, so I didn't press the matter, but during our next conversation he himself brought it up again.

"I did not," he said, "have any girlfriends in California in the romantic sense. But I had lots of female friends. Even some real *pals*. I've always regarded women as *persons*, and treated them as completely equal."

He was in some way troubled, I felt, by the implications of my question, and I supposed it had to do with speculation amid the post-arrest scandal about his sexuality. Homosexuality was at that time criminalized in Ireland, and although there was never evidence of any kind of sexual relationship between Macarthur and Connolly, some portion of the public scandal that followed the murders could be accounted for by a barely repressed prurience about the possibility. In her radio interview with David Hanley after her son's conviction, Irene Macarthur did nothing to dampen that speculation:

DAVID HANLEY: Do you think he liked female company?

IRENE MACARTHUR: I wouldn't have thought so at all.

DAVID HANLEY: Why not?

IRENE MACARTHUR: Well, perhaps no mother can visualize their own son in that, ah, light.

DAVID HANLEY: Do you think he preferred male company?

IRENE MACARTHUR: Well, I think he was so interested in the academic side of life that anyone who would talk to him on his own level probably was more acceptable, irrespective of male or female.

If this last question was one she was attempting to dodge, she did so in an oddly suggestive manner. It is as though, in her decorous way, she was invoking a sexuality that has been sublimated, rarefied into pure intellect. It is also possible that what is revealed here is simply a mother's reluctance to speak about an aspect of her son's life and identity that may have been too uncomfortable to countenance. Better to conclude that he had no interest in sex whatsoever, perhaps, than to allow that he may not have been straight.

In another interview she gave to the *Evening Herald* newspaper, she went a step further. Asked about the suggestion that Malcolm may have "had homosexual tendencies," she replied that she "would not dream of prying that much. It may be that he is bi-sexual like so many people are these days. I don't know."

《

It was always Macarthur's intention to return home eventually. He was the heir of Breemount, after all, and unlike his uncle he had no desire to relinquish that patrimony. After he finished his studies, he planned to stay a while in the United States before going back to Ireland, perhaps to travel around a bit in the vast country of which in four years he had seen so little. But soon after he graduated, he learned that, as a US resident who was no longer studying at university, his draft classification was about to go from 2-S, denoting deferment because of study, to 1-A, which meant he was available for unrestricted military service.

Ironically, given his reluctance to join the protests against the war, he was about to be forced to go and fight in it. He knew what the schedule was, and it was only a matter of time until he would have to show up at the induction center. He left with what he considered a respectable degree of haste.

EIGHT

A decade and a half passed between Macarthur's return home in 1967 and the events of 1982, and, despite his expensive foreign education, he seems to have done nothing of consequence in that time. "I was never a careerist," as he put it to me. He never felt the need to pursue an academic vocation, or to find gainful employment of any other kind. "I was lucky in that I never had to," he said. "That is the wonderful thing, by the way, about inherited wealth. You become the master of your own days."

This much he had in common with the Diggers of Haight-Ashbury: his highest value was freedom. Freedom for Macarthur meant, specifically, free time. It was not work itself that he was opposed to, but the necessity of earning a living. What would have been the point of being landed gentry, after all, if he had just graduated with his economics degree and went and got a job in a bank? He believed himself to be destined for greater things, but he did not have in mind the sort of greatness that involved working for a living. He never said as much, but it seemed to me that he saw such imperatives as essentially petty and vulgar. Just as his mother implied that he was driven by intellectual rather than sexual urges, Macarthur's own claim was that his love of learning was uncorrupted by any desire to consummate his knowledge in the form of an academic career. After Breemount was sold in 1974, and he could no longer legitimately put down "Farmer" as his occupation on official forms, he sometimes put down "Writer" instead. (He was, I would argue, at least as much a writer as he ever was a farmer.) He was usually tempted to follow it with "non-practicing," in parentheses, but he never did.

I never quite bought this business about not being "a careerist." The implication seemed to be that the only reasons for pursuing academic research, or for writing a book, were essentially mercenary, that if a person were sufficiently well off not to have to work, and had no special narcissistic desire to make an impact on the public realm, they would feel no need to do such things. In one sense, this aversion to gainful employment was very much in keeping with his aristocratic persona. But it was also clear that, notwithstanding the "criminal episode"—of which he was anything but proud—Macarthur held himself, as he might put it, in high regard. Whether he was speaking of his natural talent for golf, or his sharp and logical mind, it seemed to me that he was exactly the sort of person who would in fact aspire to achieving writerly acclaim, or to becoming a distinguished professor of something or other.

Despite the number of Macarthur's acquaintances who believed him to be some kind of academic, there seems not to have been any sort of full-blown imposture going on. It is more likely that he simply failed to correct people's assumptions about him. Acquaintances variously believed him to have been a tutor at Cambridge and a lecturer at Trinity College Dublin. After his conviction, one such acquaintance spoke to a reporter of his impressions of Macarthur, in terms so inflated as to approach mock-heroic style: "He was a nuclear and an astrophysicist. He went to the countries where he could express his ideas and do his research. He had been to Berkeley and spent a lot of time in Cambridge where he had his own research facilities. He was always in Trinity too."

«

Even his own mother was under the impression that he was an academic, and that he was, as she told a journalist after his arrest, "on the staff" at Kings College, Cambridge. It was only after the trial, when details of his life came to be widely known, that she was finally disabused of this notion. In an interview with a newspaper during that time, she spoke of her sense of her son's potential to achieve great things with his intellect and his education. She recalled something he said to her cook one day, after he received his share of the proceeds of the sale of Breemount. "I'm going to leave my mark," he said, "on Western Europe."

"He's certainly done that," his mother told the reporter.

It seems to have been true that Macarthur spent a lot of time in Cambridge, and this may have been where the perception arose from. After he returned from America, he had acquired a reader's ticket for Kings College Library. He went over to Cambridge and back several times a year and would immerse himself in the library's collections, spending days at a stretch reading up on recent developments in economics and the sciences.

He may not have been an academic, but he was a man of wide and eclectic learning—a "private scholar," as he once described himself to me. His conversation was filled with long, detailed monologues on such diverse topics as tectonic plate theory, linear regression modeling in economics, the philosophical problem of free will and determinism, the absurdities and complexities of the Irish legal system, and the root causes of the civil war in Vietnam. He treated his own erudition like a cherished possession, to be taken down off the shelf and displayed to visitors before they even had their coats off.

«

After he left America, Macarthur returned to live with his father at Breemount. His parents had been separated for some years at that point. His mother was now living in the nearby town of Trim.

I often wondered, as I have said, whether Macarthur downplayed the difficulty of his childhood, the turbulence and violence of his parents' marriage, because he wanted to remove the psychological rationale for the violence he himself later committed. Because he did not want to see his life as a tragic narrative, himself a character undone, reduced to violence and dissolution, by certain fatal pressures brought to bear on an inherent flaw in his own psyche. But there may have been another reason. It's possible he wanted to give the impression that he loved and admired his father as a means of countering a suspicion that arose around the time of his conviction, and which has since never entirely dissipated.

In 2004, amid media speculation that the prison service may have been planning to let Macarthur out on temporary release over Christmas, an article in the *Sunday Independent* reported an unattributed suspicion that he had in fact murdered his father.

"He was regularly beaten by his father Danny, who virtually abandoned him as a child," the story claimed. "Danny Macarthur died in what are now considered suspicious circumstances on the night that Malcolm made a rare visit to the family farm in Co. Meath. It was believed at the time that Mr Macarthur senior had died of natural causes in his sleep. No post-mortem was carried out, and after his father's death in the late Seventies, Macarthur received £70,000 from the estate which he squandered."

The article is full of speculation and insinuation. "It is known that Macarthur harboured deep feelings about his parents," we are told, as though any child of parents had ever harbored anything else. It's also marred by several glaring factual errors. Macarthur was not making "a rare visit" to the family farm the night his father died; he had been living alone with him at that point for some time. The author also gets the date of Daniel's death wrong by several years, as well as the name of Macarthur's second victim, Donal Dunne, whom he calls "Tom Dunne." And so it's hard to take the piece very seriously. The newspaper was, presumably, taking full advantage of Macarthur's compromised position; a convicted murderer is, generally speaking, in no position to take a libel case.

In one sense, there's no particularly compelling reason not to believe it. It is hardly absurd to suppose that a man who would kill two complete strangers in pursuit of a botched plan to commit armed robbery might also murder his violent, domineering father in order to gain an inheritance. But the reasons for suspecting him are hardly that compelling either—amounting only, in the end, to the idea that he was in a position to have murdered him, and that he was apparently the type to do so.

I asked Macarthur about his father's death. In the summer of 1971, he said, the summer he was twenty-five, he had been in the UK, spending time with family in York and visiting the Kings College Library in Cambridge. When he came back in mid-July, his father had taken to his bed with chest problems. Macarthur said he noticed blood on his father's handkerchief, and that he called the doctor, who came out for a house visit. Arrangements were made to visit a consultant in Dublin, and then he was taken for a stay in Portobello House, a nursing home in the city. His condition was deemed to be serious, Macarthur told me, and had he himself not seen the blood on the handkerchief and called the doctor, it is likely his father would have died.

"I saved his life," he said simply.

While his father was at the nursing home, Macarthur would pick him up every day and bring him for drives in the Dublin mountains, before returning him to the home. On the 22nd of October, his doctors deemed him well enough to return to Breemount. He was still weak, but well enough to take short walks in the woods around the house where he had been born, and where he had spent all his life.

One evening, a couple of days after his father returned home, Macarthur went into the city to attend an event at the Gaiety Theatre. It was a poetry reading, he told me, part of a season of performances to mark the centenary of the theater's foundation. He listed the various celebrities onstage that night: Peter Sellers, Sir Matt Busby, Peter O'Toole, Trevor Howard. Eavan Boland read from her work, as did the poet Mary Wilson, wife of the former British prime minister Harold Wilson. It was late that night when he came back to Breemount, he said, and he did not check on his father, not wanting to wake him.

In the morning, Macarthur told me, he went into his room with a tray of tea and toast. He looked very peaceful, lying there in bed. He had been dead about eight hours. When the doctor arrived later that morning, he said that it had been a pulmonary embolism, and that it would have been instantaneous. It also would have been entirely painless.

"You don't even know you're dying," said Macarthur. "It was just one of those things."

»

After his father died, Macarthur inherited two-thirds of
the estate, with the other third going to his mother. Before
long, Breemount was sold, and after death duties and other
debts had been paid, he netted about £70,000 (the *Sunday
Independent* got that detail right). This was a very significant
sum in the early 1970s, nearly €900,000 in today's money.
His father's death had left him a wealthy man, reliant on no
one else for his income.

One of the first things Macarthur said to me, that first
day I met him on the street, was that he had never been prof-
ligate with his money. Although he had a great appreciation
for wine, he was always a very moderate drinker. He was perhaps a little too generous, he told me, picking up the bill at
restaurants, and handing out loans to friends here and there,
not all of whom were as conscientious about paying him back
as they might have been. All this he said without prompt-
ing, without my asking him about money, or anything much
else.

No, he said, he was never one for what you would call
the high life. Inherited wealth was a means toward inde-
pendence and freedom. His days were his own, and he could
spend them as he wished. But it was not that he was lazy, or
work-shy. Far from it. His freedom was the means by which
he could do the work he wanted to do, become the person he
wanted to become. Time to think, time to read.

And he was over and back to London, too, of course.
Occasionally, he would open a paper in the morning and
read about a play or concert happening in London, and
would go straight to the airport; he could be in Mayfair in
time for a late lunch, see the show that evening, and fly back
the following day. Sometimes he would stay with friends,
sometimes he would take a room in a hotel. After the sale

of Breemount, Macarthur moved to Dublin. He rented a flat on Fitzwilliam Square in the south city center, about as prestigious an address as it was possible to have in the city. His neighbors were the embassies and consulates of other European countries.

His insistence that he had never lived the high life, in other words, might not have been anything so straightforward as a deception, but it certainly indicated the extent to which the claim was embedded, like so much else, in the context of his aristocratic self-conception. He lived modestly, perhaps, for a man of his social class.

«

It is the mid-1970s, the better part of a decade since his return from the United States, and I can see Macarthur as he enters his thirties. I see his tasteful tan, his thick hair neatly swept back from his patrician forehead. He is trim, and contented looking, and he has the light but unmistakable glow of affluence, as though he himself were made of some finer, more costly material than the people he passes as he walks through the city. I see his crisp oxford shirt, his jacket of soft linen, the silk bow tie which is becoming now a kind of trademark. I see his straight, slightly stiff posture, the shoulders back, the head high as he walks.

What is he thinking of? Not of crime, certainly. There'll be no need to think of that for a good while yet. And not money, either. His thoughts are on higher things. The philosophy of mind, perhaps. Some recent discovery in the field of genetic biology, which he is on his way to Trinity College to read up on at the library. Or the friends he will be meeting for lunch later. Yes, I have him now, I feel. The purposeful stride, the thoughtful air, the suede elbow patches.

And I can see him at a table in Bartley Dunne's, the

bohemian bar he frequented on South King Street. He's with his friend Victor Meally. Victor is old enough to be Macarthur's father, but they are good friends nonetheless. Victor is a Meath man himself, from Trim, but it was in Cambridge that they first met, on one of Macarthur's reading binges. Victor is himself a kind of amateur scholar, though somewhat more accomplished than his younger friend. He has edited an encyclopedia of Ireland, published by an independent Dublin publishing house. He has what Macarthur calls a "first-rate intellect"; he studied mathematics at Trinity and received a gold medal in his final exams as an undergraduate. But his intellectual gifts never resulted in the sort of academic career that seems to have been expected of him. He's in his late fifties now, and works as a bookkeeper for Bewley's café on Grafton Street. He is what they call a "confirmed bachelor," and he lives with his sisters in a house in Mount Merion.

It was Victor who introduced Macarthur to Bartley's, with its eclectic clientele of academics, politicians, punks, theater people, students, high court judges. He was a fixture there. He kept a little black book filled with names and contact details. He knew everyone. If you went away for a while, and you came back and you wanted to know where someone was, Victor was the person you would go to.

The place was hung with red velvet drapes, and there were tea chests covered with checkered tablecloths, and Chianti bottles coated with dripped candle wax. The owner, Bartholomew Dunne, handed out little cards printed with the words "Bartley Dunne's, reminiscent of a left bank bistro, haunt of aristocrats, poets, and artists." It was also known for its extraordinarily wide selection of drinks. If a patron asked for something and they didn't have it in stock, it was customary to give them another drink of their choice for free. There were sweet Hungarian wines, Japanese whiskeys, highly spe-

cific brands of ouzo. In the late sixties, a journalist who had
visited from Moscow wrote about sitting at the bar and being
quizzed by the proprietors as to the correct pronunciations of
their various Russian wines. Noël Coward had been known
to drink there, and Elizabeth Taylor and Richard Burton
were regulars when they were in the city filming *The Spy
Who Came In from the Cold*.

Bartley's was one of a tiny number of Dublin pubs at the
time that were open to a gay clientele, though it was not a gay
bar, as such. "The word 'gay' was not used then," according
to an *Irish Times* obituary of its owner. "Male homosexuality
was a criminal offence, so discretion was essential. At Bartley Dunne's there was a place for everyone. If there was a
house rule, it was that."

After the murders, Bartley's came to be associated with
Macarthur, and with the little world he inhabited. Its reputation as what the gay rights campaigner David Norris referred
to in his autobiography as "a notorious haunt of the homosexual *demi-monde*" was a major factor in how the case was
framed in the media. Macarthur had some gay acquaintances, he told me, but mostly mixed with a different set at
Bartley's. The gay people tended to congregate at the front of
the pub, the straight people toward the back.

As regards his romantic proclivities, always a subject of
media speculation, it was Bartholomew Dunne's contention that Macarthur "consorted always with female company." From time to time, he would take a girl he met at the
bar away on a weekend trip to England. On one occasion,
he took two. These were, he said, "ordinary girls with city
accents. To them, Malcolm, with his polished behaviour,
cultured accent, academic ways and plenty of money must
have seemed like Prince Charming to Alice in Wonderland."

«

It was at Bartley's that Macarthur first met Brenda Little. She was there with her sister, and they got talking at the bar; he thought her very beautiful, and he was struck by her eloquence and her strong cultural opinions. They hit it off and arranged to meet again. Though she had grown up in Finglas, a working-class suburb of Dublin, and had neither Macarthur's money nor his education, she mixed with some of Bartley's more wealthy and cultured clientele. She had lived in London for a short stretch in the early 1970s, and on returning to Dublin worked for a building company, and then took a position as a trainee hairdresser at a salon on Grafton Street.

Macarthur was impressed by Little, by her autodidact's erudition and her affinity for high culture. He was impressed, too, by the company she kept, and by the high regard in which her opinions on art and music were held. She took frequent and forceful issue with the reviews of Charles Acton, the music critic of *The Irish Times*. It was not long before she moved into Macarthur's flat on Fitzwilliam Square, and not long after that before she was pregnant. They decided that they would remain unmarried but bring the child up together. It was no small thing, in those days, to have a child out of wedlock.

«

Brenda Little's cultural interests were at the root of her (and ultimately Macarthur's) unlikely friendship with Patrick Connolly, who at that time was one of the country's most prominent barristers. Connolly had, some years previously, been part of the legal team that successfully defended Charles Haughey, the then minister for finance—and, years later, Ireland's Taoiseach (or prime minister)—when he was tried for diverting public funds in order to import arms for the IRA.

Little and Connolly had met one afternoon in the late 1960s, when she was collecting funds for a new sports center in Finglas, and Connolly had made a contribution. They got talking, and he told her that he himself had grown up not far from the area. It turned out, in fact, that he was on the board of trustees for the site on which the complex was to be built. They kept in touch, and their shared interest in classical music, and opera in particular, became the basis of a long-standing friendship. They often attended performances together at the National Concert Hall, and art-house movies at the Irish Film Theatre.

There was never any romantic attachment between Little and Connolly; they were simply friends. When Macarthur began seeing Little, he himself became friendly with Connolly. The three of them went to plays together, and occasionally to the opera. In the mid-1990s, in one of the few interviews he ever gave about Macarthur, Connolly described his friend as "a very interesting conversationalist, the sort of man you would be happy to have at a dinner party or cocktail party, in the type of company in which intelligent conversation is appreciated."

«

In October 1975, Macarthur and Little's child was born. They called him Colin. That Christmas, Macarthur went to visit his mother, who was then living in a smaller house not far from Breemount. Though he had been living less than an hour's drive away, he had not seen her since February of the previous year. Brenda did not come for the visit. The scene, which is hard to fully account for, is strange and brittle in my imagination. Irene hears the car pull up in front of the house; looking out, she sees that it is her son, to whom she has not spoken in nearly two years. She walks outside, and as he is getting out of the car, she sees a basket in the back seat, and in the basket is an infant. She asks who the child belongs to, and he says that the child belongs to him.

«

In the radio interview she gave after her son's conviction, David Hanley asked Irene whether she had had much contact with her grandson. Here is what she said:

> Oh it's a dear little child, it really is. It's what I call
> *fetching*. And when he brought it down in December
> 1975, it was then two months old . . . The child was
> in the car in a basket. I saw it. And I showed surprise.
> And he said it was his child. And I said is it a boy or a
> girl, and he said, a boy of course.

At the time Irene gave this interview, Colin was seven years old—only a little younger than my own son as I write this. I am trying to imagine a person referring to my son as "it." I am trying to imagine, specifically, my own mother, saying this of my son. "It is a dear little child." I'm trying to hear her saying "It's what I'd call *fetching*." I am struggling to imagine how I would feel about hearing that.

What does it mean to refer to a child—a seven-year-old, or even an infant—as "it"? What does it say about the speaker? It was in that same interview that Irene said she brought up Malcolm according to the tradition in which she herself had been raised: that "children are seen and not heard." To call a child "it" is, in a very obvious sense, a refusal to acknowledge the child's personhood—as though he or she has not yet attained full humanity. And to say that a child should be seen and not heard amounts to the same thing. If you learn at an early age that you are not supposed to speak, that you are not to make a fuss or a spectacle of yourself, you might also learn to build an edifice around yourself, a public facade around the pain and confusion of the real.

«

Something is bothering me about the scene above, those two short paragraphs in which Irene Macarthur encounters her grandchild for the first time. The scene demands more, I feel, than the brisk treatment I have afforded it here. But the problem is that I don't have access to the moment. Beyond the vague outline—the mother, the son, the car, the baby—I have no real idea what happened. Even had I been there, and witnessed with my own eyes this scene that had taken place before I myself was born, how confidently could I speak now of what I had witnessed? I might invoke the prestigious crunch of gravel beneath the tires of Macarthur's car as it pulled up outside the house. I might say that Irene maintained a glacial demeanor as she regarded through the window of the car her infant grandchild—that the only sign of any sort of emotion on her part was a slight flaring of the nostrils, a prideful tilt of the head.

But even if I had been there, how true could that really be? What I am trying to say is that my being there to witness it would only give me license to fictionalize the scene.

I feel here an obligation both to make the moment vivid—to bring it to life on the page—and to admit that my doing so would be an unforgivable taking of liberties. For a long time now, when I have thought about how I might handle this moment, I have had it in mind to use a quote from an *Evening Herald* interview with Irene I found in the archives.

In it, she talks about the moment when Malcolm arrived at the house with baby Colin. When she saw the child, she said, she asked her son the following question: "What is that?"

Of course I wanted to use this quote. It's a terrific bit of dialogue. It's impossible to imagine a better, more cruelly succinct, revelation of the mother's coldness. I would have her look at the baby, and say *What is that,* and immediately you would feel you understood what Macarthur's childhood had been like, and you would think no wonder he turned out that way, no wonder he did the things he did. If anything, in fact, it might be a little too blunt, a little too perfect. If I had made it up, I might want to soften it somewhat, inject a little nuance and ambiguity—to perhaps have her say "What's this?" rather than "What is that?" I would do so not out of kindness to the mother, but out of an essentially aesthetic concern, a desire not to overplay my hand. It would be an open-and-shut case. The mother did it. Or the son, at any rate, did it because of the mother.

Part of my initial attraction to Macarthur as a subject was a desire to penetrate beneath the surface of biographical facts to the inner logic of his life. I felt that I could approach him like an undergraduate writing a paper about a novel, advancing neat and satisfying arguments for the psychological motivations of a protagonist. A scene like the above would have served such a purpose handsomely. The coldness and emotional rigidity of the mother would have implied a strong psychic logic to the character and his actions.

But I can divine no such inner logic. There is no essential meaning to be found in this scene, if anywhere.

≪

One evening, on the phone to my friend Katie, I found myself telling her about Macarthur. As a writing subject,

I said, he was as vivid and complex as any character I had encountered in fiction. He had been a model for Banville's Freddie Montgomery, certainly, but the more I came to know him, the more he put me in mind of Raskolnikov, the murderer-protagonist of Dostoevsky's *Crime and Punishment,* or of Meursault, the dispassionate narrator of Camus's *The Stranger.*

Katie was less impressed with my meta-ruminations than I had imagined she would be.

"Listen," she said. "You're making a potentially major mistake in thinking of him in this way."

"What do you mean?" I said.

"What I mean," she said, "is that you need to stop thinking of him as though he's a character. He's not a character. He's a real person. He's a man who did terrible things."

"Are you worried he might kill me?" I asked, in what I hoped was a teasingly insouciant tone.

"I'm not saying that," she said. "What I am saying is that this is about power. You're talking right now as though you have all the power, in the way that you would if he was in fact just a character you had created. Right now, he thinks he's the one in a position of power, because he's telling you his story. He's deciding how much of it he's going to let you have. He's giving it to you slowly, and on his own terms. But you have to realize that eventually, if and when you're in possession of the story, and the question arises of what you're going to do with it, he's going to see that power balance shifting. And you don't know how he'll feel about that, or how difficult it's going to be."

I didn't like hearing this, but I knew she had a point. There was also an ethical aspect to this, one that had haunted my thinking about this subject long before I ever met Macarthur and began to extract the raw material of narrative. My tendency to think of Macarthur as a character, and of his crimes as constituting a bizarre and compelling story of human perversity—a story about class and Irish history, about cruelty and repression—was itself a kind of heartlessness. Because if Macarthur was a character, and his crimes were a story, then his victims were necessarily characters too, and secondary ones at that. My work, in this way, was permeated with a cold and methodical violence.

«

Toward the end of one of our meetings, as I was standing in the open doorway of his apartment, Macarthur mentioned his nervousness about the potential consequences of our conversations, and what I might write about them. It was summer, and we had been in touch by then for some months. He had told me a great many things about his life, he said, which had never previously been reported and for which he was the only conceivable source, and so even if I were never to mention in my book that I had spoken with him, it would be clear that I had done so. He was worried in particular about things he had told me about his years in prison. The last thing he wanted to happen, he said, was the tabloids getting ahold of them, because it would likely stir up a political controversy, and the prison authorities might feel they had little choice but to haul him back into custody for an indeterminate period of time. I told him that I would not include in my book anything he had told me about his time in prison, and he was reassured. But he remained anxiously uncertain about the extent of his restrictions, or the potential consequences of being seen to breach them.

He was concerned, too, about the effect of my book on the families of his victims. He had to consider how his speaking to me about what he called "the criminal episode" might impact upon them. He didn't know, he said, how I was going to negotiate these difficulties in my book, but he would in any case leave it in my capable hands, and hope that whatever route I took would result in a minimum of trouble.

The nearer we approached to the "criminal episode," the more reticent he became. His lengthy and erudite digressions gave way to a more taciturn and cautious manner of speaking. He reminded me that when I had first approached him, I had told him that what I was hoping for was a brief meeting and a very broad account of his life, and that I had already done considerably better than that. Having spoken of the beginning of his relationship with Brenda, and of the birth of their son, he made it clear that he was undecided as to whether, and how far, he would proceed.

"How much further I can go, I can't say," he said. He was leaning against the window frame and tapping the sole of his shoe slowly and rhythmically on the floor, as was his habit in moments of tension or unease. "It could well be the case," he said, "that you will never fully understand what this was all about. I don't say it *will* be the case, only that we shall have to see. I'm a normal person, after all. I'm not a psychopath. I have a full complement of healthy emotions. And anything to do with 1982, speaking about it taxes the emotions. But I may get close to it. We shall have to see."

In 1980, Macarthur, Brenda Little, and their then five-year-old son, Colin, moved to a house in the North Dublin suburb of Glasnevin. The house, a large period redbrick, had been owned by his maternal grandmother and was part of a substantial estate to which he was the ultimate heir. With his bow tie and his silk shirts and his conversation-piece hair, Macarthur was a figure of intrigue in the neighborhood. The children referred to him as "The Professor."

Colin did not attend school. His father taught him at home, just as he himself, as a young child, had been taught at home. He taught him science, and physics, and history. Macarthur was, by all accounts, an unusually hands-on father for his day, spending most of his time with his son. "He would take him into Trinity College library at the age of three or four," said one friend. "He was teaching him the rudiments of philosophy and science at a very early age."

The Glasnevin house was part of Macarthur's own inheritance, and so they lived there at no cost until the following year, when the place was sold. He received about £10,000 from the proceeds. After the sale, they moved to a flat in Donnybrook, one of Dublin's wealthiest neighborhoods. The previous tenant had been Patrick Connolly, Brenda's friend and now Macarthur's too, who had just moved to a

new place in Dalkey; there were still a few months left on
the lease, but he didn't charge his friends any rent because
the contract barred him from subletting.

Macarthur's money and connections seemed to be grant-
ing him an ease of passage through the world. But it could
last only so long.

The official story, the story told in the newspapers after
his conviction, is that—like, by many accounts, his father
before him—Macarthur was irresponsible with his money.
He entertained lavishly, frittering away his inheritance on
the best restaurants in town; he spent frequent weekends
in London, staying in hotels and attending cultural events.
Worst of all, he never considered getting a job in order to
absorb the costs of such a lifestyle. He lived like a person
with vast personal wealth, in other words, when the fact was
that, while his inheritance was substantial, it was nowhere
near large enough to fund such a life indefinitely. In the written statement he gave to the Gardaí after his arrest, Macarthur affirmed that the reason he committed the crimes "all
goes back to money." For the previous two years, he said, his
finances had been diminishing. He had spent most of the
proceeds of his father's estate, he wrote, "because of mismanagement and unwise use."

In our conversations some forty years later, he was less
stark in his self-denunciations. To some degree, he told me,
his problem was always that he was too generous. He picked
up a lot of checks at a lot of restaurants. And he was something of a soft touch. He made a lot of loans in those days,
mostly small and mostly short-term, but they all added up,
and not all of them got paid back.

There was one loan in particular, he said, that contrib-
uted significantly to the dire financial straits he found himself in. In December 1981, he got a call from an acquaintance,
a respectable figure with an established record in business.

Macarthur had lent this man sums of various sizes before, and he had always paid him back at the agreed time. He was in a particularly tight spot this time, and to get out of it he needed a significant business loan, a five-figure sum. It was a short-term situation, the man insisted, one that would be resolved quickly and efficiently. Macarthur liked and trusted the man, and so although it was a larger amount than he was comfortable loaning, he agreed to help him out. The loan was documented, and the agreement was that it be paid back the following spring.

About a month later, the man called Macarthur to say that he would be unable to pay the sum back in full on the agreed date. He had large, guaranteed bank debts, which would have to be prioritized before he could make good on his loan to Macarthur. After the call, Macarthur told me, he left the flat in Donnybrook and set out for the library at the RDS. There had been a heavy snowfall, and as he trudged carefully through the becalmed city toward the library, he began to feel that he was in trouble, that there was a real chance he would never see that money again.

Macarthur and Brenda Little had been planning for some time to spend a period abroad, somewhere hot. After some deliberation, they had settled on the Spanish island of Tenerife, off the coast of Morocco. Brenda had visited there on holiday a few times, and although Macarthur himself had never been, he happened at the time to be reading a book about the nineteenth-century German naturalist Alexander von Humboldt, and had been struck by Humboldt's rapt descriptions of a visit he had made to the island.

But now, with Macarthur's funds depleted, the plan appeared to be in jeopardy. His whole way of life, in fact, was beginning to be cast into doubt. What if the money were never paid back? He would have to temper his lifestyle, his socializing, his travel. He would perhaps even have to look for work.

Was this prospect intolerable to Macarthur? I imagine him conceiving of it as a kind of death, as the end of everything he had been born into and had been brought up to value. But whenever I brought the question up with him he was studiously vague, even evasive. It was hard for him to recall now, he said, quite what he was feeling at the time. But it was not, he said, a case of his being work-shy. It was not idleness as such that he was dedicated to; he had helped out on the farm as a child, he reminded me, and had done work here and there for his uncle in California—in the garden, at the steel plant. It was about freedom. It was about time. If he were to run out of money, and if he were forced to get some kind of job, his time would no longer be his own.

Macarthur told me that when he was preparing to travel to Tenerife, one of the things he packed was the certificate of his bachelor's degree. "I thought it might be useful to have," he said, "just in case I needed it. And so I hadn't ruled out the possibility at all of getting a job."

But then, seconds later, he said something that contradicted this, or that at any rate revealed the conflicted intensity of his thinking at the time. I asked him whether he now saw the period in which they decamped to Tenerife as part of the period of unraveling that led to the murders themselves, and he said that he couldn't be sure.

"Because Brenda had been there before and liked the place, it may be that I was thinking, well, she would be happy there with Colin, if I were to start getting up to things. I can't be sure. I may have forgotten."

I was deeply frustrated by Macarthur's reluctance to engage directly with the question of his own motivations, and the thought process that led him to the murders. I sensed that he was withholding something significant, though I could not imagine what it was—or whether it was from me or himself he was he withholding it. I felt at such moments that I was within arm's reach of the truth, or something like it, but that the very act of reaching out for it caused it to retreat into the darkness like a startled animal.

«

When I think about this aspect of Macarthur's life, his apparent commitment to preserving his freedom at any cost, I become aware of an instinct to wash my hands of him as a subject, to condemn him as a grotesque avatar of his social class and its relationship to the rest of society. No matter what frame he (or anyone else) might attempt to put on it, the fact is that he committed two murders because he wanted to protect his leisure time. What other way is there to see it, after all? He murdered a nurse, and then a farmer; he took their lives in a botched attempt to protect his own time.

This is how I see it. But I also find that seeing it in this way does not prevent me from feeling in my own gut something of the panic and despair he must have felt, or so I imagine.

Because I, too, have lived a kind of charmed life, if I look at it from a distance. I don't come from landed gentry, or anything close. But I was brought up in a context of upper-middle-class privilege that shaped my expectations and my sense of myself. I went to a fee-paying school, and from there I went to Trinity College, and though I worked after I graduated—freelance writing, a stint at a current affairs radio station—I never felt the sort of urgent pressure to earn a living that I would have felt if my parents had not been well off. I didn't pay rent any more than Macarthur did; I lived in an apartment my parents owned. I had ambitions, certainly, but they were often airy and vague. I wanted to be a writer, or at the very least some kind of professional intellectual, but I had no real plan for how to pursue that life.

When I decided in my mid-twenties to do a master's degree, it was not because I had any special passion for Irish literature, but because I quite liked the idea of returning to the security of university, where all that was required of me was to read books, and have more or less interesting thoughts about them. When I finished, I continued on and did a PhD. My research was funded by a scholarship, which allowed me a life of cautious comfort, and it seemed not entirely implausible that I would emerge at the other end of my degree into some kind of academic career.

When I graduated, and the hoped-for lecturing job failed to materialize, I spent a year doing very little. I filled out applications for academic positions, none of which led to even so much as an interview; I wrote occasional pieces for newspapers and magazines, but it never amounted to anything like livable money. I spent several months trying to write a novel, because I felt that if I did so I would then be a writer. Every morning, I would walk to my grandmother's house and sit all day at a desk in her little home office. I don't remember a lot about the novel, or how much of it got written.

Luckily I didn't need to make livable money from my writing, as my wife had a good job. I eventually got a postdoctoral fellowship, which allowed me to live and write for a further year, but there was still no sign of an academic job. By the time I got a deal for my first book, I was in my early thirties, and we had just had our first child. It was hardly a fortune, but it was more money than I ever imagined I would make from my writing, and when it came it seemed like a kind of divine reprieve. It wasn't just that I now felt I had a viable future, but that my past—the years I had spent

skulking among the stacks, trying and failing to finish novels, publishing cultural criticism on the less lucrative corners
of the internet—seemed suddenly redeemed. It had, in fact,
been leading to something all along. It had, all along, made
sense. In the years that followed, my ability to support my
family through my writing became more and more fundamental to my identity. But there have been times when that
edifice has felt fragile and unsound, when it has seemed like
the money might not stretch until the next advance payment.

The slightly shameful truth, though, is that it was never so
much financial difficulty itself that scared me at these times,
but rather what I might have to do about it—if indeed I could
do anything at all, given my lack of qualification for doing
much else. The idea that I would have to get a real job that
might take me away from writing hovered like the prospect
of annihilation. The true source of my anxiety was the possibility of losing the creative freedom and self-determination
that have always been so central to my identity.

And so when I think about Macarthur's professed justifi-
cations for his disastrous criminal venture, one of the things
I feel is a queasy, perverse sympathy—not for what he did, of
course, but for the terror at the loss of his privilege that led
him to do it. Certainly, I find it hard to imagine myself planning a robbery, and less still committing two brutal murders.
But then, I did not have Macarthur's upbringing; my parents
were neither violent nor cold. Despite his insistence otherwise, it seems to me that Macarthur's crimes are embedded
in the deep logic of his privilege.

«

But what is it that I'm doing here? Why do I want to
make so much of Macarthur's early life? The most obvious
answer is that I want his crimes to make sense. I want to

define the terms of the relationship between the murderer and the child—not in order to exonerate the murderer, but to make him add up, to balance his life like an equation. What I want is narrative coherence.

The portrait of Macarthur that emerged in the media in the aftermath of his conviction was that of a calculating psychopath, a man who knew exactly what he wanted and how to get it, and who killed with ruthless logic in pursuit of his aims. He himself did a lot to advance this view of things; in his statement to the Gardaí, quoted in the newspapers, he described his "venture" as a "heartless, cold-blooded operation." And yet there is a sulfurous whiff of madness emanating from the whole affair, a persistent sense that none of it remotely adds up.

Macarthur seemed to understand his actions as proceeding from both an excess of rationality and an acute attack of madness, as though he were at once completely in control of himself and utterly at the mercy of mysterious psychic dynamics. He described the murders to me once as "complete nonsense," which struck me as remarkable. He said this as though he were still cross with himself for some old error of judgment, some flagrant youthful folly that had continued to haunt him into old age. It made me think of Patricia Highsmith's novel *Ripley's Game,* of a moment toward the end of the book in which Ripley looks back on his first killing, the murder of Dickie Greenleaf. "Hotheadedness of youth," he thinks. "Nonsense!"

As the terrible return of some long-repressed childhood trauma, the murders can be forced to make a kind of sense. But isn't this also a little too neat, a little too satisfying? And who is it that I am most interested in letting off the hook: him or me? Am I averting my eyes from the gap between the damage that was done to him and the damage he himself did? And even if my parents had mistreated me, even if my father had bitten me on the hand—either maliciously or accidentally—and I had needed stitches, would this have made me capable of murder?

«

In March, not long before the move to Tenerife, Macarthur received another call from the acquaintance to whom he'd loaned the money. He was in a position to pay a portion of the sum. This enabled Macarthur and Little to go ahead with their Tenerife plan. They flew out, and found a reasonable apartment, which Macarthur paid four months' rent up front to secure. He said nothing to Brenda, or to anyone else, but he had come to see that his circumstances had changed dramatically, and that he could be in serious trouble. They had been there a few weeks when he received a call from his creditor back home. His business was going under, he told Macarthur, and the bank was taking everything. There would be no further installments.

For weeks, Macarthur baked in the dry heat of the Tenerife sun, silently tormented by his situation. His inheritance was almost gone. What remained was held in a trust he had set up with his mother, and he would not see any significant portion of it until she died. He wondered whether perhaps he could find some kind of work at an economic think tank, or as a journalist of some sort. But he was almost thirty-seven years old, and he had never had a job, unless you counted helping out the workers on his parents' farm as a child, or the short time he had spent at the steel plant in California. For all his education, he had no practical training for anything. No profession. What was he going to do? Start a business?

No: he needed money now.

There had in recent months been a number of stories in the news about armed robberies around Ireland; the IRA had been staging post office and bank raids in order to fund their paramilitary campaign. The previous December, Ben Dunne, the owner of the Dunnes supermarket chain, had been abducted from his car by the IRA on the main Dublin-Belfast road and held for seven days until a ransom was paid. Macarthur was very aware of these events, and although he told me that he never formulated any kind of plan while he was in Tenerife, he acknowledged that these robberies were on his mind as he struggled to imagine a way out of what he referred to, in his written confession, as his "obsessive financial situation."

Six weeks after they arrived in Tenerife, Macarthur decided he had to return to Ireland. He says he had no clear idea, at that point, of what he was going to do there, but he knew he wasn't going to solve his money problems lying around on beaches and reading about Humboldt. For once in his life, it was not reflection that was required, but action.

He was not, he told me, in a state of panic at that point. He had by his reckoning about a year's worth of funds left, if he spent more or less wisely. In the meantime, he said, there were some further sums of money owed to him by people back in Dublin; they were smaller sums, he said, but if he were to recoup them it would certainly buy him a little more time.

And so he left Brenda and Colin behind in Tenerife, with sufficient funds to get by for the period he intended to be away. He told Brenda only that he had to leave to settle some pressing financial matter—not what the matter was, or how he proposed to settle it. He assured her that he would return in two or three weeks, and that he would have money with him.

PART THREE

THE CRIMINAL EPISODE

TEN

It is at this point, as he approaches the definitive moment of his life—the thing that cannot be negotiated or reinterpreted or forgotten—that Macarthur's memory becomes partial, slippery. His manner of speech, ordinarily so precise and purposive, becomes hesitant, and a kind of nervous dreaminess takes hold. He is an unreliable narrator at the best of times, but now he is barely a narrator at all.

This is strange, for a man with such extraordinary powers of recollection. Countless times during our conversations, I have interrupted him to remark upon the uncanny accuracy with which he is capable of recalling events from early childhood. He speaks of things that happened long before he was born, and includes details of startling specificity. He is able to tell me, for instance, not just the name of the ship his uncle Jack sailed to the United States on when he first traveled there in the 1930s, but the name of the friend he traveled with, the port they landed in, their time of arrival.

He knows he has an unnaturally vivid and powerful memory, and he is proud of it. He got it from his mother, he says. (In prison, he was a highly valued teammate for table quizzes; if you had Macarthur on your table, you were as good as victorious.) But when it comes to the actions by which his life will always be defined, there is only so much he can tell me. It is as though he is trying to recall a dream from which he has lately awoken, or the plot details of a novel he read a long time ago.

I could never quite decide whether this whole period was really a blank for Macarthur, or whether he was staging a failure of memory because he didn't want to talk about his own premeditation of the crimes. Did he know what he was going to do? He says that he didn't. Not consciously, at any rate. Frankly, he can't say for sure. But something, he tells me, may have been taking form within.

«

On the 8th of July, Macarthur flew back to Dublin. He did not want any friends or acquaintances to know that he was back in the country, so he took a bus straight to Dún Laoghaire, a suburban coastal town just south of the city, and booked himself into a guesthouse. It was a small, pleasant bed-and-breakfast run by an older woman who took minimal notice of her guest. Among the first things he did, he told me, was to call his mother. They hadn't spoken since he'd left for Tenerife, and she was living alone in Mullingar, about thirty miles west of Breemount; he wanted to check in on her, see if she needed anything. She was fine, and there was no need to visit. He told me he never mentioned his financial situation to her, and she herself said later that he never asked her for money; she would have helped him, she said, had she known he was in trouble.

Had Macarthur been planning to murder his mother, as the written notes found after his arrest were often thought to indicate, it surely would have made sense to ask her for money first. As with so many things that have to do with Macarthur's "criminal episode," his own motivations and reasoning seem only hazily delineated in his memory. He is unable to say why he never went to his mother for financial help—or for that matter to his wealthy uncle in California.

"I'm not sure," he told me, when I asked him about it. "Possibly it never occurred to me. Possibly it was inhibition."

I suggested to him that it may have been shame that prevented him asking for help—shame at his profligacy, shame at revealing himself to himself as the sort of person who needs a handout from his mother—but he gently rejected the notion. He himself had loaned many people money, he said, and he had not thought any less of those people for it. He had little more to say on the subject; in his way, he seemed as bewildered by it as I was.

«

After his arrival in Dublin, he made inquiries into some of his outstanding loans, but they came to nothing. A plan was germinating in his mind, taking form under pressure in the darkness.

One day, he took a bus into the city. He passed a sporting goods shop on Parliament Street and stopped to look in the window. His eye was drawn toward a poster advertising forthcoming events. There were listings for clay pigeon shoots at gun clubs around the city and its surrounding areas. Of these he made careful note. Inside the shop, he bought a tweed fisherman's hat. He also bought a crossbow, a short-stocked little weapon with a pistol-style handle. Not having a hunting license, this was the closest he could come, for now, to acquiring a firearm.

He returned to Dún Laoghaire and lay low at the bed-and-breakfast. For the first time in his life, he stopped shaving, and his beard grew fast and thick, making of his own

face an unfamiliar mask. He used a small saw to remove the
end of the crossbow, and used wood filler to build the barrel
back up. He sanded it down and painted it black, so that it
might look plausibly like a gun to a person who did not dare
ask to see it more closely. He had no great faith in it, but he
was growing desperate, and it was all that he had.

«

When Macarthur was arrested, he had in his possession
two books. One was an academic volume called *A Materialist
Theory of Mind*, by the Australian philosopher David Armstrong. The other was the textbook in which his handwritten
notes were secreted, a medical textbook on forensic pathology. These are the things he was reading, it seems, at the
time of the murders. What interests me is the jarring juxta-
position of these two books: one a dry philosophical analysis
of the functions of the mind, the other an encyclopedic guide
to the destruction of the body.

I am succumbing here, of course, to the temptation to
encounter reality as a fiction, to read it as though I were a
critic; but I cannot help thinking that the presence of these
two particular texts suggests a frame for thinking about
Macarthur and his crimes.

Armstrong was known for a theory of mind called "central state materialism," which claimed that mental states—
thoughts and emotions and so on—were in fact physical
states of the brain. His contention was that this idea could
explain consciousness itself. One of the means by which
Armstrong attempted to explain consciousness was what he
referred to as the phenomenon of "autopilot." You're driving
a car on a long journey, and suddenly you become aware that
you have not been aware of what you're doing. You've been

steering the car, changing gears, stopping at intersections, and so on, but you have been totally unaware of all of it. In this way, it's possible for the mental processes, the thinking, to unfold without our conscious experience of them. Consciousness, he argues, is no more or less than "perception or awareness of the state of our own mind," or what he calls a "self-scanning system in the central nervous system." The mind, in such "autopilot" circumstances, does what it does whether we pay attention to it or not.

For a time, I wondered whether this book, and Macarthur's possession of it at the time of his arrest, might somehow serve to explain his actions—or if not to explain them, then to provide a way of thinking about them. The psychiatric professionals who examined him following his arrest, after all, unanimously concluded that he was acting as an "automaton," that he was not fully in control of his actions. Macarthur's defense team were pleased with this consensus, because it prepared the way for them to pursue a plea of "guilty but insane."

This plan was soon undone, however, by the discovery of the handwritten notes between the pages of the second book, the forensic text. The belief that Macarthur was meticulously planning the murder of his own mother apparently removed any grounds for the claim of insanity—as though meticulously planning the murder of one's own mother were the exclusive preserve of the impeccably sane.

Irene Macarthur never said definitively whether she believed her son had been planning to murder her. Perhaps she was genuinely unsure what to think, or perhaps she did not wish to discuss family business in the media. In his RTE radio interview with Irene, David Hanley raised the speculation, based on the discovery of the notes, that she herself was to be his next victim. Her response was strangely detached,

and perfectly composed. The Gardaí, she said, had not given
her any information about the matter, and so it would be
wrong of her to speculate.

"But of course," she said politely, "like other things in
life, everything is possible."

On the internet, I found a copy of the forensic medicine
textbook, a later edition. Its table of contents included: "The
medical aspects of death"; "The appearance of the body after
death"; "Firearm and explosive injuries"; "Immersion and
drowning"; "Injury due to heat, cold, and electricity." Inside,
the various entries were illustrated with horrifyingly graphic
photographs of autopsied bodies—burnings, dismember-
ings, heads blown off by shotgun blasts. The longer I spent
perusing its pages, the more I felt as though I were reading a
clinical report on the fallen condition of humanity.

In a chapter entitled "Regional Injuries," I saw a photograph of a human head, shaven clean, with a large ovoid
depression at the very center of its crown, from which radi-
ated a series of jagged fractures. "Depressed skull fracture,"
read the caption, "with rounded contours, closely replicating
the dimensions of a round-headed hammer." Aside from the
color of the skin, which was white, the image was devoid of
any kind of personalizing detail: no hair, no indication of
gender, no glimpse of facial features. The deceased person
whose skull was depicted here was reduced to a disembodied
wound.

Then, in a section on child physical abuse, I found a reference to the frequency with which bites occur in such situations. Bites to the arms of children, I read, were especially
common.

In a newspaper article from 2002 with the headline
"Macarthur: Outsider Who Never Did a Day's Work," I
found a detail about the days before the murders that I had
not come across anywhere else. The article, published at a

time when Macarthur was up for parole, claimed that he "had a fragile relationship with reality" and that "it is thought he was slipping into a psychotic state as he planned a cold-blooded operation in Ireland to get money." These apparently paradoxical claims—that he was in a state of psychosis; that he was acting in a calculated, cold-blooded manner—struck me as fairly typical of the coverage in the Irish press, in which pretty much anything could be said about Macarthur, regardless of internal contradiction, as long as it made him seem more monstrous and strange. More interesting to me was a story the journalist offered, without attribution, of how Macarthur psyched himself up for armed robbery by walking in and out of hotel lobbies in the city, carrying a brick.

I imagined him finding this brick on the street somewhere, beside a building site perhaps, picking it up, hefting it in his hand. I imagined him holding it conspicuously inside the breast of his tweed jacket. I imagined him walking through the front door of a hotel—the Shelbourne; why not—and nodding curtly at a liveried doorman. I imagined him standing in the lobby a long moment, catching a glimpse of himself in a large mirror on the wall: an uncanny face, with its startled eyes and thickening beard. I imagined him feeling the coarse weight of the brick against the soft skin of his right hand, before turning and walking out. I wondered about the story's credibility, given that it was unattributed and appeared nowhere else that I could find.

A few days later, I was walking along the quays toward the city center. Life was gradually returning to the streets, and I was on my way to work in the library, which had opened again for the first time in many months. As I passed the entrance to the Four Courts, I thought of Macarthur, and I took out my phone and called him, as by then I had done many times. He answered almost immediately. He seemed pleased and a little surprised to hear from me; being constitutionally incapable of small talk, however, he launched straight into asking after the progress of my book—a line of questioning the real point of which I understood to be his own fate.

I told him about the story I had come across in an old newspaper article, about the hotel lobby and the brick, and asked him whether it was true. He had not been aware of the article but seemed to know immediately what I was talking about, and asked me who the source was. The article didn't quote any source, I told him. Someone with inside information, he said, must have tipped the journalist off anonymously.

"So it's true, then? This is something you really did? The brick, the hotel lobby?"

"No, it's a complete fabrication."

"Then why would you say that the source for it was someone with inside information?"

"Because it was something I had been saying at the time. It was a joke. To illustrate a point."

"What point was it was illustrating?"

"Well, that's a little too complex to go into," he said, and I let the matter go.

This was a frequent gesture of Macarthur's, perhaps even an obsessive one. Things that were difficult to account for he very often attempted to explain away as jokes—as pranks, or games. The attempt to explain the notes found inside the forensic medicine textbook, for instance, as part of the whole *Kind Hearts and Coronets*–rewriting parlor game with his friends. If he thought he could have gotten away with explaining the deaths of Bridie Gargan and Donal Dunne as the result of a misjudged jape, I suspected he might have given it a go.

«

As the months passed, Macarthur began to feel more comfortable in my presence, and I came to see that, in a wary sort of fashion, he liked me. He was surprisingly earnest about this, saying that he held me "in very high regard" and that he could see that I had "a first-rate intelligence," and even that I was "a very decent fellow."

He saw me as a worthy interlocutor. It sometimes seemed to me, in fact, that I was precisely the kind of person—a person who made a living, for better or worse, through thinking and writing—he himself, as a younger man, might have wanted to become, had he not become a murderer.

One day he was making a passing reference to his time in prison, when he paused and asked me not to mention this particular story in my book. He was wary, he said, of doing anything to irritate or embarrass the prison authorities. But if I wanted to hear more about his years behind bars, he said, he would be happy to speak to me about it on what he called a "friendly basis," by which I understood him to mean off the record.

"We may even *become* friends," he said then, with a slightly nervous laugh. "If you would consider the possibility."

"Yes," I said, with a nervous laugh of my own. It was an insufficient response, I realized, but it was as much as I could manage. I had certainly considered the possibility that a measure of ease, and even a kind of intimacy, might eventually enter into our exchanges. I knew that he was lonely, and that he was flattered and intrigued by my interest in him.

Until that point, I couldn't quite tell whether what appealed to him about me was the prospect of conversation alone, or of my turning those conversations into a piece of writing about him. He had, as I had suspected, been approached by writers in the past, but these had tended to be crime writers and tabloid journalists, people whose interest in him he saw as puerile and exploitative. (Some of these journalists had, he said, offered him extraordinarily large sums of money to speak to them, six-figure sums. He had not, he told me, been tempted even for a moment: for one thing, he would have been sent directly back to prison for profiting from his crimes, and for another, he no longer needed any money, ironically enough, because the state provided for his needs.)

In any case, I was aware of the risk of his coming to think of me as a friend. And this possibility was unnerving to me for two reasons. The first was simple enough: I had no wish to be friends with a man who had murdered people, no matter how long ago this had happened, and no matter what stance he took toward it now. The second was slightly more complicated. I felt uneasy about the degree to which I was already benefiting from Macarthur's openness, and I had no desire to manipulate him by seeming to be his friend.

I had reminded him a number of times in our first few meetings that, although I would respect his wishes that I not write about certain things, and that the last thing I wanted was for him to wind up back in prison as a result of my book, I could not offer him any reassurance that he would *like* what I ended up writing. Chances were, I said, that he would feel wrong-footed or even betrayed by what I wrote, because what I wrote would after all be my view of him, and by no means an exoneration or apologia. He seemed entirely at peace with this prospect. He had seen and done worse things in his time, I supposed, than an unfavorable portrayal in a work of literary nonfiction. He could hardly have been hoping for a favorable portrait, I felt, given that he was, in the final analysis, a murderer. In any case, he continued to talk.

In our early conversations, I had surprised myself by the uncharacteristically professional approach I was taking. I had sat at his little frosted glass table, taking note in my notebook of everything he said, interjecting at certain points with judicious questions, seeking clarification of timelines and so on. At first, it had seemed to me that I was doing this because I wanted to access the truth, or at least his version of it, his narrative. But I realized quickly enough that this rigidly professional approach—the notebook and pen, the voice recorder, the strangely formal line of questioning—was in fact an elaborate defense against the possibility that he might warm to me as a human being. It took a little while longer to realize that it was also, and perhaps more pressingly, a defense against the possibility that I might warm to him.

As the weeks and months progressed, we spoke fairly regularly on the phone. Often I would call him, but just as often it would be he who called me. Hardly anyone else, in fact, ever called me out of the blue; he tended to call in the evenings, so that if I felt my phone buzz with an incoming call in my pocket anytime after dinner, I could always be reasonably certain it was either my father or Malcolm Macarthur. He would always have some reason for calling—often to revise, or to strike from the record entirely, some remark he had made the last time we spoke. But I sometimes suspected that these were just pretexts for getting a monologue going, for talking about a film he had seen years ago, or for delving into some matter of philosophical or scientific interest.

One evening, in the long days between Christmas and New Year's, he called me to tell me about an article he'd read in the paper. He thought I'd be interested to hear, he said, that a German literary scholar claimed to have discovered the exact date on which Joyce had set *Finnegans Wake*. I was interested to hear this, I said, although mostly I was interested in the fact of his telling me about it.

Not long after that, he called one evening to say that he'd

been discussing me with his probation officer. He wanted to prepare her, he said, for the fact that my book would be coming, and that he'd been talking to me for it.

"She's a very reasonable person," he said. "Swedish, luckily, not Irish. Very practical people, the Swedes."

He was always talking about this probation officer. He had great admiration for her, and his admiration was clearly bound up with her being from Sweden, a nation he associated with rationality and fair-mindedness.

"I told her," he said, "that it was very important that this whole thing was dealt with by a person such as yourself. A serious person. A person with very high *intellectual standards*."

I said I was glad to be thought of in this way, as a person with high intellectual standards, although in truth I wasn't sure what it meant.

And then he said: "You know, you have become a very important person in my life."

"And vice versa," I said. "As I'm sure you're aware."

He raised once again, tentatively and almost shyly, the prospect of our association evolving into a friendship. I said, by way of evasion, that he should defer any decision on that until my book came out.

One evening, I had just put my three-year-old daughter in her pajamas and brushed her teeth, and we were lounging on her bed for a while before I read her story. I had caved to her persistent demands and given her my phone to look at, and I was reading a book. She liked to look through the photos and videos on my phone, probably because most of them were of her. She was swiping with practiced ease, gazing fondly at images of her slightly younger self, when I heard the buzz of an incoming call. I glanced over at the phone in her hands, and I saw the word "Macarthur" on its screen, and I felt a wave of dread pass through me. I put out my hand for the phone, saying that I would fix it for her. I let it ring out, and at length his name disappeared from the display; the photo my daughter had been looking at rematerialized, a photo of her and her little dog hugging on the couch. I put the phone on silent and pocketed it, telling her it was time to read her story. All the rest of that evening, I couldn't get it out of my head: his name on the screen, the unsettling thrum of the phone in her little hands.

«

The Saturday after he arrived back in Ireland, in July 1982, Macarthur decided to take a bus to Swords, a coastal suburb to the north of the city. One of the clay pigeon shoots he'd seen advertised at the sporting goods shop was taking place at the local gun club that afternoon, and it had presumably occurred to him that it might be a likely place to acquire a shotgun. He did not himself participate in the event. According to one gun club member, who took note of his strange manner and unusual clothing, he spent most of the afternoon sitting alone on a bench, watching the shooting. He had an overnight bag with him, in which he carried the crossbow fashioned into the crude likeness of a handgun, along with a shovel and a hammer.

Another gun club member, a local doctor, saw Macarthur loitering near his car. He didn't much care for the look of him—the beard, the fisherman's hat, the intense stare. He locked his car, a thing he would not ordinarily have done. The doctor remarked on what a fine day it was and asked Macarthur whether he himself was interested in shooting. He replied that he was, that he had often taken part in hunts and clay pigeon shoots as a younger man. His accent must have gone some way toward allaying suspicion, but he was giving off powerfully strange vibes, and for the rest of the afternoon, the doctor kept an eye on him. He noted that he was standing for unusually long periods of time, staring intently, and for no obvious reason, at the scoreboard.

Some days later, reporting this suspicious character to the Gardaí, the doctor remarked that he had "a vacant look about him, and he moved slowly when walking." He noted, too, that although the man was wearing a pair of spectacles, he angled his head resolutely downward, so that he was at all times peering out over the top of them like a stern schoolmaster. It was clear, he said, that he was not able to see with these glasses, and that his reasons for wearing them were at the very least somewhat eccentric.

The hat, the glasses, the beard. The hammer, the little shovel, the crossbow. There is no clear demarcation here between the ridiculous and the sinister. I imagine it would have been difficult to know whether to take Macarthur as a joke or a threat. He spent the entire rest of the day at the shoot, arousing unease and suspicion, and perhaps some amusement, but encountered no opportunity to take a gun. Over the following week or so, he attended other clay pigeon shoots—at Ashbourne in Meath, and Ardee in Co. Louth. There may have been others, too, he says, though he can't be sure.

I asked Macarthur whether, at this point, he had formulated his plan to commit armed robbery.

"Something must have been going on in my head," he said. "I must have been processing something. But I can't explain it. It may have been, with these shoots, that with each successive attendance, I was becoming a bit more interested in the idea."

I didn't know what to make of this, this claim that he didn't quite know what he was doing—or that he did know, but that he was not fully conscious of knowing. On the one hand, it didn't seem credible that, without having a clear sense of why he was doing so, he would travel to a gun club in Co. Dublin, and then to another in Co. Meath, and then yet another in Co. Louth. But on the other hand, why would he lie about such a thing? It hardly mattered much, in the end, when exactly it was that he formulated a plan to commit armed robbery—whether he had it all worked out in his mind before he started showing up at the clay pigeon shoots, or even before he went to Tenerife with Brenda and Colin. It didn't change the fact of what he had done, or the magnitude of his guilt.

The official version of the story—the story that was put together by detectives, and endlessly repeated in the media—followed a simple trajectory: Macarthur's funds were running low, and so he decided to rob a bank, and for this he needed a gun and a car. This story makes perfect sense, in its way. It encapsulates the brutal, remorseless logic of Macarthur's crimes. I also think it happens to be true. And yet I also believe that Macarthur is not lying when he says he is unsure when he began to formulate his plan, that he doesn't know what he was thinking as he sat on that bench watching the clay pigeon shoot. The law, by its nature, privileges narratives in which people have clear motivations, in whose service they act in comprehensible ways. The pursuit of truth, in a legal sense, is necessarily reductive. It is possible that Macarthur both did and did not know what he was doing.

There was a great deal of walking in this time, a great deal of standing around. He walked and he walked, and when he got to where he was going, or was simply tired of walking, he stood. He stood around at the clay pigeon shoots. He walked around the city. He stood at corners. He sat on benches, in parks. He walked so much, his feet began to develop sores. He was wearing heavy brogues, ill-suited to the heat of the summer and to the endless traipsing, the endless standing.

There is a sense, here, of a kind of aimless urgency. This is a man who knows he is going to do something drastic but

has no clear sense of how he might go about it. He knows by
now that he is going to rob a bank, and that he needs a gun
and a car to do so. But how does one get a gun? An ordinary
criminal will typically hire a gun from a contact, a weapon
that cannot be traced back to them. Macarthur didn't know
any ordinary criminals; he had never knowingly encountered
a person who had used a gun for anything other than shooting pheasants and foxes. In a way, it stood to reason that
he would take the clay pigeon shooting route to sourcing a
weapon, and that when that didn't work out, he would buy
a copy of the *Farmers Journal* at a newsstand near the guesthouse in Dún Laoghaire and go through the classified ads.
The route that he followed toward murder was determined
by a cartography of class.

«

When he saw the ad, he knew what he was going to
do. A farmer in Edenderry, about forty miles west of Dublin, was advertising a shotgun for sale. His name was Donal
Dunne. He was looking for a thousand pounds, too high a
price for Macarthur even to consider forking out. But that
was not an insurmountable obstacle. He called the number listed. Dunne's sister Carmel answered the phone. He
announced himself as a Mr. Ryan.

"It's for you, Donal," she said.

The conversation was brief. Dunne suggested that this
Mr. Ryan come to Edenderry the following evening, take a
look at the gun, try it out if he needed to.

Macarthur must have seen then the path that lay ahead.
Once he was holding the loaded weapon, he would have no
need to pay the farmer. An elegant solution, in its way: an
armed robbery in which the means and the end were one and
the same.

Dunne gave him directions to his house, and he jotted them down. He knew he needed to get his hands on a car by the following evening—to get to Offaly, and to get back to Dublin, having stolen the shotgun, and to pull off the armed robbery he was planning. And he needed a car that could not be connected to himself, or to anyone he knew. Thus began the "criminal episode."

«

At some point during this interlude, Macarthur did something that reveals a higher level of calculation and premeditation than he himself might want to suggest: he went to a bank in Dún Laoghaire and opened an account under a false name, John Eustace. He had previously taken note of an abandoned building not far from the guesthouse where he was staying, and he gave this address as his own. These are the actions, it seems to me, of a man who knew exactly what he was doing, and what he was going to do.

On Capel Street, in a large hardware store, he bought a smallish shovel and a large lump hammer. "I wanted this hammer," explained Macarthur in his written statement, "to intimidate somebody, to get a car, to travel down the country to get a gun, because I had no transport." The shovel, he continued, was a necessary precaution. "My attitude was that I wanted this venture to succeed, and if by chance I did kill anybody in this venture, I would use the shovel to dispose of the body."

I have always found the language here chilling. *I wanted this hammer to intimidate somebody. I wanted this venture to succeed.* It encapsulates the psychological paradox of the whole affair: ruthless logic in service of a deeper madness. What we have here is a man who knows exactly what he is doing; and yet this is a man, just as clearly, who has absolutely no

idea what he is playing at. The shovel seems a good example.
I have seen a photograph of this shovel, and it's obvious even
to a layman like myself that a person would struggle long
and hard to dig even a smallish hole with it, let alone a pit
deep enough to contain a body that would never be found. It
is essentially a gardening tool. Macarthur is by no means a
stupid man, but he seems to me to be exhibiting here, as elsewhere, the peculiar foolishness of the intellectual. If there is
such a thing as a criminal dilettante, this is what he is.

I am reminded here of Tony Hickey, a former assistant commissioner of the Gardaí, whose work as a detective
on the Macarthur case was instrumental in leading to his
arrest. In one of my conversations with Hickey, he talked me
through the timeline of the events. He had been speaking of
Macarthur's heist plan, its chaotic execution, its disastrous
aftermath.

"It was," he said, shaking his head with amused contempt, "a frenzy of tomfoolery."

ELEVEN

On July 22, the day after Macarthur spoke to Donal Dunne on the phone, Dublin was in the middle of a heat wave. The city, on such days, assumes an air of festive indolence. Everything opens out, becomes looser and more fluid. Men in the inner city swagger abroad unclothed from the waist up, their shirts slung casually across a shoulder, their backs reddening in the sun's heat. People drink beer on benches, in parks, on the banks of the canal. There is the sound of small radios turned up full blast, a tinny blare of reggae and other musical styles appropriate to the temperature.

Macarthur must have looked bizarre in such a setting, this patrician oddball with his beard and his rounded spectacles. The heavy military sweater, the fisherman's hat, low over the brow. The hat—and this was something he made a point of mentioning, for whatever reason, in his statement—had an orange feather in the side of it. This getup he referred to as his "disguise outfit." He must have looked as though he had dressed to go hunting. (Later, Macarthur insisted to me that the fisherman's hat was never intended as a disguise; before he'd left Tenerife, he said, he'd gotten slightly sunburned on his forehead, and the fisherman's hat was to protect against exacerbating the sunburn in the heat wave.)

He'd taken a bus from Dún Laoghaire into the city center. The bus stopped at the quays, and when he got off, he stood for fifteen minutes or so, watching the dull stagnant water of the Liffey.

"I stood there at the wall," he said in his statement, "admiring a sort of floating wooden house which was on the river. I was particularly admiring two lads who were sitting on two chairs on this barge."

He carried with him a blue overnight bag he'd brought from Tenerife. In it was the hammer, the retooled crossbow. The shovel was too large to fit in the bag, so he carried it separately, wrapped tightly in a black plastic sack. So that the sharp corners of the shovel would not tear the wrapping, he had covered them thickly with masking tape. (I can't but think, as I write this, of this man's dismal living room, some forty years later, with its television and bookshelves wrapped tightly in black plastic bags, taped together. The bizarre meticulousness. And I can't but wonder what, if anything, this business of wrapping things in black plastic is all about.)

Walking along the river toward the park, he stopped into a small shop on the quays and bought an orange.

When he got to the park, he walked along its broad central thoroughfare. He walked past young couples, past people walking their dogs, past families with young children on their way to the zoo. He would not, I imagine, have been looking just yet for a car, for a victim, this being the busiest part of the park, closest to the city center.

When he got to the Wellington Monument, he stopped and put down his bag. He peeled the orange and ate it unhurriedly. Did he pause to look at the monument? I believe Macarthur when he says he doesn't remember such things, that his prodigious faculties of recall fail him when it comes to these strange days, and the terrible acts at their center. But if I had to guess, which I do not, I would say that he did pause, and that he did think about its significance, there in that place.

There's a famous quote about Wellington's Irish origins that is often attributed to the duke himself, but which was in fact a joke made in a speech by Daniel O'Connell, leader of the movement for Catholic emancipation in the nineteenth century: "To be sure, he was born in Ireland, but being born in a stable does not make a man a horse."

I can't resist the symbolism of the scene: Macarthur pausing to eat his orange, the monument rearing up behind him as he does so, an obelisk as toweringly intransigent as history itself. Around the granite base of the 203-foot-tall structure is a series of plaques, depicting Wellington's various military glories—the Indian Wars, the Battle of Waterloo— supposedly cast from cannons captured from Napoleon's defeated army.

I pass the monument several times a week—out on a run, walking the dog, bringing my children to play in the park. And when I do, I see him there, in his bad disguise, his heavy clothes, perched on the black iron railings running alongside the footpath. I see him peeling the orange. I see him eating each segment slowly and deliberately, an absent look in his eyes. Thinking about what he is about to do.

«

Macarthur walked on. Past the tea rooms, past the cricket club. Past the entrance to the zoo, and the children giddy with excitement for the animals they would see. He walked alongside the jogging track. He took his time. And as he walked, he scanned the area for opportunity. He checked out some parked cars; none of these were, as he would later put it, "easy prey."

He passed the polo grounds, and the Papal Cross, and
Áras an Uachtaráin, once the residence of the viceroy and
now the home of the Irish president.

And then, just a little farther along, near the entrance
to the US ambassador's residence, he saw a small silver car, a
Renault 4, parked beside a row of trees, its door wide open.
This was it: the car he would take to Edenderry to get the
gun, the car he would use to do the heist. Easy prey. In the
long grass beside the open door was a young woman, lying
on her back, basking in the heat of the afternoon sun.

«

Bridie, that was her name. Bridget Gargan, but everyone
called her Bridie. She was twenty-seven. She was a nurse,
and she worked in St. James's Hospital just across the river.
She lived at the far side of the park, in an apartment building
in Castleknock. She had been on her way home through the
park after a long shift when she decided, on a whim, to stop
the car and sunbathe awhile, because the day was so perfect,
so lovely and warm. I imagine her feeling free and at ease,
the way you feel on a summer day when work is finished, and
you are young, and the world seems open, alive with possibility and pleasure.

Macarthur looked around and saw that there was no
one else nearby. He bent to prop the shovel against a tree.
He removed the imitation gun from his bag, and he made
his approach. He kept low to the ground, walking at a low
crouch.

He stood over the woman and pointed the weapon at
her, and she looked at him. He told her to get into the car.

"Is this for real?" she said.

"Yes," he said, "it is."

She asked him if she could put her clothes back on before she got in the car. He told her that she could, and she reached for her blouse and pulled it on, buttoning it hurriedly.

He noted, in his statement, that she seemed calm. He noted, too, that she was not wearing a bra.

He made a gesture with the weapon, motioning her toward the back seat of the car. Like a man with a gun in a film. He told her that he was only interested in the car, that she had nothing to worry about. That was all he wanted, just the car. But unfortunately he was going to have to tie her up. And when he said this, she panicked, and she would not lie down. And because of this, Macarthur himself panicked. At least he says that he panicked, that he was afraid that she would draw attention to them. Afraid that she would scream, and make a scene. This, he believed, should not be a scene.

«

There is no telling what happened. I don't mean this in the sense that we don't know what happened. We do know, more or less. We know that he hit her in the head with the hammer, many times and with tremendous force, and that although she didn't die there in the car, in his presence, she did die, four days later, from the injuries he inflicted.

We know that Paddy Byrne, a groundskeeper in the gardens of the ambassador's residence, noticed what was happening in the car. Byrne saw through the rear windshield the first blows, and thought that what he was looking at was a man hitting a woman with his fist. He saw him clutching her hair, holding her like that as he hit her head. He jumped a low wall and ran toward the car, and when he got there, he saw Macarthur sitting in the driver seat of the car, calmly reading *The Irish Times*. Then he saw Bridie Gargan in the back seat, partially covered by the pages of the newspaper Macarthur had placed over her in an attempt to hide her wounded body. We know that Byrne thumped on the roof of the car with his fist, and that Macarthur thrust aside the newspaper and pointed his prop gun at him through the window of the car and told him to keep his distance, and that Byrne, who had no idea the gun was fake, made a lunge at Macarthur and grabbed at the arm that was holding the gun, and that Macarthur then got out of the car and pointed the gun at his face, and that Byrne stepped back and saw Bridie starting to slip down sideways, the dark blood matted in her hair, saw that she was barely conscious and yet still attempting to speak. According to Byrne, Macarthur told him to "back off, or I'll put a bullet in you." We know that Macarthur kept moving toward him with the fake gun, and that Byrne stepped backward until he stumbled into a ditch at the perimeter of the embassy, and that Macarthur went back then to the car, and that he drove off, fast, along the jogging track that ran parallel to Chesterfield Avenue.

But there is also no telling what happened in the sense that it is, in some real and irreducible way, impossible to tell. How can I tell it? I wasn't there. And even if I had been there, could I tell it even then? Bridie Gargan's death was hers alone, and it would be obscene to attempt to take possession of it by imagining myself into her thoughts in those final moments.

I mean that there is no right way of telling it. How could there be? All I have is the testimony of a man whose words I can't take as truth, even if he believes them himself.

Macarthur sped through the park in the little Renault. There was a near miss with an ambulance coming in the opposite direction. He was having trouble with the unfamiliar transmission, and the engine emitted a wretched howl as he floored it in second gear.

As the ambulance swerved to avoid being hit by the Renault, its driver took note of the blood-spattered side window, and of the passenger in the rear, holding her head in her bloodied hands. He noted, too, on the windshield, a parking permit for St. James's Hospital, and assumed that what he was seeing was a doctor taking a badly injured patient to the casualty ward. By the time the ambulance turned around and caught up with the Renault, Macarthur had driven out of the park, and he was stuck now in late-afternoon traffic. The ambulance driver motioned as he passed for Macarthur to follow him. And so it was that Macarthur was granted a sudden reprieve from his situation; he sped through the streets after the ambulance, its lights and sirens blaring, a motorcade of murderer and victim.

A detail I find particularly hard to contemplate: As they drove, Bridie Gargan managed to signal out the window to a number of other drivers. They saw her, these drivers, horribly wounded and bleeding and distressed. As one newspaper report put it, these drivers "saw her dying effort but made no attempt to interfere when they saw the ambulance in front of the car."

Macarthur followed the ambulance into the grounds of St. James's Hospital. As its driver turned off for the casualty ward, Macarthur did a swift U-turn and went back the way he had come. He started to head toward the city center, but it quickly became clear to him that the afternoon was not going to work out as he had intended. He needed to extricate himself from the situation he had created, and he needed to do it immediately. The woman in the back was in a very bad way. She was alive, but he must have known that her injuries were very serious. And so he pulled the stolen car into a narrow lane. He got out, and he closed the door behind him—on Bridie Gargan, and on the hammer he had beaten her with.

«

One afternoon, a few weeks after I first met Macarthur, we were speaking in general terms about the aspects of his crimes he felt had been misreported and misinterpreted, when he began to speak about the murder of Bridie Gargan. He brought it up almost out of the blue, and I was caught a little off guard by his talking of it so openly. Although the murders were the sole reason for our conversations, he had never spoken directly about the killing itself; he had warned me, from our first conversation, that he might not ever speak of it. It had been by no means clear until that moment that he ever would.

It was not a sadistic, motiveless attack, he told me. He spoke slowly, his voice quiet and tentative. He had expected to take the car easily, he said. It was possible that she didn't take him seriously, because he was not threatening in demeanor. She asked whether it was a joke, or something along those lines, and when he made it clear that it was not, she asked to get her possessions. And instead of getting them for her, he invited her to get them herself, and he couldn't get her out of the car. That, he said, was the triggering mechanism. This happened in the middle of the park. He couldn't see anyone. If it had been a built-up area, he said, he probably would have disappeared.

He paused a moment, and when he spoke again his voice was lower still. The blows were to subdue, he said. To subdue, and to extract. It was a terrible word to use, he said, but the blows were *calibrated* to knock out.

There was a short silence, during which Macarthur

remained perfectly still, leaning against the windowsill that was his frequent perch, gazing downward at his shoes. His feet were crossed at the ankles, in a manner that might have seemed casual, were he not so clearly discomfited by what he was saying, or by having to say it. It had been very wet all that afternoon, and as he spoke droplets darted fitfully down the length of the glass behind him.

The blows, he said, were not intended. His words trailed off, their meaning hovering irresolutely in the darkening room.

I asked him whether he was trying to say that the blows he dealt Bridie Gargan were not intended to kill her.

He seemed lost, as though he was not sure what he was trying to say, or whether anything could be said at all. He said, at length, the word *no*. He said, more quietly still, the words *not to*. Because the blows did not have the desired effect, he said, they were repeated. Those were his words: *they were repeated*. And when a small amount of blood appeared, he said, he stopped, because he was horrified.

There was another silence of almost intolerable length, during which I forced myself not to interject. His expression was difficult to judge, because as always he was wearing a medical mask, but his eyes looked suddenly tired, as though something in him had gone momentarily slack. He tapped the sole of his leather brogue against the laminate wood of the floor, his hands gripping the windowsill as he leaned against it. He continued tapping for a while, a stately and pensive legato.

All at once then he seemed to rally his energies and began to speak again, more animatedly now. He told me how he struggled with the gardener, how the ambulance appeared as he drove out of the park, how he pulled the car into the lane near the hospital. Before he got out of the car, he said, he turned around and was relieved to see that she was sitting up, and that she seemed relatively unharmed. She was not exhibiting any distress, he said. And then he told me that he spoke to her, one final time, and that he told her that help would arrive shortly.

These words, *help will arrive shortly,* he pronounced with a kind of breathy, pleading precision. And as he did so, I felt a crawling sadness in the flesh of my neck and shoulders, a compound horror and pity. The phrase was absurdly officious, as though even when faced with the dire consequences of his own savage irrationality, he was maintaining a performance of sensible authority, of what he had called, in one of our previous conversations, *a good balance of responsiveness and control.* It was possible that he had erased the memory of her injuries from his mind, and it was possible that he was straightforwardly lying to me, but it was not possible that, in the minutes after he battered her skull with a lump hammer, Bridie exhibited no distress.

He said then that the death was caused by something called "*contrecoup,*" which was, he explained, an injury that affected the side of the brain opposite from that on which an impact has occurred. It was the brain moving inside the skull, that is to say, rather than the blows themselves that had caused the death. (This was how he put it, avoiding the use of the possessive pronoun: *the brain, the skull, the death.*) If your brain moves very rapidly, he explained, it can be damaged by the bone surrounding it. That was the official cause of the death, he said, which happened four days later.

His use of arcane medical terminology seemed to me to be both profoundly strange and entirely characteristic. I wondered whether he had made a point of telling me this because he imagined that it somehow lessened his culpability, that it was not, technically speaking, his hitting her repeatedly in the head that had killed her—his clutching a fistful of her hair in one hand as he dealt blows of the hammer with the other—but the resulting impact of her brain against the side of her own skull.

I didn't think he could consciously have been trying to convince me of this, but it occurred to me that he may unconsciously have been trying to convince himself, or to already have done so, long ago. And what about the language itself, the medical terminology, which he wielded like a diagnosing neurologist? Was he retreating into the comfort zone of science, a technical language in which he could talk about a thing too horrible to be otherwise expressed, a thing which he himself had done, and would always have done, no matter what language he used to speak of it? As unsettling as I found the use of this language, I understood that this was the only means by which he could speak, in that moment, of what he had done.

«

Macarthur ran. He ran away from the abandoned car, with its dying owner, and out onto the South Circular Road. He kept running, in his fisherman's hat and his thick wool sweater, and the day was still hot, and he was sweating, and his breathing was heavy. He was in the grip of a terrible panic now. I cannot say with any confidence whether he was panicked because of what he had done to Bridie Gargan, or because of the likely consequences, but my sense of it is that the latter was at that point more a concern than the former. He saw that his sweater was stained with her blood, and so he pulled it off quickly over his head, and the hat came off, too, and he ran up another quiet laneway, and he took the garments that had been stained with the blood of the woman he had beaten, and then he dumped them, too, balling them up and shoving them under some wire fencing into an empty lot, a waste ground.

Back on the South Circular, he tried to flag down a bus to take him out of there, anywhere out of the city, but had no luck. The police would be searching for him, he knew. The gardener would have phoned them by now. He kept running, his brogues slapping against the concrete, his feet already sore from the walking he had done in previous days.

He passed an open door, and he went through it, into the house. If the police were after him, it was surely better to be off the street. He looked around. There were leaflets every-where, brochures. He was in a travel agency.

Sweating still, struggling to catch his breath, he asked the woman behind the counter if she would be good enough to fetch him some water. She went in the back and returned with a glass of tap water. He knocked it back and asked for another. She obliged. He drank it and requested a third. He had been running, he said, by way of explanation. Thirsty work, running in this heat. Again, she refilled the glass, and again he drank. The woman took him in—the beard, the slacks, the leather brogues. The odd, hyper-refined manner of speech.

He felt it would be unwise to go back out onto the street. He cast about for something to say to this woman, some-thing to justify, even momentarily, his presence here.

"Do you happen to be an agent for the Magic Bus?" he asked.

The Magic Bus was a bus tour. You got on in the city center, and it took you to some mystery destination—to the mountains, the sea, maybe farther afield. Usually there was a pub involved. You went wherever the Magic Bus took you.

The Magic Bus, she said, had been discontinued some years back.

He asked her to call him a taxi. She didn't care for his tone. He could get a bus right outside on the street, she said. He handed the glass back to her and walked out. The woman stood there watching him a moment, and then took the glass into the back and washed it.

«

Macarthur got off the bus in Finglas, the working-class North Dublin suburb where Brenda Little had grown up. He had no particular reason for being there, other than that the first bus that had come along happened to be going in that direction. He found a shop and bought a three-pack of disposable razors. He went into the nearest pub and headed straight for the toilets, where he began to shave off his beard. There was no hot water, and he had no shaving soap. People came in and out of the toilets as he worked away at the beard. Remarks were made. It took a long time to shave, and the result was imperfect.

Was his face visibly bleeding when he exited? I don't know, but it seems hard to imagine that he shaved off a full beard without soap or hot water and managed not to shed any of his own blood.

He emerged from the toilets, and went to the bar and ordered a sparkling water. There was a pay phone in the back. He got some change at the bar and called a taxi. He drank his water, and he waited.

«

At around this time, a thirteen-year-old boy was walking home from the nearby sports trophy shop where he worked, and he passed the stolen Renault in the lane where Macarthur had abandoned it. He saw, first, the rear passenger window with its drying spatters of blood, and then Bridie Gargan, laid across the back seat, where Macarthur had left her earlier that evening. (Was this what he had meant in telling her that help was on its way? That somebody, eventually, would find her?) Her hair was slick with blood, the boy later told detectives, and she kept pushing it back with her hand. He ran back to the trophy shop and announced what he had just seen. The paramedics came, and then the Gardaí, and within a short time Bridie Gargan was in hospital, being kept alive by a machine.

«

When the taxi came, Macarthur told the driver to take him back into the city. When he got there, he changed his mind and asked to continue on to Dún Laoghaire. He got out at the ferry terminal, a short walk from the guesthouse. He couldn't stay there much longer, he knew. He would have to find some other lodgings while he hid out, and decided what he was going to do next.

When he got to the guesthouse, he went to his room and inspected himself in the mirror. A quantity of the woman's blood had stained the back of his shirt. He changed into fresh clothes. He put the shirt and trousers in a bag and slipped again out of the guesthouse. It was evening now, the air still warm. People strolling, eating ice cream from a nearby van, enjoying the fading glory of the day. The smell of the ocean, sharp and brackish. He walked downhill to the water, his bloody clothes in a bag. He walked the length of the long East Pier, and when he got to the far end, he flung his garments, stained with the traces of his violence, into the Irish Sea. They floated awhile, drifting out on the tide, before sinking beneath the surface. Then he threw the imitation gun into the water, too, flinging it as far out as he could.

«

According to interviews the Gargan family gave to the media after Macarthur's conviction, Bridie had been planning to go home to Meath that weekend. Her parents, Vincent and Bridget, were adding a new bathroom to the farmhouse where they had raised Bridie and her ten siblings, and she was helping them with it. It was she, rather than any of her brothers, who handled the DIY jobs in the house. Her parents had once hired a team of carpet layers to carpet one of the rooms. Bridie had watched them doing the job—rolling, cutting, fitting, stapling—and when they left, she told them that if those men could do it, she could do it too. Since then, she'd done much of what needed to be done around the house. She laid the carpets, put up wallpaper, painted the walls and the skirting boards. She had been working on the shower unit in their new bathroom and was hoping to finish it that weekend.

Vincent Gargan was out milking cows when a guard from the local station arrived at the farm. The guard asked him whether Bridie's car was a Renault, and he said that it was. The guard read out some letters and numbers to him, and asked whether these letters and numbers were the registration of Bridie's car, but he didn't know. They went into the house and checked with Bridget, and she said that yes, this was her daughter's car. The guard told them that the car had been found abandoned in a lane in South Dublin, with a woman in the rear seat who had been seriously injured in an aggravated assault.

Vincent and one of his sons, Philip, drove to Dublin, but when they showed up at the hospital Bridie was in surgery. They sat in a waiting room, hoping and dreading to hear more, until a detective came in and told them that yes, the woman undergoing surgery was definitely their daughter.

Later, when he was interviewed by the Gardaí, her father

said that he had been out drawing hay at the exact time she was attacked. It was a beautiful evening, he told them, warm and clear and with a fine golden light in the air. It could hardly be borne, he said, to think that while he was working the field and enjoying the waning warmth of the day, some bastard was killing his daughter with a hammer in the park.

"Everywhere there are memories," he later told a reporter, "the reminders that a link in the family chain has been broken and cannot be re-forged. All over the house are the pictures which include her. We will always remember the way she would organise the household for going to weddings or other events, even getting our clothes prepared for us. I often wonder if there'll ever be a day again—if there'll ever be fifteen minutes that pass without the whole thing coming into our minds, if we'll laugh heartily, or ever tell a good yarn again."

She was, at the time, three months from the end of an eighteen-month midwifery course at Richmond Hospital—the same hospital, in fact, where she died of her injuries.

The Gargans were a political family, grassroots Fianna Fáil people. Vincent was director of elections and party council chair for their area. In recent years, Bridie herself had gotten involved; she and her sister Mary, in fact, were the only women in the area to have any kind of active political role. On Friday evenings, she would finish work and drive home for the weekend; she'd sit down for a late dinner with everyone, and someone would bring up politics, and they would all go at it, laughing and squabbling fondly. There was a lot to talk about that year, with a new government, led by the Taoiseach, Charles Haughey, and its various scrapes and scandals.

«

I am wary of going further here; in fact I may already have gone too far. Let me try to explain.

The moral imperative in contemporary writing about crime is that of centering the victims. The thinking is that, for too long, the genre has focused on the figure of the killer, ignoring the irreducible selfhood of the victims, who are rarely presented as anything more than pasteboard figures, blank masks of innocence, suffering, and horror. We learn next to nothing of their childhoods, their families, their successes and failures, their friends and lovers.

And so a writer who wants to produce something more than mere exploitation is under an ethical obligation to tell the story of the victims. They must not be reduced to a series of disembodied wounds, like images in a forensic pathology textbook. They must have names and faces. They must have stories. It was, in this sense, my intention to give Bridie Gargan and Donal Dunne a faithful portrayal in these pages.

And yet, the more I try this, the more wrong it feels. The story I am telling is about Malcolm Macarthur, and Bridie Gargan and Donal Dunne had nothing to do with him other than the grave misfortune of their encountering him during his criminal spree. They were not the victims of a serial killer, selected on the basis of some or other aspect of their identity. Their deaths were, in a deep and crucial sense, a violent aberration from the context of their lives.

Writing about Macarthur himself is fraught in its own way. My relationship with him is, after all, an inherently extractive one, as though I were a prospector who had struck a rich vein of crude oil. With this, I can reconcile myself. Because to understand Macarthur, or to attempt to do so, is to attempt to understand the darkness and violence that run beneath the surface of so many lives, and which has shaped so much of human experience.

Macarthur's story, his life and his terrible crimes, has cast a long and oblique shadow over the city of Dublin. And he is, in various ways, the protagonist of that story: he has lived a life defined by decisions he himself has made. The murders were, at the most basic and unambiguous level, a series of choices. Inasmuch as any action can be taken in freedom, Macarthur freely chose to commit these acts of terrible violence.

The same cannot be said of the people he killed. What happened to them happened against their will. He, in his freedom, chose to bring an end to their freedom, to their futures, to their being. And so I cannot apply this extractive approach to their lives. For me to incorporate those lives into his story—into my story about him—is a liberty I am not willing to take. To do so would be to compound the violence that has already been done to them.

TWELVE

The following day, Friday, Macarthur made a call to Donal Dunne, the farmer in Edenderry. Again, his sister answered. Macarthur apologized for not having made it down the previous evening as agreed. Something had come up, he said; his brother, unfortunately, had been in a car accident. He should be able to get there that Saturday or Sunday, he said.

Then he made another call from the guesthouse, to Tenerife. When Brenda asked him where he was calling from, he told her he was in Ostend, in Belgium. He was sorting out some financial matters there, and it would all be wrapped up in a matter of days. He would be back with her and Colin in about a week.

Early on Saturday evening, he got on a bus in central Dublin, and a couple of hours later, he got off on Edenderry's central square. He walked the long main street, away from the center of the town, toward the banks of a canal. "I forgot about what I was down there for, for the time being," he said in his statement, "and I just enjoyed a walk along the canal bank."

He realized he had no idea where exactly Donal Dunne's house was, or how he might find it. Eventually, he waved at a car, and the driver stopped, and he asked him if he happened

to know where the Dunne family lived, and the driver said
he had a vague notion of the area, but that he couldn't tell
him exactly. He gave him a lift to a stretch of road just outside of the town and let him out. It was somewhere around
here, said the driver. Macarthur went to the nearest house, a
bungalow, and the door was answered by a young man who
looked to be in his twenties, and Macarthur asked him for
directions to Dunne's house. He pointed to another house,
just a little farther up the road. Macarthur thanked the man
and continued on up the road toward the house. He could
see the lights in the windows. But about halfway there, he
stopped. It was after 10:00 p.m. now, and the night was
thickening about him. He stood in the road, staring at the
lights of the house, feeling all of a sudden overwhelmed by
exhaustion. He had been on his feet so long. Walking, endlessly. Standing. He was not sure if he had slept since that
dreadful business in the park, the girl, the car, the hammer.

Here is how he puts it in his statement: "I got cold feet.
The determination wasn't there."

I can hear him say this. *The determination wasn't there.*
Rueful, matter-of-fact, impersonal. His voice in my head,
saying these words.

«

In talking about his "criminal episode," Macarthur
repeatedly used a phrase which struck me as remarkable.
The phrase was "fixity of purpose." It had originally been
employed, he said, by a barrister on his defense team, Michael
McDowell. (Years later, McDowell would become minister
for justice and be forced to recuse himself from the decision
as to whether Macarthur should be allowed probation.) It
was McDowell's contention, on behalf of his client, that he
had at the time of the murders been in the grip of a moral

blindness, whereby all that he could see, all that he could think about, was doing what he felt was necessary to solve his financial problem. "Fixity of purpose," he told me, "can become a kind of lucid insanity. To be insane doesn't mean that you don't know what you're doing. It can mean that you are so completely fixed on a particular purpose that nothing will get in your way. Nothing. No setback, no inconvenience, can stop you. You neglect your health. Your feet might get sore from too much walking, and you just carry on. Fixity of purpose. Lucid insanity."

He spoke of how his mind had been "trapped" by this fixed idea. All his instincts, he said, had been overridden by this fixity of purpose. Listening to him talk in this way, I wondered whether he was somehow trying to absolve himself for what he had done. He had done it, absolutely; there was no question about that. But the impression I got was that he almost believed that it wasn't *he* who had done it—that he was somehow controlled by this fixity of purpose, that his own obsession was acting through him, as a demon acts through the body of a person possessed.

But it was also a good deal more complicated than that, both morally and psychologically. Because he insisted that his actions were not those of a mentally unstable person, but a man who was entirely too in thrall to a cold rationality. His insanity, such as it was, consisted of a violent surfeit of reason. Whether he felt this made him less or more of a murderer was never clear to me. But I do think it allowed him to separate himself from the things he could not deny having done—a separation which must, for him, have been psychologically necessary.

And what was this purpose upon which Macarthur was so fixed? The superficial answer is money. But money was never, in his mind, anything other than a means toward the end of freedom. And freedom, for Macarthur, meant time.

The reason for his crimes, for beating Bridie Gargan to death with a hammer and for shooting Donal Dunne point-blank in the head with his own shotgun, was time. This is the true nature of his offense. He robbed them of their time—their freedom, their possibility, their lives—because he could not countenance relinquishing his own.

«

To speak with Macarthur in any depth was to understand that his sense of self had its foundations deep in a layered bedrock of class distinctions. The first time we met, he spoke at length about his commitment to a kind of pure freedom, a life of the mind untethered to any financial or career imperatives—to being master, as he put it, of his own days.

But his wealth was never sufficient to allow him an indefinite pursuit of this life, this fiction. As his inheritance steadily diminished, so, too, did his insulation from reality. The prospect of having to relinquish his life of intellectual self-determination and languid liberty must have loomed like an existential threat.

Perhaps this can explain not only the fact of the killing, but also the inscrutable savagery of its style. I cannot help but think that there was an element of narcissistic rage at work behind his "criminal episode," a blind fury at the collapse of a protective facade. I cannot help but think, that is, that although the violence was carried out in service of a fiction, it was realer than anything he had ever done in his life.

«

The word that several psychiatric professionals used to describe Macarthur's mental state at the time of the crimes was "automatonism." It's a concept in sympathy with his own preferred phrase, "fixity of purpose." And there are moments, in Macarthur's telling of the story, when it becomes hard not to picture him as a weird, malfunctioning robot. In Edenderry he was, as he put it to me, "behaving very oddly." He would stand still "like a statue" for hours on end—six, seven hours at a stretch, he said. At one point he came across a little tin hut near the banks of the canal and stood inside it for many hours. He did nothing in this time. He didn't think. He didn't move. He just stood there.

The night before he killed Donal Dunne, he slept under a stone bridge over the canal. Or at any rate, he spent the night there; as with so much else about that time, he has no recollection of whether or not he slept. I find this detail especially haunting, for reasons that are not entirely clear to me. Perhaps it is the slight fairy-tale resonance of the scene: the troll beneath the bridge.

There is a shape-shifting quality to him now: a broken robot in his tin hut, a troll under his bridge, a vampire abroad in the shadows. Something of this protean instability emanates from the descriptions collated by the Gardaí of their chief suspect, from various witnesses, in the days after the killings. In one description he is "twenty or twenty-five years old, with a good strong build, athletic looking." In another he is in his mid-thirties, "pale and sickly looking," with a peculiar gait, "as though he is walking against the wind."

"Appears to have a craze for the sport of clay pigeon shooting."

"Likes water, i.e. rivers, canals, and boats."

"Quiet, and will not speak unless spoken to."

This wandering presence with his soft, cultured accent and his "good white teeth." His pale complexion, his unusual walk, his "well-kept" hands and fingernails. What is he, this creature? I know him. I have walked around the city with him. I have felt the buzz of a call in my pocket as I dressed my daughter for bed, and seen his name on the screen of my phone, and felt an uncanny chill of transgression. I have seen his hands, still well kept, and his teeth, no longer good or white. I don't know what he is, other than a man. I don't know what he is, other than what he did.

«

In the morning, he awoke early, from whatever sleep he may have had. He spoke briefly, and pleasantly, with the few people he encountered by the water: A man out for an early morning walk. A farmer checking on his cattle. A group of boys who had camped nearby asked him the time. It was still only 8:00 a.m., too early yet to call to Donal Dunne. At 9:00, the local shop opened, and he bought a copy of the *Sunday Independent*, a pint of milk, and some oranges. He went back to the canal bank and read the paper at his leisure. He drank the milk, ate the oranges. He saw a story in the paper about his assault of the woman in the park the previous Thursday. She was in hospital, he learned, in critical condition. He found a bin and shoved the paper into it, along with the empty milk carton and the orange skins.

For a half hour or so he did nothing. Three people were preparing to take a barge out on the canal. He watched them for a while. Did he think about the time he had spent looking at a barge on the Liffey that previous Thursday, admiring the two lads on the two chairs, before he had gone to the park? Did he ask himself whether it meant anything, these barges, the rivers, the canals? Did he wonder whether the woman he had beaten with the hammer had died since the paper had gone to press? Was his purpose so fixed that such thoughts did not occur to him?

At 11:30 or so, he left the canal bank and headed toward the town. He found a pay phone and called Donal Dunne's number. He was here, he said, and ready to see him, ready to see the gun. Dunne told him to wait where he was; he would drive in and pick him up.

A few minutes later, Dunne pulled up at the phone booth in a silver Ford. He was a young man, the same age as Bridie Gargan, with a mane of reddish hair and thick sideburns. I am tempted to say that he had a friendly, open expression, but I would be basing this solely on the one photograph I have seen of him. I don't know what his expression was like, in truth, or whether Macarthur made note of it.

Dunne said he had the gun in the trunk of the car, but that it would probably be a bad idea for him to take it out and show it to Macarthur there on the street.

If he had done that, would he have lived? Would Macarthur have shot him right there, in the middle of the town, at noon on a Sunday, with people around to see him do it? Did he know what he was going to do to Donal Dunne? Did he see it all play out in his mind as they drove out to a nearby field? Did they make small talk? What did they say to each other? (These questions remain unanswered, because Macarthur would not, for the most part, speak of these moments. He gave different reasons for this at different times: his memory of the period was vague because of the extreme mental stress he was under at the time; he did not want to risk upsetting the families of the people he had killed. In any case, his extraordinary memory and volubility deserted him when it came to the moments, the decisions and actions, by which his life has been defined.)

A few minutes outside of the town, they came to the edge of a bog, and Dunne stopped the car. This, he said, was where the local gun club came for clay pigeon shoots. Macarthur could try out the shotgun here, to see how it handled.

He went round to the trunk, took out a long canvas case. He unzipped it. He didn't need the gun, Dunne said, but he didn't particularly need to sell it either. He opened the breech. He put a couple of cartridges into the chamber and handed it to Macarthur.

Macarthur aimed the gun across the bog at a white post in the middle distance. He fired, but it was too far away to know whether he'd hit it or not.

Dunne said that the shotgun had cost him £1100, and he had no desire to sell it at a loss. It was an unusual brand, he said, Japanese. Miroku.

Macarthur, in his statement, said that he was desperately trying to think of a way to get the gun without paying for it, and that he was stalling for time.

What are we to make of this claim? He was standing there, with a shotgun in his hand, and there was one bullet left in the chamber. Dunne was at point-blank range. The obvious thing to do, within the logic of the situation Macarthur has engineered, was to point the gun at Dunne and tell him to walk across the bog, and keep walking. The keys were still in the ignition of the car.

This, surely, is how you get the gun without paying for it, and the car into the bargain. This is not a racking-your-brains situation.

What Macarthur said in his statement, and what he said to me when he spoke about his killing of Donal Dunne—as he eventually did, despite his expressions of uncertainty as to whether he would—was that Dunne started to get impatient with him. He started to get angry. Just as with Bridie Gargan, it was the victim's emotional reaction to the situation that served as the proximal cause of Macarthur's violence.

It is Macarthur's claim that Dunne, in his rising impatience, reached out his hand to grab the gun, and that he,

Macarthur, took a step backward, and that he squeezed the
trigger. He shot Donal Dunne in the face with the bullet he himself had loaded it with just moments before. He
watched him fall backward onto the soft surface of the bog.

«

Some newspaper reports of the murder include a detail
that, if it were true, could only have come from Macarthur
himself: that in the moment before he shot Donal Dunne, he
said to him, "Sorry, old chap."

I have read that Macarthur himself mentioned this to
the detectives who interrogated him. I don't know why he
would have told them this. For the same reason, possibly,
that he told me of the whispered assurance he'd offered to
Bridie Gargan, two days previously, as she lay dying in the
back seat of her car, that "help is on its way." Because he felt
it made him seem somehow more humane.

But "Sorry, old chap"? That is something different. It
seems calibrated, to use Macarthur's own terrible word, to
sound as chilling, as casually cruel as possible. One does not
say "Sorry, old chap" to someone one is about to accidentally
shoot in the face, in the midst of a struggle for a shotgun.
They are not the words of a person committing manslaughter. They are the words of a murderer. More than that, they
are the words of a murderer in a film. It's easy to imagine
them being spoken, in fact, by Louis D'Ascoyne Mazzini,
the tenth Earl of Chalfont, as he dispatches yet another of
his victims in *Kind Hearts and Coronets*.

Macarthur, when I asked him about it, told me that
he never said anything of the sort to Donal Dunne. It was
something that he had said in a later attempted robbery, and
which had been transposed, in the newspapers at the time,

onto the scene of the Dunne murder, either because of an
error of reporting, or because it made for an irresistible bit
of dialogue. For what it's worth, I believe him. Though it
makes for a less cinematic moment, it makes more sense.

«

Macarthur went back to the car and propped the gun
against a door. He returned to Dunne and saw the result
of his actions: Dunne's head, as he later put it in his statement, "was in a mess." He grabbed the young man's feet
and dragged him across a short stretch of bogland toward
some nearby bushes. He broke some branches off the bushes,
and he laid them across the body, concealing it as well as he
could. He went back to the car and laid the gun at an angle
between the two front seats. Then he got behind the wheel
and he drove.

By the time he got back to Dublin, he knew that he
would have to abandon the car. If the guards weren't looking
for it now, it was only a matter of time before they started.
He parked it on Eustace Street, took the gun in its carry case,
and got on a bus headed for Dún Laoghaire.

«

Lying at the heart of these crimes is a contradiction. On
the one hand, there was an obvious, brutal logic to them.
Macarthur wanted to maintain his lifestyle, his freedom,
and for that he needed money, and so he decided to rob a
bank, for which he needed to steal a gun and a car. But on
the other hand, there was no requirement, even within the
enclosed logic of this personal necessity, that anyone die. He
could easily have taken Bridie Gargan's car without harming

her. He could, even more easily, have taken Donal Dunne's shotgun without shooting him. Something here is not right. Beneath the cold, computational logic of the crimes, there is something chaotic and strange, a violence reducible to neither reason nor circumstance. A violence that is itself alone.

THIRTEEN

The day after he returned from Edenderry, Macarthur went to a paper stand near the guesthouse in Dún Laoghaire and bought a copy of *The Irish Times*. On the front page, beneath the headline "Man Shot Dead in Offaly," he read of the discovery of Donal Dunne's body. A family from Dublin had been picnicking; one of the sons, a man in his early twenties, wandered off to pick raspberries and found, lying facedown and partly concealed in some bushes, the body of the murdered farmer. The article also featured a photograph of the hammer with which Macarthur had assaulted the young woman in the park four days previously. (The article made no suggestion of any link between the murder in Offaly and the Phoenix Park assault; it also mentioned a number of other unconnected recent murders.) Turning to page 6, Macarthur learned that his first victim's name was Bridie Gargan, that she was a nurse, and that she was in her late twenties. He also learned that she had suffered severe brain damage from the blows, and that she was being kept on life support. He read that the hammer he had used was "similar to the type used by brick layers," that it was made in China, and that it had the figure "1000" embossed on its metal head. The Gardaí, he read, had made "an urgent appeal for retailers of this sort of tool to contact them in an effort to trace the attacker."

The following day, Macarthur returned to the paper stand. He bought the *Times* again and scanned down through the front page. "Nurse attacked with hammer in park dies," read the headline.

When he told me of his horror at learning of her death, I pointed out to him that, even if he did believe she would live, he had not two days previously shot a man point-blank in the face, and so it was not as though he could have been experiencing a sudden apprehension of himself as a killer. He already knew by then that he was a murderer.

"Yes," he said. "I already knew that I had killed a person. But for some reason, reading the paper that day, learning of it—that seemed to have an effect. I can't recall exactly, but it was one of surprise, or of shock. I suppose 'shock' was the word. It was unexpected news. Because when I left her, she was sitting in the back seat, not exhibiting any distress."

I am struck once again by Macarthur's description of Bridie Gargan, in the moments after his terrible assault. I find it deeply implausible. We know for a fact that he hit her in the head with a hammer many times, and with sufficient force to cause fatal brain injury. We know that she was bleeding a great deal; he said in his statement that "there was blood all over her and some on the window and more on the seats." And yet here he was, telling me that when he left her in the back seat of the car, she was exhibiting no distress.

There are times when I believe that he is simply lying. But there are times, too, when I think that there is no such thing as a simple lie, and that there are situations in which a lie can lay bare the truth of a person more clearly than a mere fact ever could.

This is a man who has always shaped his own reality. "A

Walter Mitty type," as one of the detectives who investigated him once put it to me. "A bit of a dreamer," as his mother called him. What would it do to him to acknowledge that he beat a woman in the head with a hammer, brutally and without mercy, and that he knew he had caused her grave and horrific injuries, and that he left her alone to die in a lane, in the back of her own car? What would he see of himself if he faced that truth, plainly and without delusion?

It is worth remembering here what Irene Macarthur said in that radio interview, when David Hanley asked her whether Malcolm was a fantasist as a child. He had inherited from his father, she said, a certain kind of relationship to the truth. "When they got something into their mind," she said, "and when they thought about it long enough, they literally believed it themselves."

Macarthur seemed to me to be extraordinarily capable of shaping memory to suit his purposes. If something was painful to recall, he would fashion it into something more easily assimilated. I witnessed this happen in real time once. It was nine months or so after we had first met, and Macarthur was recalling our first conversation on the street that day. He felt that I had been effectively stalking him, and he would sometimes mention it in a manner that was not quite playful, but perhaps a little pleased. In recalling that first meeting, he reminded me that I had stopped him on the street and that we had spoken there for a time, and that we had then moved to the foyer of his apartment building, because "it was very noisy on the street."

I was startled by this. Could he really be forgetting something as dramatic as what had actually happened?

"It wasn't because of noise that we moved away from there, to the foyer of your building," I said. "Don't you remember? It was the man with the camera. The man who approached us and confronted you about Bridie Gargan."

Macarthur paused very briefly but did not seem particularly flustered or confused. He didn't attempt to deny the fact of what had happened, but neither did he seem interested in dwelling on it, or on the meaning of his having seemingly erased it from his memory of that afternoon. He simply moved on with what he had been saying.

«

In the days that followed Dunne's murder, his behavior became more erratic still. He could have gotten on a boat and left the country, never to return. He could have gone back to Tenerife. But he stayed. Despite everything that had happened, despite everything he had done, he was still maniacally fixed upon the plan to acquire money through violent means.

Because of descriptions they had gathered of the suspect, and because both murders had involved the theft of a car, the Gardaí had by then come to believe that there was a connection between the two killings, and an increasingly public manhunt was now underway. Within a week of the death of Donal Dunne, a reconstruction of the crimes was filmed and broadcast on RTE television; the part of the murderer in the tweed hat was played by a detective in the murder squad who happened to bear a resemblance to the man described by witnesses.

Still Macarthur chose not to abandon what he called his "venture." He checked out of the guesthouse in Dún Laoghaire, and for a few nights he was on the streets. He spent a lot of time sitting on benches, staring into space. One night, in Sandycove, he sat by the low, squat Martello tower—the tower in which the opening chapter of Joyce's *Ulysses* is set—and stared out at the sea until dawn. When it was light enough to see, his gaze rested for a long while on a ship, a Nigerian cargo vessel. The ship had been embroiled in some kind of dispute over customs, and had been anchored in the bay for several weeks now. It was entirely white, save for a blue funnel. For hours on end he stared, entranced, just as he had been entranced by the little floating house on the Liffey on his way to the Phoenix Park the week before, and by the barge on the canal in Edenderry.

I write that he was entranced, but in truth I am the one who is entranced—by the image of the murderer, sitting for hours on end, staring out at this vessel, with its pale blue funnel, this vessel which itself is becalmed out in the bay, with nowhere to go, at once floating and firmly anchored. I feel it must mean something, that he sat there looking at this ship for so long, and that he remembered it so clearly, and that he told me about it forty years later. It must mean something, all this staring out at the water—the river, the canal, the sea.

«

Not long after his arrival back in Dublin, Macarthur had called an acquaintance of his to whom he had loaned a sum of money. The acquaintance had told him that he'd written him a check sometime back, and that he'd posted it to the flat on Fitzwilliam Square, not realizing that Macarthur was no longer at that address. There were, by then, new tenants in the flat, but Macarthur still had a key to the front door of the building. He let himself in and checked the post. There was nothing.

As he let himself out the door again and headed down the building's stately granite steps, he was hailed by a former neighbor. This man, Mr. Fawcett, lived at number 46, a grand, ivy-covered house, which was known for its remarkably ornate Edwardian door. Macarthur and Fawcett got talking about this and that, and Fawcett invited him in.

Macarthur accepted and stayed awhile, talking knowledge-
ably about the original Georgian features of the building.

According to one of Fawcett's adult children who was
also there, Macarthur was wearing a pair of thin white rub-
ber gloves at the time, which he explained by saying he was
suffering from dermatitis on his hands. But later, when plates
of smoked salmon and bread were passed around, Macarthur
took the gloves off in order to eat, and his hosts noted that his
hands seemed completely smooth and unmarked.

Fawcett noted, too, that Macarthur had a long canvas
bag with him. Only after Macarthur's arrest did his former
neighbor release what was in it: the shotgun with which, a
few days previously, he had killed Donal Dunne.

(When I asked Macarthur about this, he told me that he
was wearing only one glove, on his left hand. He did indeed
have a skin condition on the palm of that hand, he said, and
he had been given a cream to treat it; the pharmacist had
recommended he wear a glove. The skin condition would
not have been particularly noticeable to anyone looking at
his hand, he said. And as for the canvas bag containing the
gun, that was completely false—yet another example, he
said, of how, when it came to stories like his, people had a
tendency to embellish and outright fictionalize the reality of
their experience.)

When Macarthur left number 46, it was late. He let himself back into his former building. On the ground floor was
a GP's surgery. He settled himself into a comfortable chair
in the waiting room and drifted off. The following morning,
he was awoken by the doctor's receptionist, a Mrs. Westby,
who knew him from his time living upstairs. He muttered
something about a lost key and headed out the door.

FOURTEEN

One of Macarthur's acquaintances from the Bartley Dunne days was an American named Harry Bieling. In the late 1960s, Bieling had been working for the US diplomatic service in London, when he took a trip to Ireland with some friends and was so taken by the place that he decided to move. The two men were not close, but they had moved in the same social circle at Bartley's; they'd met in the mid-1970s, through a woman Macarthur had been seeing at the time, a good friend of Bieling's. Macarthur would not tell me this woman's name, referring to her only as C.M.; she was from a working-class background, he said, and had grown up in Ballyfermot. He felt that they had too little in common, and that the relationship would not last. But she was, he said, very keen on him, and very reluctant to let him go. "I was kind to her," he said. "In my view, that is the quality women find most attractive in a man. Kindness."

Bieling lived in Killiney, in a sort of miniature castle overlooking Dublin Bay. The house was called Camelot. An absurd name, certainly, but the sort of thing that houses around Killiney Hill tend to be called. (There is, for instance, a much larger house next door to "Camelot," for which it had once served as the gate lodge, and which is now the home of the singer Enya, who named it Manderley Castle, in tribute to the large West Country estate that is the setting of Daphne du Maurier's gothic novel *Rebecca*.) Macarthur had been to Camelot on quite a few occasions, back in the mid-seventies, for parties, and the occasional dinner. He'd stayed the night there once.

Bieling had come from money in New York and in his early retirement in Ireland lived a fairly lavish lifestyle. As Macarthur later put it in his statement to the guards, "I thought that he would have money." He decided he would tell Bieling that he just happened to be in the neighborhood, and that he wondered whether perhaps he would mind if he took some photographs of the spectacular view of Dublin Bay from Camelot's living room window, which he remembered from parties he'd been at there.

But as soon as Macarthur arrived at Bieling's door on August 4, things began to go awry. There's a persuasive account of the incident in *The Boss*, a 1983 book about Charles Haughey, by the Irish journalists Joe Joyce and Peter Murtagh. The encounter was framed, according to Joyce and Murtagh, by the fact that Bieling did not remember who Macarthur was. Macarthur reintroduced himself, and gave him the line about the view of the bay, the photographs he wanted to take. Perhaps Bieling didn't recall, Macarthur said, but he was a keen amateur photographer. In fact he had his camera equipment with him, he said, nodding to the bag he was carrying.

"Is it just you here?" asked Macarthur. "I could come back another time if you have company."

No, said Bieling, it was just himself. He still had no firm sense of who Macarthur was, and the situation was becoming awkward. It seemed that this was someone he really should remember, and it would not have been entirely unlike him to forget such a person. The man was a little disheveled, it was true, but he was very polite and spoke in the unmistakable

accent of the Anglo-Irish ascendancy. (It's hard to imagine
Bieling giving this man he did not recognize the benefit of
the doubt had he spoken with a provincial accent, or with
the agile drawl of Dublin's inner city. Macarthur's upper-
class manner had a way of opening doors for him, even when
it came to crime.) Bieling told him to come inside, and he
crossed the threshold.

Macarthur went to the French doors and gazed out at
the sea. It was a hazy late summer evening. The conditions,
said Bieling, were not exactly ideal for the kind of crisp shot
Macarthur was presumably looking to take.

No, said Macarthur. This was exactly how he remembered it from before. These were the precise conditions he
was hoping for. And the light was perfect.

They made small talk for a while. Macarthur mentioned
the names of a few other people who had been there, at the
party, the last time he was in the house. This must have set
Bieling's mind at ease, reassured him that this was not just
some random interloper with a tweed jacket and a bow tie.

The last time he was here, Macarthur reminded Bieling, he, Macarthur, was being "pursued by some slut from
Ballymum."

They chatted a short while longer, and then Bieling, perhaps eager to reclaim what remained of his evening, pointed
out that the light would not remain so perfect for so long.

Here Macarthur put his bag down on a table and
unzipped it.

"I hope you have a sense of humor," he said, and removed
the shotgun from the bag. He told Bieling to sit down in a
chair on the far side of the room. He took a seat himself, and
sat with the shotgun in his lap, pointed in Bieling's direction.

Bieling went pale and began to tremble. He asked if he
could go across the room to the drinks cabinet and fix himself
something to settle his nerves. Fair enough, said Macarthur,

as long as he wasn't keeping a gun in there. Macarthur could follow him if he wished, he said, to make sure he didn't try anything. Macarthur kept the gun pointed at him, and Bieling poured himself a vodka.

Bieling returned to his chair and asked Macarthur what all this was about.

Money, he said. It was about money. He knew Bieling had a lot of it, and he wanted a thousand pounds, at the very least.

Bieling asked if he had been doing this for long, this sort of thievery. About a year, Macarthur said, presumably to give the impression that he was more practiced in the craft of armed robbery than he actually was.

Bieling said a thousand pounds was out of the question, as he didn't keep much money in the house. There was a total of twenty-three pounds on the premises, and Macarthur was welcome to help himself.

In that case, Macarthur said, he'd accept a check. Because even if Bieling didn't remember him, Macarthur remembered Bieling. He recalled very clearly how Bieling used to spend at least a thousand pounds a week in bars and restaurants around town. He was known to be the beneficiary of a healthy trust fund. So: a thousand pounds it would have to be. He should make it out, he said, to one John Eustace—the name under which Macarthur had opened a bank account some days previously.

Macarthur talked a little more, keeping the shotgun leveled at Bieling all the while. The truth was he'd mismanaged his funds, Macarthur told him—a characteristic moment of candor amid a tangled profusion of lies. His inheritance had all but dried up, and this robbery business, unfortunately, was the only way out of the mess he was in. He told Bieling that he was working with an accomplice.

Macarthur asked where the phone was. Bieling pointed

him toward it and said he would really appreciate it if he didn't yank the cord out of the wall, because it could be a good six months by the time the phone company sent a man around to repair it. That was fine, said Macarthur. He just wanted to call his accomplice, to get him to come and watch Bieling overnight, until the bank reopened in the morning and Macarthur was able to cash the check.

Macarthur continued to bullshit about this nonexistent collaborator. This was his second such coconspirator, he said. It was getting harder and harder to find dependable people to work with. At some point, Bieling made an attempt to talk him out of the robbery, to appeal to his good sense. Macarthur had committed no serious crime at this point. If they called it quits right now, he said, that would be the end of it; he would never mention the matter to anyone.

No dice.

The evening was wearing on; Bieling needed another drink. He went and fixed one, and stood at the far side of the room. Listen, he said. It had just gone seven o'clock, and his housekeeper was due in half an hour to make his dinner. He would go upstairs now and get his checkbook; it was in his bedroom, he said. Bieling's room was at the top of a spiral staircase.

Macarthur agreed; he followed Bieling up the staircase, the shotgun aimed at his back. The place was a bit of a mess, with clothes and books and various other personal items strewn about the floor. Bieling made a show of looking around for his checkbook, going through drawers, lifting piles of books, and so on. Perhaps it wasn't up here after all, Bieling said. It must have been downstairs in the living room all along. Macarthur was losing his patience at this point, and he accused Bieling of trying to pull a fast one on him. Bieling told him by all means to have a look for himself.

Macarthur had no intention of leaving prints all over Bieling's house. He declined the offer.

They descended the spiral staircase, Macarthur following a few steps behind Bieling with the shotgun leveled at the back of his head. When Bieling got to the bottom of the stairs, he ran for it—down the hall, through the front door, and out onto Victoria Road. As Macarthur later put it in his statement: "Mr. Bieling made good his escape. I don't know whether I would have shot him or not."

In any case, he never got the chance. By the time Macarthur made it to the road, Bieling was out of sight, and he was not going to chase him down Killiney Hill with a shotgun. There was a limit to these things, even for him. He went back inside, grabbed his overnight bag, stowed the weapon, and left.

«

Despite the Camelot fiasco, Macarthur remained doggedly committed to the broad outline of his plan, haphazard though it may have been: his "fixity of purpose," in his own preferred terminology, was unshaken. He walked down the street a little and rang the bell of a neighboring house. The door opened slightly, revealing the wary face of an old woman; she had secured the door with a chain. There'd been an accident, said Macarthur, and his brother had been injured. He asked whether he might use her telephone. The woman looked at Macarthur for a moment. She told him her phone was out of order, and closed the door firmly in his face.

On Killiney Hill, a car came toward him and he flagged it down. There were three men in the car, a father and two sons, and they were on the way back from a fishing trip, headed toward Dalkey. He made up a story about a friend who had been in an accident, and said he needed to get to Dalkey to tell this friend's mother about what had happened.

Despite the refined accent and the elegant manner of dress, something was palpably off about this man. The driver dropped him off at the Pilot View apartment complex, where he said this friend's mother lived, but he kept the car idling a moment to see whether Macarthur walked through the entrance. He and his sons watched as Macarthur walked past the gates and disappeared instead down a nearby side street.

They abandoned their fishing trip, went straight to the nearest Garda station, and made a report about this breathless character who had flagged them down. In their descriptions, they insisted he was wearing an Inverness cape—the sort of sleeveless outer-coat associated in the popular imagination with Sherlock Holmes. There is no evidence that Macarthur ever owned such a garment, but the fact that these men described him as dressed in this manner is, if nothing else, testament to this peculiar quality of his—that even a passing stranger was compelled to imagine him as a fictional character.

«

Macarthur had, at this point, already been in touch with Patrick Connolly, the old friend of Brenda's who had by now risen to the position of Ireland's attorney general. He'd phoned him a couple of weeks previously, not long after his return to Dublin. Macarthur was in Belgium, he claimed. (When he'd spoken to Brenda, he'd said he was in Ostend; he told Connolly now that he was phoning from Liège.) He was heading to Ireland shortly, he said, and suggested meeting. Connolly would be glad to see him; he told Macarthur that he'd had a call from Brenda, however, and that she seemed not to know where he was. Macarthur said he'd tried phoning her, but had for whatever reason failed to get through. In any case, he would be home only for a few days, sorting out some financial matters, before heading back to Tenerife. Connolly asked whether Macarthur would care to stay with him while he was in the country. Macarthur at first declined, telling him that "a friend from Trinity" had offered to put him up, and in any case he didn't wish to intrude. (In reality, Macarthur was, as he put it to me, "sleeping semi-rough.") Nonsense, Connolly said, he wouldn't be intruding in the least. Macarthur would have the apartment to himself, because he would be in the city all day, at his government offices. In that case, said Macarthur, he would be glad to accept Connolly's generous hospitality.

And so it was that, on the evening of August 4, 1982, the Irish government's most senior legal official had his house-keeper prepare the spare room for his friend, a man who had just days previously murdered two strangers, and who had that very evening botched an armed robbery at the home of an acquaintance.

«

I was fourteen when my widowed grandmother left Pilot View and moved closer to the city center. But I remember the place with sensory clarity: the low electric gates; the squat, angular buildings; the sloping lawn down toward the rocks and the sea beyond. I can hear the throaty drone of the intercom, and I can see my grandfather's name on the printed card beside their buzzer: "E. O'Neill, Capt." And it gives me a jolt of cognitive dissonance even now to think of Macarthur walking through those gates, walking up the flagstone steps to the door, pressing the buzzer.

«

The following morning, Connolly left for work in the city, chauffeured by a Garda in his state car, and Macarthur was left alone in the three-bedroom apartment overlooking Dublin Bay. He browsed through Connolly's collection of classical records, selected a recording of Beethoven's Seventh Symphony, and put it on the turntable. He sat for a while on a chair in the living room, gazing out at the glistening sea, the clear blue sky, listening to the symphony. (Was the Nigerian cargo ship still there? Was it visible from the large window of Connolly's living room?) His thoughts turned to the previous evening's fiasco at Camelot. Bieling would almost certainly have reported the incident to the police by now. The thing to be done, he decided, was to phone the man and see whether something couldn't be worked out.

«

When Bieling had returned home the previous evening, in the company of a Garda, the place was empty, and Macarthur was nowhere to be seen. After the Garda left, he found that he was too shaken to be alone, and he phoned a friend to come around and keep him company. They'd stayed up drinking until 4:00 a.m., Bieling getting progressively drunker as he recounted, again and again, the bizarre events of that evening. All night, he'd tried and failed to remember the name of the man with the gun, whom he felt he should know, and who clearly knew him.

At about 9:00 a.m., the phone rang, and woke him from an unsettled sleep, gravely and unambiguously hungover. In an interview he gave after Macarthur's conviction to the authors of *The Boss,* the book about Haughey, Bieling provided an account of the call.

He could hear, on the other end of the line, the stately strings of Beethoven's Seventh blaring, tinnily but insistently. Macarthur announced himself as Bieling's friend from yesterday evening. He wanted to know why Bieling had run away. He was just messing about, he said. It was a joke, although he saw now that it was in poor taste, and that it had not gone over.

Macarthur asked which of them should phone the Gardaí to let them know that it had been a misunderstood jape? Bieling suggested that it should probably be he, Macarthur, who should do it. Macarthur said that he would, and then asked if he might call around again to Bieling sometime next week.

Was this a threat? It's certainly hard to see how Bieling could have taken it any other way. I imagine him holding the receiver to his ear, his hand trembling from the compound effects of the hangover, the horrifying events of the previous night, and now this bizarre and terrifying conversation.

He said that he didn't mind if Macarthur wanted to call around again, but that he would prefer if he telephoned in advance.

«

Later that morning, Macarthur made another call, to the Garda station in Dalkey. He told the guard on duty, Sgt. Pat Fitzgerald, that he was calling in relation to an incident last night in Killiney. An American chap by the name of Bieling would have been in touch about it, he said. Fitzgerald asked what it was he wanted to report. Well, there was nothing to report, as such, said Macarthur—other than the fact that it had been a joke, and that it had gone awry. Bieling had misunderstood his intentions, he told him, but they had just spoken on the phone, and the whole thing was cleared up now, so there was really no need to pursue the matter any further.

Fitzgerald asked who it was that he was speaking to.

"This is Malcolm Macarthur," he said.

The name would have meant nothing to the guard, it is true, but it would be hard to argue that the decision to give it was anything but a massive unforced error. He could very easily have introduced himself as John Eustace, or some other assumed name. But this is classic Macarthur: just when he seems to be at his most sinister and calculated, he reverts to chaos, to farce.

When I asked him why on earth he'd given his name to the police, he told me that it had not occurred to him that they wouldn't already have it. He had no idea at that point, he said, that Bieling didn't remember him. As far as he was concerned, they'd already have been looking for a man named Malcolm Macarthur. Had Bieling not been too polite to tell his intruder that he had no idea who he was, Macarthur would never have given his name to the police.

«

Almost forty years later, the botched joke version of the story is one to which Macarthur still holds. His reasons for showing up at Bieling's house that evening did have to do with money, he told me, but he had no intention of robbing Bieling. He'd gone to inquire about a mutual acquaintance, to whom he had made a loan—not huge, he said, but significant—and who had disappeared, as is so often the case with such people.

Macarthur told me that he did not actually pull a gun on Bieling—not in earnest, at any rate. He had a camera with him, he said, in his bag, and he did in fact want to take a photo of the view from the balcony. He had no intention of using the gun, but unfortunately Bieling happened to see it when he opened the bag, and asked Macarthur what he was doing with a shotgun. Macarthur did take the gun out and point it at Bieling, he admitted, but he was doing it ironically. He acknowledged that it was in poor taste, to be horsing around with a gun mere days after having used that same gun to shoot a man dead. But he was not himself at the time, and could not properly account for his actions or his motivations.

The joke, such as it was, had to do with a conversation he and Bieling had had years previously, he said, about a holdup Bieling had once witnessed in New York. In taking out the gun and pointing it at Bieling, Macarthur was in fact making a playful allusion to this previous conversation. (It was, in comedic terms, a "callback." Not that Macarthur used this term; it's difficult to imagine him ever having heard it.)

"It was a humorous thing on my part," he told me, "which he mistook to be real."

"What exactly was humorous about it?" I asked.

"The fact that I was referring back to this old conversation, in a slightly humorous, or even clownish way."

"So what was it that you said? What was the joke?"

"Oh, I said something about his checkbook. And of course Bieling's checkbook was famously useless, you see, because he was kept on a very short leash. A family trust paid a small weekly sum of money, just to keep him sensible, because otherwise he would have spent it. This was a reference to a conversation we had had about his checkbook eight years earlier. I remembered all of this, and he misunderstood it. But the key point here is that he didn't recognize me, according to him. And I accept that. But that would have given a wholly different meaning to the encounter for him, because rather than being an acquaintance with a gun, I was a stranger with a gun."

"Surely," I said, "even an acquaintance with a gun is quite an intimidating thing."

"Well that depends," he said, "on whether it's just being

waved around. If it's being pointed directly at one, of course, it's a different matter."

We agreed to differ, as we so often did.

«

I have said before that the question Bridie Gargan put to Macarthur as he approached her with his imitation gun is one that seems to me to hover insistently over this story I am telling, this monstrous farce. Is this for real? The events, or in any case an attempt to recount them, can seem like a joke in feverishly bad taste. (Did you hear the one about the wealthy socialite who tried to pull off an armed robbery, and wound up murdering two people and nearly bringing down the government?) This is what makes the story so uncomfortable, this strange tonal instability. It is a terrible tragedy, involving the brutal killing of two young people by a stranger. And yet there is no getting around the fact that it is also a terrific yarn.

Is this for real? It's an insistent question, an important question; Macarthur himself was constantly blurring the line between reality and fiction, between actions undertaken in earnest and in jest. It was the question I asked myself, certainly, whenever Macarthur told me anything about his life, whenever he offered an account of the things he had done, or an explanation of his reasons for doing them.

«

Here the story opens out onto two diverging narrative paths. There is Macarthur, lying low in Connolly's apartment, and there are the detectives investigating the murders. Certainly the Macarthur narrative does not lack for intrigue: the murderer, skulking around the attorney general's apartment, gazing out at the glistening sea. As always, there is the problem of information: I don't know all that much about what he was up to while he was there. He is reluctant to speak about this period, and claims in any case not to remember much of it. A certain amount of imagination might be necessary here, on the reader's part and my own. What does a man like Macarthur get up to while he is alone, hiding out from the police, from the consequences of his horrific actions? (He is not planning to leave the country; that much I know. He said it never entered his head.)

Maybe he reads that book on the philosophy of mind. Maybe he listens to Connolly's extensive collection of classical records. Maybe he passes my grandmother in the hallway, at the front door, and nods politely to her. Maybe he works out the details of a plan to murder his mother. Maybe he does no such thing, because maybe he is telling the truth about the provenance of these notes. Maybe he stands at the end of the lawn behind Connolly's building, the same lawn I played on with my sister and my cousins as a child, and stares out to sea. Maybe he thinks about what he has done, about the feel of the hammer in his hand as it strikes the young woman's skull, the weight of the young man's body as he drags it across the bog. Maybe he thinks about nothing at all.

PART FOUR

GROTESQUE, UNBELIEVABLE, BIZARRE, AND UNPRECEDENTED

FIFTEEN

For now I will leave Macarthur and his uncertain doings and direct my attention toward the men who were trying to find him. Sometime before I met Macarthur, I got in touch with John O'Mahony and Tony Hickey, both of whom had been involved in the investigation as detectives, and both of whom had subsequently served as assistant Garda commissioner before retirement. We spoke over the course of several months, nearly always the three of us together, and their account of the investigation unfolded as a kind of two-hander, with Hickey delivering long monologues before ceding the narrative to his former colleague. They had stayed in touch since their retirements, and even when we spoke over Zoom, their jokey, teasing affection was clear. Hickey was the older of the two, and he had been the more senior detective at the time of the investigation.

As it happened, they were both on their way home from funerals when they learned of the vicious assault in the Phoenix Park, a crime that had not yet become a murder investigation. Hickey had been at a funeral in his native Kerry. O'Mahony had been in the West of Ireland with his then-partner Frank Hand, the two in their mid-twenties, having only been made detectives three months previously. (Hand was killed in a shoot-out two years later, on duty during an

IRA armed raid on a post office van.) Returning to the city, O'Mahony and Hand drove through the Phoenix Park, and as they passed the US ambassador's residence, they noted a Garda presence in the grassy area directly outside it. This, they quickly learned, was the scene of the assault on Bridie Gargan.

Within days, it had become a murder case, and both Hickey and O'Mahony were assigned to investigate, part of a group of about thirty detectives—the so-called Murder Squad, led by Superintendent John Courtney. Courtney was an experienced detective in his fifties, who had three years previously led the investigation into the IRA's assassination of Lord Louis Mountbatten, the uncle of Prince Philip. (One of the reasons the Macarthur case was so shocking, O'Mahony and Hickey told me, was that in the early 1980s, before the explosion of hard drugs on Dublin's streets led to a rise in organized crime, there were relatively few murders in the Republic, and those that did occur were often linked to the paramilitary campaigns of the IRA.)

The detectives operated out of an incident room in Kevin Street station, in the south inner city. O'Mahony made a point of recalling that photographs of Bridie Gargan and Donal Dunne were prominently positioned on the walls of the small room. "That would have been the case with most murder investigations," he said. "Those photographs were there so that you were constantly reminded that these were human beings whose lives had been taken."

The frenzied and chaotic nature of the assault on Bridie Gargan led Courtney and his detectives at first to consider that their culprit might be a patient of a psychiatric hospital. O'Mahony and Frank Hand were dispatched the following day to visit the city's psychiatric facilities. When they called to St. Patrick's, the general hospital just across the river from the park, the medical director told them that he was certain the killer was a patient of his hospital. A man had checked himself in on Thursday evening, he said, just hours after the assault, and he seemed to match the description offered by O'Mahony and Hand. They thought, for a few giddy hours, that they had the case cracked; it turned out to be a dead end.

When the detectives went through the contents of the handbag left behind in Bridie Gargan's car, one of the things they found there was a prescription for a cold sore cream, written by a doctor at a family planning clinic. Given the Catholic Church's near-theocratic level of influence over reproductive matters in Ireland at the time, such clinics were extremely controversial. Contraception of all forms was illegal. (Gardaí, most of whom were Catholics, were at the time expected to attend Mass on Sunday as part of their duty.) Some of the older and more senior detectives speculated, based on scant evidence, that she might have been secretly involved with a man, and that this person might have had a hand in her death.

The detectives who went to interview the doctors at the family planning clinic asked about the reason for her prescription. Bridie Gargan, they were told, had developed cold sores on her mouth from sunbathing in the heat wave. Why, then, had she gone to a family planning clinic for a cold sore treatment? It was, they learned, simply the most convenient place for her to consult a doctor. She worked there as a nurse on a voluntary basis.

«

After the murder of Donal Dunne in Edenderry, it didn't take long for Courtney and his team to become convinced there was a link with the attack in the Phoenix Park. There was, first of all, the fact that both killings involved the theft, and subsequent abandonment, of a victim's car.

Witnesses who had encountered the stranger wandering the streets and canal banks of Edenderry, and those who had seen a man acting oddly at clay pigeon shoots around Dublin, both described this man peering out over the rim of his spectacles while talking, as though unable to see properly through them. When a set of prints taken from a newspaper retrieved from a bin by the canal in Edenderry was found to match prints found on the polythene-wrapped shovel in the park, there was no longer any doubt that they were looking for a single suspect for both murders.

Paddy Byrne, the gardener at the US embassy who had attempted to intervene in the assault of Bridie Gargan, had described a well-spoken man, with dark, wavy hair, wearing a cravat. The travel agent gave a similar description, and suggested that the somewhat imperious manner in which he had asked her to fetch him glasses of water and call him a cab suggested that he had grown up with servants. These descriptions were, in turn, remarkably consistent with Harry Bieling's account of the vague acquaintance who had shown up at his house with a shotgun, and whose name he could not for the life of him recall.

The day after the Bieling episode, Superintendent Mick Sullivan from Dalkey Garda station called Courtney at the incident room in Kevin Street. Sgt. Pat Fitzgerald, who had spoken on the phone to Macarthur, had immediately told Sullivan about the call. The more Sullivan thought about it, he told Courtney, the more convinced he was that his suspect in the Bieling double robbery attempt (well dressed, well spoken, oddly decorous) and Courtney's double murderer were one and the same. Even better, the apparent perpetrator had been kind enough to give his name.

The killer's manner of speech was a matter of persistent interest to the detectives. Along with the cravat (or the bow tie, depending on the source), it was invariably among the first things witnesses mentioned in their descriptions. After his conviction, Superintendent Courtney, a Kerry-man, described Macarthur's accent to *The Irish Times:* "Oh, a high-flown accent," he said. "Very cultured altogether. You'd never miss it."

«

The day after the reconstruction of the crimes was shown on television, a man in his early twenties named John Monks showed up at the station in Dún Laoghaire. He'd seen the broadcast and had a hunch that he might have seen the guy they were looking for. John O'Mahony went to talk to him and took a statement. Monks worked a newspaper kiosk on Marine Road in Dún Laoghaire, and he'd noticed a peculiar character who'd been showing up on and off the last few weeks. He generally came by the kiosk twice a day, for the morning papers and later for the evening editions. This guy had a polished air, but there was something off about him. When he'd first started coming, he'd had a beard, but then more recently he'd shown up completely clean-shaven. He wore glasses, but he'd push them down low on his nose, or sometimes rest them high on his forehead, as he stood looking through the papers. He'd take the *Evening Press* and the *Evening Herald* off the rack, Monks said, and go straight for the ads. What Monks didn't know, but what O'Mahony understood, was that the man had likely been looking through the listings for someone selling a gun.

And then there were the heavy clothes, wildly inappro-priate for the hot weather: a tweed hat, of all things, and a fawn sweater, military style, with cloth patches on the shoul-ders. O'Mahony showed him photos of various different sweaters. He immediately identified the sweater the guards had found abandoned near Bridie Gargan's car as the sweater worn by the customer.

O'Mahony, like most of the detectives in the incident room, was not afforded a high-level understanding of the investigation. There was a small number of detectives in an inner sanctum to whom all the information flowed, and for whom seemingly trivial details might form part of a larger composite picture of the case. John Courtney was the person who, each evening, went through the day's statements and gathered evidence, and isolated relevant details. The key detail from Monks's statement, it turned out, was the sweater. Courtney was confident that this regular customer of the kiosk was the man they were looking for. He assigned two plainclothes detectives to a surveillance detail on Monks's kiosk, in the hope that the man would return.

He never did, at least not in person.

«

The reason he never returned was that he was now comfortably established in Connolly's apartment in Pilot View. I've said I don't know that much about what Macarthur got up to while he was there, but I do know that he got into the habit of phoning a cab company in Dún Laoghaire and getting a driver to pick up certain things for him—takeaway meals, the daily newspapers, sparkling water, and so on. At one point, apparently, he got a cabdriver to pick up a copy of *Private Eye* from a newsagent in Dún Laoghaire and bring it around to Pilot View. Even if we bracket the larger issue— always looming, always irresolvable—of whether this detail is even true, there are some baffling aspects here. This is a man whose financial situation is apparently so dire that he has killed two people in a botched effort to resolve it, and yet he is paying for cabdrivers to deliver him expensive bottled water and satirical magazines. (Here we might glimpse the attitude toward money that led Macarthur to this impasse in the first place.)

Once or twice, instead of staying behind in the apartment while Connolly went into work, Macarthur accompanied him into the city. As a perk of his job, Connolly was driven everywhere by a Garda in a state car. And so we must pause here to picture a scene of superlative absurdity: the most wanted criminal in the country, sitting in the comfortable leather-upholstered rear seat of the attorney general's car, being chauffeured across the city by a cop.

A further absurdity: On Sunday the 8th of August, Macarthur attended a match in Croke Park with Connolly. It was the All-Ireland hurling semifinal, Kilkenny versus Galway. Connolly was a serious fan of the game and had secured VIP tickets. He'd been planning to go with his brother, Anthony, and his nephew, Stephen, but managed to secure an extra ticket for his houseguest.

The four men were chauffeured across the city by Connolly's driver. Macarthur didn't have a VIP ticket, so he parted company with his friend and went to sit in the stands. In the VIP box, in the area reserved for government officials, Connolly happened to be seated close to Pat McLaughlin, the Garda commissioner. Connolly hadn't been in the job very long at that point, and he had not yet met the commissioner. He introduced himself, and the two men chatted amiably for a short while. They talked about the game: the championship so far, the prospects for the two teams.

"Tell me this," said Connolly then, shifting the tone. "Are you making any progress at all on those dreadful murders?"

They were, said McLaughlin. They had some strong leads, and they were hopeful they would get their man.

And so it was that, in a spirit of collegiate interest, the

attorney general discussed the most notorious murder case in many years with the head of the police force, while the man responsible, his friend and houseguest, sat in another area of the stadium, watching the match.

When the match ended, Macarthur made his way down toward the VIP parking area. While he waited for the others to show up, he leaned against the passenger door of Connolly's state car, taking in his surroundings. He was wearing dark glasses, confident—rightly so, it turned out—that no one would connect him to the composite photo of the murder suspect that was all over the newspapers that weekend, or to the description of him that had been broadcast in the television reconstruction. A woman in her early thirties was standing beside the car next to Connolly's in the VIP car parking area, waiting for her own driver to arrive. Macarthur recognized her as Máire Geoghegan-Quinn, a junior education minister in Taoiseach Charles Haughey's recently formed government, and the first woman in the history of the state to have been appointed to a ministerial position. She noticed Macarthur standing beside the attorney general's car, but the two did not speak.

Less than a week later, Macarthur's image was all over the news, and Geoghegan-Quinn was profoundly shaken by the realization that this was the man she had silently stood next to after the match. Eleven years later, she was minister for justice, and a peculiarity of Irish criminal law meant that the question of Macarthur's probation was at her discretion. She did not grant it.

SIXTEEN

One morning later that week, Tony Hickey and a fellow detective named Kevin Tunney were sent to check out Pilot View, the upscale apartment complex where a driver had reported a strange man he'd picked up asking to be dropped off, before disappearing into a nearby estate. The detectives walked in past the electronic gates and started pushing buzzers. They had a bunch of facial composite images with them, which they showed to whomever they managed to speak to, but they weren't getting much traction. Mostly, people were taken aback to be talking to the police at all. Pilot View was not the kind of place that criminal investigations ordinarily led to.

At the front doors, the buzzers had little plates next to them with the names of each apartment's resident. One particular name caught Hickey's eye—a retired army colonel, according to the title: exactly the sort of upstanding character who would make for a reliable witness. As he was pressing the buzzer, it so happened that the colonel's wife appeared at the door, on her way into the building with some shopping.

Hickey explained the situation to her and showed her the composite images. She personally had not seen anyone who looked like the face in the images, she said, but suggested he should talk to a Mr. Solomon, who lived in the building next door. Mr. Solomon was head of the residents' association, she said, and he made it his business to know who was coming and going in the building, who had visitors and so forth.

Hickey thanked the woman, and headed for the apartment block next door.

«

This, I admit, is a scene of only modest significance to our story. The woman at the door is hardly a crucial player. But ever since Hickey mentioned her to me, I have had a lingering suspicion—a conviction, in fact—that this woman was my grandmother. To be clear, Hickey mentioned her to me with the specific caveat that she was *not* my grandmother. He couldn't remember her name, or her husband's name, but he was fairly confident it wasn't O'Neill, my grandparents' surname. Also, I had specified to him that my grandfather was a retired army captain, and he was certain that this woman's husband was a retired colonel. He wasn't sure why, he told me, but he remembered that quite clearly. And so this woman can't have been my grandmother.

And yet I am not quite willing to give up the idea that she was. Not long after I decided to write about Macarthur, I visited my grandmother for what turned out to be the last time. She was by then on her gentle but inexorable descent into senility. But when I asked her about her memories of the investigation and the arrest, she told me that both she and my grandfather had been questioned by the police—almost everyone had been, she said.

How likely is it that there would have been a retired colonel and his wife living in the same complex as a retired captain and his wife? Not that likely, but then hardly inconceivable either. Whether or not the woman at the door was my grandmother is yet another thing I will never know.

«

Alfred Solomon was in. Hickey described the suspect to him and showed him some of the facial composites. No, he said, he couldn't think of anyone in Pilot View, anyone who lived here or whom he'd seen around the place, who matched that description.

Hickey turned to go.

"Actually," said Solomon, "hang on. Run that description by me one more time."

Hickey ran through it again. Wavy hair. Posh. Well turned out. Cravat.

"Patrick Connolly, the attorney general, lives in this building," he said. "He's had a nephew staying with him the last while. Now that you say it, the nephew is very like that description you've just given. Wears a cravat as well."

The nephew, he said, had been here before, too, a while back, maybe a year ago. They'd met on the stairs a few times but never spoke. He'd struck him as somewhat rude, in fact. At one point, Solomon said, he had seen him out front, having trouble starting his car. It was a cold morning. He went to his own car and got a can of Easy Start spray, and sprayed it on the man's engine for him, and he was able to get it started. "There was no conversation," Solomon said. "The most he said was thank you."

Hickey thanked the superintendent and kept going. It didn't strike him as a particularly compelling lead, this thing about the attorney general's nephew. It sounded, in fact, completely daft. But you had to keep an open mind about these things. You never knew. He made a note of it, and

when he got back to the incident room he passed it on to
Courtney.

«

Obviously, you didn't just turn up on the doorstep of the
attorney general and demand to question his houseguest,
nephew or otherwise, about a series of murders. Not, certainly, on the strength of a statement by a solitary, tentative
witness. They needed to find out more about this person, and
the nature of his connection with Connolly.

When the detectives interviewed Harry Bieling, they
were especially interested to hear the names of mutual
acquaintances that had come up in his conversation with the
gunman. One of those names, an especially useful one, was
Betty Broughan. Broughan was part of a group who drank
in Bartley's, he said; they'd been friendly back in the mid-
seventies, though they'd since fallen out of touch. The gunman had mentioned her; it was she who had organized the
party he said he'd been at.

Broughan was living alone now, in a suburb on the
Northside, with a young child. Hickey went to see her with
another young detective, Denis Donegan. They told her only
that they were investigating an attempted armed robbery at
the home of her old friend Harry Bieling. They said nothing
of the likely connection between that incident and the two
recent murders; nor did they mention that the man they were
looking for had given his name to the guards. They passed
on the details of the description Bieling had given them. "A
good-looking lad," said Hickey, "swanning around the town
with wavy hair. A lord of the manner type of a fella." Could
she think of anyone who attended that party, and who would
correspond to that description?

"Oh yes," she said. "That's probably Malcolm."

"Malcolm who?"

"Malcolm Macarthur."

She had known Malcolm pretty well, she said, back in those days. He'd been romantically involved for a while with a good friend of hers, and he had once taken them both to Cambridge on one of his trips. He'd been very generous and put Betty herself up in a hotel. The two women did some sightseeing, though Macarthur spent most of his time in the library, reading books and journals. He was something of a playboy, certainly, but also very much an intellectual.

She was surprised to be told that he might have been involved in some kind of armed robbery, but then again, he was a peculiar man. He had said something to her once that she would never forget, she claimed, something utterly inexplicable. They should get married, he said to her, and they should have a child together, and raise it until the age of seven, and then just abandon the child, let it go feral. When she asked him why he would suggest such a thing, he told her that this was what his own parents had done to him at that age.

She had not seen much of him since then. He was in a relationship now with a woman named Brenda Little. She'd known Brenda, too, back in the Bartley's days—another young woman from a working-class North Dublin suburb, whose lifestyle had markedly improved since taking up with Macarthur.

They had a kid now, she said, a little boy who must be nearly seven.

Hickey asked Betty whether she happened to know the attorney general, Patrick Connolly. She told him that she did know him, though not well. He and Brenda Little, she said, were good friends.

Did she happen to know, asked the detectives, where they might find Macarthur now?

The last she'd heard, he and Brenda were somewhere in Spain, or maybe the Canary Islands, with their son. She wasn't in touch with either of them these days. But if anyone was likely to know what he was up to, and where he was, it would be a mutual friend of theirs named Victor Meally.

«

One evening in early autumn, I called Macarthur. It had been a while since we'd spoken, a month or maybe six weeks. He had a tendency to be terse on the phone, because of what seemed to me a somewhat paranoid concern that someone— maybe the guards, maybe the press—might be listening in on his calls. But for whatever reason, he was more voluble than normal that evening, and I got him talking about Betty Broughan. He adopted a tone of lawyerly hauteur, saying that she had very little "evidential value" as a witness, given that she had known him only for a short time, and only slightly, many years before the "criminal episode."

"She was an habitué of Bartley Dunne's," he said. "But I stopped going there in 1976, when my son was born. I had better things to do. And I saw very little of her after that. She was a friend of Victor Meally's. A sort of hanger-on, really. She came into my orbit briefly, and then around the time Brenda and I began seeing each other, she ceased being in my orbit. I didn't think she had much to offer, intellectually."

I mentioned this strange proposition he had supposedly made to her. This was not the first time we had discussed this proposition; he had brought it up himself, in fact, the very first time we'd met, invoking it as an example of the groundless and often deranged stories that had found their way into the press after his conviction. My sense was that Macarthur was right about this. He seemed to me to have been, if anything, more hands-on and progressive in his parenting than most men of his generation—at least in his own telling. Even after he went to prison, he continued to be involved in Colin's upbringing, and had a great deal of input into decisions around the boy's education.

After his arrest and his conviction, he said, everything became a kind of narrative free-for-all. When you were as notorious as he was, almost anything could be said about you, and it would be reported as fact in the newspapers, and people would believe it. But this story was especially absurd, he said, and he had no idea where she could have gotten the idea to say such a thing. For one thing, he had always had a deep philosophical aversion to the concept of marriage.

I told Macarthur that, for what it was worth, I found it difficult to imagine him saying such a thing. Then again, I said, I also found it difficult to imagine him bludgeoning a woman to death with a hammer, or shooting a man in the face at point-blank range. I don't know whether the story of their conversation is too implausible to have happened, or too implausible to have been fabricated. Or perhaps it isn't so much implausible as inexplicable; perhaps, as with so much else to do with this whole affair, it is simply impervious to rational analysis. There are times when I imagine certain readers—Macarthur himself, or Brenda Little, or any number of legal and political figures whose names I have not even encountered—turning the pages of this book and shaking their heads in weary amusement at all the things I don't understand, all the things I haven't even realized I don't know.

«

The morning after Hickey and Donegan spoke to Betty Broughan, they showed up at the house Victor Meally shared with his sisters in Mount Merrion, an affluent suburb on the Southside. Conroy came along, too, and another detective named Joe Shelley. They revealed as little as possible to Meally about their reasons for wanting to find his friend Macarthur, because they had no idea what the nature of their relationship was. Meally and Macarthur could have been family, accomplices, even lovers. They made it clear only that it was imperative that they speak with him. (They did also ask whether Macarthur was gay. Meally said he had never known him to be interested in men.)

Meally was visibly shaken by this turn of events—four plainclothes detectives turning up and asking about his old friend, who had clearly gotten himself mixed up in something. But he was willing to help, in the one small way that he could. He reached into an inner pocket of his jacket, removed a book—an actual little black book—and flipped through its pages. He didn't have the address for Macarthur and Little's former flat, he said, but he did have a number. They took this number down, thanked him, and went on their way.

As a superintendent, Courtney had access to a registry of phone numbers at the post office, and found the address that corresponded to the number they'd just been given. Donegan called to the apartment. A Malaysian doctor was living there now. Donegan asked her if she knew anything about the previous tenant, and she told him that the attorney general, Patrick Connolly, had lived there before her. She gave him the number of her landlord.

When Donegan called the landlord, he was not pleased to be talking to the police, but he confirmed that the previous tenant was in fact Connolly. And yes, in the time between his leaving for a new apartment in Dalkey and the lease period elapsing, a young couple had lived there with their son. Connolly had continued to cover the rent, he said, for that period.

The more they talked, the more imperiously irate the landlord became. He was a friend of Charles Haughey, he said. A close friend, in fact. Perhaps he should call the Taoiseach right away and inform him that the Gardaí were making spurious inquiries involving his attorney general?

Donegan persuaded the man to hold his fire for twenty-four hours, while they made some further inquiries. The last thing the investigation needed now was the leader of the country being made aware of the suspicion pointing toward his own attorney general. Who knew what kind of political pressure might be brought to bear, and how it might affect the investigation?

They were closing in on their suspect. They had the head of the residents' association talking about the man with the cravat staying in Pilot View. They had Betty Broughan linking Macarthur's partner to Connolly. And they had the link with the Donnybrook apartment. As bizarre as all of this seemed, and as circumstantial, it was pointing in a definite direction. And because one of the murders involved a shotgun, possession of which was covered in the Offences Against the State Act, the guards were entitled to a warrant to enter and search the premises.

It was time to go to Pilot View.

SEVENTEEN

Hickey and Donegan got there first and waited outside the building in a van, watching the door. Connolly's apartment was on the top floor of the building, and its front windows could be seen from the parking lot at the front. They'd been there maybe an hour when a figure appeared in the window, peered out through the curtains a few moments, and disappeared again. Corduroy jacket, cravat, wavy hair.

Hickey went to the door and pressed the intercom button for the apartment, announcing his presence. No answer. He tried a second time, a third. Nothing. He got back in the van.

A few minutes later, more detectives from the murder squad showed up. Frank Hand, John Courtney, Noel Conroy. There was a chance, they figured, that Macarthur could escape by climbing out a rear window of the apartment onto the roof. Hand went around the back to keep an eye.

Courtney was still talking through the choreography of the thing when a taxi pulled into the car park and sounded the horn. The guards descended on him, told him to state his business. One of the residents here had called him and asked for a few things to be delivered, he said.

Was this person by any chance in apartment number 6? they asked.

He was, said the driver. He'd picked this man up a few

weeks back, outside a pub in Finglas, and driven him to Dún
Laoghaire, and since then he'd gotten into a habit of calling him for delivery purposes. It was a peculiar business, all
right, but the money was good.

He gestured toward a miscellany of purchases on the
passenger seat. There was the September issue of *Town &
Country* magazine, the cover of which bore an image of
a model in a long white coat against the backdrop of the
Chrysler building. ("Manhattan: The Pleasure of Having it
All.") There was a bottle of high-end sparkling water. And
there were two hacksaw blades, such as might be used in an
attempt to saw off a shotgun barrel by a person who knew
nothing about saws, or shotgun barrels.

This was their guy, all right: their cravat-wearing,
sparkling-water-drinking, lifestyle-magazine-reading suspect. The hacksaw blades indicated to them that he still
had the stolen gun with him, and that he was not finished
using it.

Conroy and Hickey got access to the foyer of the apart-
ment building by pressing the buzzer for another apartment.
They decided to wait there until Connolly showed up. With
Frank Hand at the rear of the building, there was no chance
Macarthur was getting out.

«

Then there was stasis. Macarthur did not appear at the
window again, and the guards made no further move until,
an hour or so later, a black Mercedes drove through the gates,
chauffeured by a uniformed guard, and pulled up outside the
building. As soon as Connolly emerged from the rear of the
car, Courtney was on him, explaining with brisk efficiency
what was happening—who he was, who these men with him
were, and why they were here. He told him there was a man

in his apartment they wished to speak to in connection with an attempted armed robbery in Killiney nine days previously. Of the murders, he said nothing, feeling that he had given him enough to think about for the present.

The attorney general could barely speak. When Courtney asked him to confirm that the man in his apartment was Malcolm Macarthur, he confirmed that it was. Was this man his nephew? they asked. No, not his nephew, he said. A friend.

Throughout this exchange, Hickey later recalled, it was as though Connolly was physically shrinking into himself. He was in shock, of course, and had probably not even begun to calculate the damage that was about to be done to his career, his life.

He produced a small diary out of an inner pocket and began to flick through it. He pointed to an entry for August 4. Yes, he said. Macarthur had been staying with him since that Sunday evening, the evening of the armed robbery Courtney had just spoken of.

«

I find this detail unaccountably touching. Perhaps it has to do with the strange, futile officiousness of the gesture; it's as though Connolly is attempting to use his diary, this meticulous register of daily comings and goings, as a means of staving off the chaos that has already begun to engulf his world. I find it touching despite the fact that I have no real idea who Connolly is. I know some facts about him, certainly—more than the average person, I imagine—but not nearly enough.

«

Connolly wanted to go in himself and talk to Macarthur, and convince him to come out and speak to the guards, but they were insistent that this would not be a good idea. He had a shotgun in there, they said. Connolly was disturbed to hear this, but persisted: Malcolm and he had been friends for eight years, and he was hardly likely to turn the gun on him.

Courtney was unconvinced. He didn't say as much to Connolly, but it was entirely plausible that, before the cops arrived, Macarthur had been planning to rob him, much as he'd attempted to rob Harry Bieling. Connolly was due to fly to New York the following morning, for a holiday. Macarthur must have known this, and must have anticipated Connolly's arrival home that evening with a lot of cash in US dollars. Better to hand over the keys and let the detectives deal with it. These men were armed, and they knew what they were doing.

Connolly gave the keys to Courtney. The detectives made their way into the buildings, their guns drawn. Hickey tried the keys in the door, but it was locked from the inside with a safety bolt. He heard someone moving around inside.

"This is the Gardaí," he shouted. "Open the door, please."

Macarthur's voice, from the other side of the door: "I will not. Is Mr. Connolly with you?"

Courtney went and got Connolly from the foyer and brought him up. He pleaded with his friend to open the door. There was a short pause, then the sound of the bolt being turned. They hustled Connolly down the corridor, away from the line of fire. There was a push at the door, a struggle, some shouting, and the detectives were in.

Macarthur was just standing there, apparently unarmed. They grabbed him and wrestled him to the floor. Connolly came in then and saw his guest, his friend, flanked by two detectives, hands cuffed behind his back.

«

And what about Macarthur? What was he thinking as they applied the cuffs; what was he feeling? He claims that he was calm. It wasn't that he knew that this was coming; if he had known they were as close to catching him as they were, he would almost certainly have left the country, he says, an idea he had so far not entertained. But there was nothing to be done now. What was happening was happening, and the only way out of it was through. Did he know then that it wasn't just the armed robbery at Bieling's place they wanted him for? Surely he must have hoped that they had not made the connection.

I imagine a lingering silence here, punctured by the shrieking mockery of a gull. And then Connolly spoke.

"I don't know what this is about, Malcolm," he said. "But whatever it is, you're on your own."

"That's fine," said Macarthur. I don't know how he said these words, but, knowing what I know about Macarthur, I suspect that he did so with stiff composure.

Connolly turned to the cops and told them they could use the living room to speak to Malcolm, to interrogate him. He was going upstairs, he said, and would be in his room.

Exit Connolly.

They asked Macarthur where the gun was then, and he brought them upstairs to the landing, showed them a little alcove door. Behind it were stacked cardboard boxes, papers from a long and hitherto distinguished legal career. Macarthur told them to look behind these boxes. Court- ney directed one of his men to crawl into the space, and he emerged a moment later with a bag—a black plastic bin liner, such as Macarthur had used to conceal his shovel and, decades later, his books and papers, his television. The butt of a shotgun protruded slightly from the open end of the bag.

They asked him how he came to be in possession of this gun. He had chanced upon it, he said, while out walking on Killiney Hill, of all places. It had been lying under some bushes. He'd also found a box of cartridges. They were in there too, he said, next to where he'd hidden the gun.

"If I'd known you were coming," he said, "I'd have been long gone from here."

"We made sure you didn't know," said Courtney.

Courtney took a good look at the gun. The Miroku, the brand that Donal Dunne had listed for sale. The serial number confirmed it: this was Dunne's weapon, the one that had been used to kill him. On the strength of unlicensed possession of a firearm alone, they could get Macarthur to the station for questioning and keep him for forty-eight hours.

And so then they were out, into the warm August evening, the sea air. They bundled him into a car and made haste along the coast road for Dún Laoghaire. From the front passenger seat, Courtney turned to face Macarthur. What, he asked, was he really doing in Killiney that evening? What really went on up at Camelot?

It was just as he'd told the guard on the phone the morning after, said Macarthur. It was all a misfired joke.

"Funny sort of a joke," said Courtney, turning back to face the road ahead.

«

Hickey and Conroy sat with Macarthur at a table in a small room in the station. For much of that evening, their suspect parried questions with a kind of pompous bewilderment. He knew nothing about the murders they were investigating, he told them, other than what he had read in the papers, and he certainly had no personal connection with them. He spoke about his privileged childhood, his intellectual pursuits, his humanistic principles. He told them of his deep and abiding passion for the arts and sciences, for philosophy and economics. His was a life of the mind; he was not some ravening brute with a lump hammer and a lust for blood.

They brought him a hamburger from a nearby fast-food place. I imagine Hickey, a man of wily irony, apologizing to Macarthur for the low-grade fare, which was not the sort of meal a man like him would be accustomed to. And I imagine Macarthur replying, with stiff formality, that he was as receptive as the next man to the uncomplicated charms of a grilled beef patty. (Always wary, Macarthur, of being taken for a common snob.)

The hamburger consumed, and a cup of milky tea along with it, Hickey and Conroy renewed their questioning. They were turning up the heat now. What was the motive for the murders? Did he know Bridie Gargan, or Donal Dunne? At this, Macarthur's performance of imperviousness was beginning to show signs of structural distress.

Why, asked Hickey, would a man like him be in such dire need of money that he would attempt a robbery?

He offered them a small truth then: that he had squandered his inheritance. Money and position meant nothing to him, he said. Money was simply the means to buy time—time to think, time to explore his interests, time to discover himself. It bought him freedom, for independent study and research. But he found himself running out of money, running into debt, and therefore running out of time itself.

"Was that what the gun was for?" asked Hickey.

"Yes," said Macarthur. "Desperate situations require desperate measures."

«

When Tony Hickey told me about the night of Macarthur's arrest, he mentioned a detail which, the more I think about it, seems more deeply ambiguous. Macarthur had shown almost no emotion, Hickey said, the entire time he had been in custody. But as he sat across the table from Hickey and Donegan now, after several hours of questioning, he began to lose his composure. He gripped the edge of the table tightly, and his knuckles began to tremble, and his face suddenly lost all its color, as though he were becoming the ghost of himself; his head went back and his eyes rolled upward into their sockets. Hickey was concerned, he said, that their suspect was having some kind of seizure or stroke, that the stress of the questioning had triggered a grave cascade of neural misfortunes.

"I'm regressing!" said Macarthur. "I'm regressing!" He repeated these words, said Hickey, a number of times. And then he stopped, and regained his composure.

It was close to midnight now, and the suspect was legally entitled to eight hours of rest while in custody. He would need some time to assemble his thoughts, he said, to put his recollections in chronological order. In the morning he would tell them everything.

EIGHTEEN

The previous night, as the detectives left Connolly's apartment with Macarthur, they told the attorney general that he was not himself a suspect, and that, from their point of view, he was free to leave the country for his holiday the following morning if he wished.

More detectives arrived and began to go through the apartment for evidence. Connolly was already in shock when he was informed that Macarthur was wanted in connection with not just an attempted armed robbery, but also the murders of Bridie Gargan and Donal Dunne.

In 1995, some thirteen years after the Macarthur affair, Connolly did an interview for a television docudrama. It's the only such interview I could find with Connolly, who died in 2016. He was in his late sixties at the time, although he could easily have passed for ten years older: what remained of his hair was yellowish white, wispily combed across the top of his pale head, his eyebrows angled and unkempt.

We see Connolly, sitting on the sofa in his living room, wearing a black three-piece suit. He takes out a small black notebook—the same diary that he produced in that conversation with the detectives outside his apartment building. Fingering the pages of the diary with nervy fastidiousness, he speaks slowly, and with a practiced lawyerly drawl: "In the context of the effect which the thing had on me in the immediate," he says, "I wrote in my diary at the time, by which I mean not necessarily that night but certainly within the next day or two, the following entry."

He produces then a large magnifying glass, and, peering through it at the tiny diary in his lap, he begins to read from its pages: "When I came home this evening, ready and packed for holidays, I found that there were detectives waiting to arrest Malcolm Macarthur. Stop. Absolutely stunned. Stop. The most shattering day of my life. Stop. He was wanted for two murders of a violent nature. Unbelievable news."

His voice betrays no obvious emotion, though he is talking about the events that not only ended his tenure as attorney general, but very nearly brought down the government for which he was chief legal advisor.

«

When I asked Hickey about whether the Gardaí ever considered that Connolly might be involved somehow in Macarthur's crimes, he told me that it was never taken seriously as a possibility. It was clear to anyone who had seen Connolly's reaction to his friend's arrest that he was utterly in shock, and that he was an entirely innocent party in the whole affair.

"Connolly would have been the type of fella," he said, "even though he came from North County Dublin, he would have been living in a rarefied atmosphere. He'd have gone to private school, the Kings Inns, the Law Library. He was a nice man. But they'd be floating around, them sort of fellas. They'd be a bit removed from reality. He said afterwards that he'd never really asked your man what he was at. He was independently wealthy, was all he knew. And it never occurred to him to ask, you know, what are you doing all day? What are you working at?"

«

The first person Connolly called was his brother, Anthony, who had met Macarthur just days previously at the hurling match. When he told him the news, Anthony got straight into his car and drove to Dublin.

When Anthony arrived, a couple of hours later, there was some minor discord between him and the police. According to an account of the arrest contained in a book published by Courtney after he retired, a family member of Connolly's—presumably Anthony—subjected him to "a barrage of criticism for not tipping off the Attorney General. When he confronted me I explained to him that I was doing my job as a policeman and was not in the business of cosying up to anyone, however elevated their position."

There was, then, another, more difficult call Connolly felt he had to make. He had a number for a phone in the foyer of the apartment building Macarthur and Brenda Little had been staying in in Tenerife. It was up to him, he decided, to tell Brenda what her partner had done—or stood accused of doing. He called the number; another resident answered and agreed to pass on a message to Brenda. Minutes later, she returned the call, and Connolly told her everything he knew: that Malcolm had been arrested, and that he was currently in police custody, where he was being questioned in relation to two murders. I can only imagine that she was badly shaken; she did not for a moment, however, doubt the truth of what she had been told, given that it was Connolly who had told her.

At about ten o'clock that night, Connolly called his boss, the head of government. Haughey was out of the city, in his house on the private island he owned off the coast of Kerry. (The conflict between Haughey's lavish lifestyle and the relatively modest remuneration of public office was at that point a subject of discussion in political and media circles, but only in later years, after he left office, did it become a subject of open speculation and eventual investigation.)

There are a couple of theories as to how this conversation went. The first is that, because the phone line to the island was patchy, Haughey was able to understand only the gist of what Connolly was saying to him: he gathered that an arrest had been made in the double murder case, but not that the suspect was a personal friend of Connolly's, and that the arrest had been made in his apartment.

The other version is that Connolly, for whatever reason, simply didn't tell Haughey the whole story—possibly because he hadn't quite been able to process the reality of it himself. According to an *Irish Times* article published after Macarthur's conviction, Connolly "could not speak very freely, as there were other people, most likely Gardaí, in the flat. He told the Taoiseach little more than that a friend had been arrested, and would most likely be charged with murder."

Either way, Haughey gave Connolly his blessing to fly to Heathrow the following morning as planned, then on to New York that afternoon. It is basically inconceivable that the Taoiseach would have done so had he been fully aware of the implications of the news.

«

Connolly was preparing to leave for the airport the following morning when John Courtney and Noel Conroy showed up again. They wanted a statement, but Connolly took a firm stand against the idea. He was the attorney general, and he knew precisely what his rights were; he was entirely innocent in all of this, and furthermore he had booked an expensive holiday which was now long past the point of any possible refund.

Attorney general he may well have been, said Courtney, but the more relevant context here was that a man who was about to be charged with two murders had been hiding out in his apartment. Perhaps, in the interest of assisting the cause of justice, there was some later flight he could catch. No, said Connolly. He was going to London, and the following morning to New York, and he would give them a full statement when he returned in a fortnight's time. As much as the guards might have wanted to detain Connolly, he was not a suspect; they were satisfied of his hapless innocence in the whole affair. The attorney general got in his chauffeured state car and headed for the airport, perhaps justifying his decision to himself on the grounds that no one could possibly be more in need of a holiday than he was at that moment.

«

That morning, Macarthur awoke at 6:00 a.m. and announced that he was ready to give a statement. Not long later, he was back in the same room he had been questioned in the previous evening, sitting at the same table, across from detectives Joe Shelley and Denis Donegan.

Speaking calmly and with languid deliberation, he dictated to Shelley a long and detailed account, in which he outlined how he had killed Bridie Gargan and Donal Dunne, and how he had attempted to commit armed robbery at Harry Bieling's house in Killiney.

Having read over and then signed his statement, Macarthur's thoughts turned toward the likely consequences of his actions on the life of his friend, the attorney general. Because of an act of kindness and plain hospitality on his part, Connolly's career and reputation were now in grave jeopardy. Some form of mitigating action, he felt, was necessary. He requested a pen and paper. Watched over by the detectives, he wrote the following note, for the attention of the Taoiseach himself.

> *Dear Sir,*
>   *I have already stated to the police and wish now*
> *to state to you also, that my good friend, Mr Patrick*
> *Connolly, Attorney, had no knowledge whatsoever of any*
> *wrongdoings of mine and must be considered to be utterly*
> *blameless. I earnestly hope that the career and happiness*
> *of this splendid man shall not be adversely affected.*
>   *Yours sincerely,*
>   *Malcolm Macarthur*

Of all the things I have learned about Macarthur, that he composed this note, at this time, seems to me to be the most revealing of his particular strangeness. Here is a man who, having just confessed to two murders and an armed robbery, sees fit to write what is essentially a letter of recommendation, pleading the innocence and good character of his friend, the attorney general, to the man's boss, the leader of the country. Even as he is confessing to having committed the most terrible of crimes, for the most abject of reasons, his understanding of himself as a person whose opinion might influence the Taoiseach remains intact. Even now, forty years after the murders, having spent much of his life in prison, he retains an abiding sense of himself as an associate member of the establishment, albeit one who went seriously rogue. A man whose terrible actions—actions which he does not for a moment deny—fail, in the end, to obscure his fundamental probity.

From my earliest acquaintance with Macarthur, I was struck by how important it seemed to be to him that he was held in high regard by others. "High regard," as I have said, was a signature expression of his; he was always talking about the high regard he was held in by some or other person, or about the people—including, occasionally, myself—he held in high regard. Once, he told me about a letter of recommendation a former school principal had written for him when he was applying to colleges in the United States, in which he described him as "a boy of excellent character, whom I would unhesitatingly employ in a position of responsibility and trust," and who was possessed of "an uncommonly good balance of responsiveness and control." It was clear that this letter of recommendation was, sixty years on, a part of the structure of his self-conception. Despite everything that had since happened, everything that he had done, he remained in his own mind a boy of excellent character.

He took a distinct pride, too, in the confession he gave to the police that morning. He spoke of it as though it were generally regarded as a classic of its kind. It was an unusually detailed statement, he said, and from the point of view of the Gardaí an extremely good and reliable one. A senior detective, he told me, had once remarked to him that there were fifty-six points of corroboration in the statement. "In other words," he said, "I independently told them fifty-six things they already knew, thereby proving that I had to have been speaking from experience." Even his confession to a brutal double murder was, to Macarthur, evidence of his own intellectual rigor and moral seriousness.

«

When the detectives searched Paddy Connolly's spare room, they found the forensic medicine textbook, and inside it the notebook pages that they believed to be evidence of Macarthur's plan to kill his mother.

«

Right after Macarthur dictated his statement, the detectives took his photograph. Tony Hickey told me that Macarthur wanted his bow tie on for the photo, and asked him to tie it for him. "I said something to the effect that the bow tie was part of his image," he said. "And he looked at me as the photograph was about to be taken, and said, 'This is one for your archives.' So he was thinking to himself at that stage, Oh, I'm famous. Now, Jesus, that's an abnormal piece of behavior from a man that has been arrested in the attorney general's apartment, and is facing two murder charges and an aggravated burglary, and all the rest of it."

But I am struck less by Macarthur's odd arrogance than by what I imagine as a discordant note of tenderness in the detective tying the murderer's bow tie. It's tied imperfectly, but when you look at the photograph—which was soon all over the newspapers, as Macarthur knew it would be—it's clear that Hickey made an effort to get it right. There is a kind of surreal inversion here: the criminal and the lawman momentarily become gentleman and valet—an association I find it hard to imagine did not at least cross Hickey's mind.

He was, surely, well aware that he was assisting Macarthur in completing a costume. *It's a part of your image.* And the bow tie did become a central element of Macarthur's aristocratic persona as it was constructed in the media. His insistence on wearing it for the photograph, and for the court appearance later that day, hints at a deeper dissimulation. His entire identity, it seemed—the apparel, the accent, the endless days of cultivated leisure—was rooted in a fiction, a performance.

NINETEEN

Connolly's holiday did not pan out. By the time he got to London, Haughey had been more fully apprised of the details of the arrest, and had come to see its dire political implications. He called Connolly at his hotel in the West End and asked him to come back to Dublin. Again, Connolly refused; he told his boss he'd phone him again to check in once he got to New York. Haughey let it slide, possibly wanting to avoid the kind of conflict that might result in his having to fire his attorney general, thereby giving the media grounds to speculate about the nature of Connolly's relationship with the murderer, and possible involvement in the crimes themselves.

"Those who believed in conspiracy theories had a field day," wrote Haughey's press secretary, Frank Dunlop, in his memoir *Yes, Taoiseach*. "Ultimately any neutral assessment of the affair would show that, apart from the discovery of the suspect in the apartment of the Attorney General, any connections with the government were tangential. But at the same time, though nobody would say it publicly, many journalists and politicians [. . .] were prepared to believe that the Attorney General's departure on a pre-arranged holiday was some sort of set-up and that, notwithstanding his complete and total innocence in the affair, this was yet another example of there being one law for those in power and another for everyone else."

By the time Connolly arrived at JFK Airport the following day, the story had exploded in the Irish media and was already a subject of interest in the British and American press. At arrivals, reporters hounded him for quotes. The following day the *New York Post* ran a story with the headline "Irish Biggie Flees Here After Slay Scandal," which strongly implied that Connolly was on the run from the law himself.

When he got to his hotel on Madison Avenue, there was another call from Haughey; it was clear he would have to fly back as soon as possible. And so the following morning, despite his best efforts not to get embroiled in the growing scandal back home, he flew back to London by Concorde. He spent the three-hour flight reading the British newspapers the consulate in New York had given him, and drafting a statement for the press, clarifying the nature of his relationship with Macarthur. He explained why, from his point of view, Macarthur had been staying in his apartment, and why he himself had decided to fly to New York rather than stay at home to deal with the fallout from the arrest. The Gardaí, he wrote, had told him he was within his rights to depart; "I had already furnished them with all the information I had concerning Mr. Macarthur's presence in my home," he wrote.

When he landed at Heathrow, a television crew from BBC News met him at arrivals; he ignored their questions and headed for the Irish Air Corps jet that had been sent to fly him on to Dublin. From there, he went directly to Haughey's house, to work out the details of his resignation.

«

The Macarthur affair—the murders, the investigation, the public scandal and political fallout—is often viewed as essentially a long and bizarre footnote to the career of Charles Haughey. The arrest, after a very public manhunt, of a murder suspect in the home of the attorney general was by no means the immediate cause for the fall of Haughey's government, just nine months after it was formed. But it fed a growing public mistrust of the Taoiseach and the people around him.

The full extent of Haughey's corruption would not be revealed until after he finally left office. (He was returned for a third term in office in 1987, which lasted until his retirement in 1992—a testament to the Irish electorate's enduring indulgence of venality.) But even in 1982, it was obvious to anyone who cared to think about it that he was on the take. He was, though a career politician of fairly humble origins, a conspicuously wealthy man. He lived in a vast Georgian mansion on a 250-acre estate in Dublin, which he bought in the early 1960s when he was minister for finance. He owned a racehorse named Aristocracy. He owned a private island off the coast of Co. Kerry, which he purchased for five times his official annual salary. He owned a yacht called *Celtic Mist*.

In 1997, five years after he retired, a tribunal uncovered the lurid particulars of his corruption: he had received a total of some eight million pounds in bribes from various businessmen throughout his time in office, which money he hid from his own government in Cayman Islands bank accounts. All this at a time when Ireland was one of the poorest countries in Europe. Throughout the 1980s, the economy was in perpetual recession, unemployment was as high as 17 percent, and the top rate of income tax was 60 percent.

The day after Connolly handed in his resignation, Haughey gave a press conference. It was intended to be about a public sector pay dispute, but the assembled journalists were much more interested in Haughey's attorney general, and the outrageous circumstances of his resignation. In describing the events surrounding Macarthur's arrest, and the fiasco that had befallen his own attorney general, Haughey used a series of expressions that quickly became synonymous with his own leadership. The entire affair, he said, was "a bizarre happening," a "grotesque" and "unprecedented situation," and an "almost unbelievable mischance."

The following day, *The Irish Times* published a column by Conor Cruise O'Brien, a deft and prominent critic of the Taoiseach, in which he coined the acronym that immediately came to be synonymous with the Macarthur affair and, in a broader sense, to define Haughey's political career: "If the situation was Gubu—that is to say, grotesque, unbelievable, bizarre and unprecedented—then the greater the credit due to Mr Haughey, for dealing with it. The more heads the Hydra had, and the more fangs they bore, the more highly we think of Hercules."

The press conference became notorious for another reason too: Haughey very nearly derailed Macarthur's trial. At one point, he was asked why there had been no official government statement congratulating the Gardaí on their work. (The implication was that Haughey was deeply embarrassed by the arrest, and that he was trying to avoid giving it oxygen; there was even some speculation that the Gardaí had deliberately chosen to arrest Macarthur inside the attorney general's apartment rather than outside the building specifically to damage Haughey himself.) It was, he said, a very good piece of police work; they had done an excellent job, "slowly, painstakingly, putting the whole thing together and eventually finding the right man."

It wasn't immediately apparent to Haughey what he had done, implying the guilt of a suspect who had yet to be tried, but Frank Dunlop, his press secretary, knew a prejudicial remark when he heard one. As soon as the press conference ended, he explained it to him in as delicate terms as he could.

"Oh God," said Haughey. "I didn't, did I?"

«

If he had sought to curb the growing political controversy, Haughey succeeded only in escalating it. The remark didn't make it into the Irish media, because reporting on it would in itself have amounted to contempt of court, but British journalists were subject to no such restrictions. After Haughey's comment was broadcast by the BBC—available in many Irish households—Macarthur's defense lawyers, having only just been assigned to him, went to the High Court to argue that the Taoiseach should be held in contempt, and that the case was irredeemably prejudiced.

"In the highly charged atmosphere," wrote Dunlop, "there were those who insisted on believing that it had been no slip of the tongue but a deliberate attempt to pervert the course of justice."

Although the court concluded that Haughey had made a genuine error, suspicion remained among the general public that something was being covered up, that the connection between Macarthur, Connolly, and Haughey's government was not as random as it first appeared, and that Connolly might not have been as hapless in the whole affair as the official story had it.

"It was all too Haugheyesque," as the Irish journalist Fintan O'Toole later put it. "Only a fool could believe that there was in fact nothing much to see here. By far the strangest thing was that there really wasn't."

«

The summer ended, and while the murderer awaited his trial early the following year, the Macarthur affair faded from the headlines. In October, members of Haughey's own Fianna Fáil party called a motion of no confidence in him, both as Taoiseach and as leader of Fianna Fáil. The motion was defeated, but Haughey's leadership position had clearly been weakened. His was a minority government, propped up by the support of the Workers' Party and independents. In November, Haughey put forward a motion of confidence in his leadership. The motion was voted down; he had lost the support of his coalition partners, and he had no choice but to call an election. By the end of that year, his government would be no more.

«

I am not sure what to do with the following fact, other than to note it as another example of the endless strangeness of this case, and of the smallness and intimacy of this country: the farm where Bridie Gargan grew up, and where her family still lived at the time of her murder, was previously owned by the parents of Charles Haughey. It was here, on this same farm, that the Taoiseach had lived in early childhood.

TWENTY

There's a photograph of Macarthur that was taken outside the Bridewell District Court a few days after his arrest. Macarthur himself is entirely obscured by a beige corduroy jacket over his head, held in place by the hands of plain-clothes detectives—Hickey, Conroy, and Donegan among them—as they bundle him into a squad car after his remand hearing. Crowded with cops and onlookers, the scene is a chaos of hands and faces. There is anger and contempt on these faces, but there is also curiosity and even amusement. Two boys stand at the entrance to the station, looking as though they are enjoying the spectacle; the man standing beside them, perhaps their father, bears an expression of focused, queasy inquisitiveness. In front of them is an older man, heavyset and stolid, his nostrils flared, his mouth set in fascinated disgust. The image gives off a charge of feral intensity, and something like repressed hilarity.

In another photo of the same scene, Conroy and Donegan are flanking Macarthur. Conroy is looking directly at the camera in stern reproach, while Donegan repels a man who is attempting to speak to Macarthur. The man—middle-aged, balding, disheveled—is bent low in front of the shrouded murderer, his face angled upward in order to see him through a gap in the corduroy jacket wrapped around

his head. The man's hand is raised in what might be a gesture of entreaty, or of violence.

Mary Kotsonouris, the district court judge who presided
over the hearing, wrote in her memoir about the sound of
the crowd as Macarthur was brought into the court to stand
before her. "Through the barred windows," she wrote, "I
heard a sound that was neither human nor animal, a low,
thunderous swelling of noise that was as inchoate as it was
meaningless. It was a sound I hope never to hear again—the
baying of the crowd."

And there was violence that day, of word and deed. The
courtroom itself was rammed; those who couldn't get into
the public gallery crowded on the stairs, hanging over the
banisters, waiting to catch a glimpse of the captured killer as
he was brought up. They wanted to see him in the flesh, this
paradoxical creature, this highborn savage. According to an
Irish Times report of the court appearance, he looked "acutely
nervous," his eyes darting furtively as he ascended the stairs.
Bodies surged toward him, held back by the Gardaí escort-
ing him.

Inside the courtroom, he stood in the dock, holding in
his hand a small white card. He twisted the card nervously in
his hands, looking down at it often, as though about to read
from it, but he never spoke.

"The slightly rakish elegance of his white shirt, grey silk
bow tie, gold silk handkerchief and white knitted waistcoat,"
wrote the *Times* reporter, "contrasted oddly with the beige
corduroy jacket he wore in Dún Laoghaire court, now creased
and grubby, creased grey trousers, unpolished brown shoes.
His hair, very thick, very dark, very well brushed, curled over
his jacket collar. He looked singular, intelligent, worried."

The hearing was swift. Justice Kotsonouris remanded
him in custody until September 9, and he was bundled out,
back down the stairs and out again into the crowded street. A

crowd of perhaps thirty, almost all men, pressed in on him as he was brought to the waiting squad car. Someone shrieked the word "bastard" a few times. Someone else shouted at the guards to take the jacket off his head so that they could see his face.

A woman roared at him as he passed. "Pig! Pig! Swine!"

The crowd worked itself to a pitch of righteous rage, and then fists emerged from the chaos, ferocious and determined. One fist got under the protective arms of the detectives, connecting glancingly with Macarthur's face. Another thumped him in the small of his back. Out of nowhere, a woman emerged—the woman who'd called him a pig, perhaps—and held back though she was by a detective, she swung her handbag with spiteful skill over his shoulder and landed an authoritative blow on Macarthur's neck.

An article in the *Irish Independent* quoted a woman standing on the courtroom steps: "I saw him go in. The cheek of him. He knew he did it, and I knew he did it, and he went in there in cold blood with not a bother on him."

The article mentioned, too, a group of farmers who were "preparing to express their outrage more tangibly." "I'm going to take a swipe at him now," said one of them, "a swipe that'll put him into Kingdom Come."

Macarthur had begun a new life, finally and unequivocally. He was a man, now, who could be abused with moral certitude: punched, spat upon, hit with a handbag. He had arrived at a state of abjection from which he would never be redeemed.

«

During the five months that Macarthur was awaiting trial, he had to attend regular remand hearings, and these public scenes became an almost weekly fixture. Macarthur knew, of course, that the signifiers of his class—his accent, his appearance, his social connections—were an aggravating factor. But he resented the way in which the press focused on this point of tension between himself and the assembled crowds. He accepted that he would have to live with being seen as a murderer, because that was what he was, but he didn't like to be thought of as an elitist.

More than once, he brought up with me an article he said had appeared in one of the papers after one such scene outside the courts. "Some columnist," he recalled one day, "wrote that my presumed attitude towards the protesters was, *Oh, it was one of theirs that I killed.* That it was a class thing. But I'm not a snob. I treat people as individuals. Oh, I'm aware of class, of course, of what are called *class distinctions.* Manners and accent and so on. But I've never been a snob."

I told him that I had read everything I could find on "his case" in the archives, and I had not come across an article making any such claim about Macarthur's attitude to the crowd. But there was something naggingly familiar about it all the same.

Later, I searched through everything I could access about the hearings, in all the major papers, and found nothing. And then I realized why it was familiar: it was a line from *The Book of Evidence.* I took down my copy of the book and found the passage where Freddie is mobbed outside the court after a hearing. "They shook their fists," it read, "they howled. One or two of them seemed about to break from the rest and fly at me. A woman spat, and called me a dirty bastard. I just stood there, nodding and waving like a clockwork man, with a terrified grin fixed on my face. That was when I realised, for the first time, it was one of theirs I had killed."

Macarthur had, it seemed, confused himself—and in a more literal fashion than he normally did—with a fiction based on his life.

«

After he was charged, Macarthur's free-legal-aid solicitor appointed a senior counsel to represent him in court. This barrister, Paddy McEntee SC, was at the time the country's most prominent criminal lawyer. According to a report on Macarthur's legal defense in the current affairs magazine *Magill*, McEntee was initially considering pursuing a plea of guilty but insane. And so a few days after his arrest, McEntee went to visit Macarthur in Mountjoy Prison, where he was being kept on remand. He wanted to get a feel for how he would come across in court, according to the article, and to see whether the insanity plea would convince a jury. When he met Macarthur, though, he seemed perfectly lucid. The reports of the psychiatrists who had met with him in prison also undermined this initial strategy: they could find nothing to suggest that he had any kind of psychiatric condition, or that he was not in control of his faculties.

A guilty but insane plea would, too, be highly reliant on a sympathetic jury, and the press coverage of the trial meant this was an unlikely prospect. With every passing day, Macarthur's image as a sneering dandy and a louche playboy was etched more deeply into the public consciousness. On top of all this, Connolly's involvement in the case was driving paranoid speculation among an increasingly cynical and disillusioned electorate that some kind of cover-up was in the offing, and that Macarthur would be acquitted due to the government's tampering in the legal process.

According to the report in *Magill*, McEntee looked at the evidence and advised that Macarthur should consider a guilty plea: "A not guilty plea would have ensured a three week trial and an accompanying media circus. Not only would all the gory details be known, the most sensational evidence would be highlighted day after day after day. The evening papers would vie with each other for the most grue-some headline, with each edition giving an update on the trial. The early editions might tell how the gardener at the American Embassy saw the car shaking and the blood drip-ping out. Later editions might tell of the car chase and Bridie Gargan's pathetic efforts to catch the attention of passers-by." The more lurid the press coverage, the less likely Macarthur would be to get a fair hearing—or, when the time came, to get an early release.

A peculiarity of the Irish justice system at the time was that, when it came to prisoners serving life sentences, the decision to grant release ultimately rested with the minis-ter for justice. An elected politician would never choose to release a murderer if the press and the public remained strongly against it. McEntee's view (which seems, in the end, to have been vindicated) was that the less publicity Macar-thur's case got, the sooner he would eventually be freed.

Just minutes after the trial got underway, McEntee asked the judge, James McMahon, for a twenty-four-hour adjournment. Harry Hill, the barrister acting on behalf of the state, had apprised him of certain documents that he planned to present to the court: psychiatric reports attesting to Macarthur's sanity, and the written notes, found by detec-tives between the pages of the forensic medicine textbook, which seemed to suggest that he had been planning a third murder. McEntee told the judge he needed to consider this evidence, seek expert advice, and consult with his client. The adjournment was granted.

Macarthur's legal team knew where things were headed. The following morning, Macarthur pleaded guilty to the murder of Bridie Gargan. With a conviction in hand that promised a life sentence, the severest punishment the Irish government could impose, the prosecutors decided not to proceed with the Dunne charge.

Harry Hill requested that he be allowed to read a statement of evidence, and to call Superintendent John Courtney as a witness. The idea here was to ensure that some basic information about the case was entered into the official record, to satisfy at least to some small degree the public's desire to know about the murders, and perhaps to offset concerns about a cover-up. Judge McMahon insisted, however, that such gestures were pointless. Macarthur had pleaded guilty to murder, he said, and a murder conviction carried a mandatory life sentence.

And so, with not a word of testimony spoken, Macarthur was given life for the murder of Bridie Gargan. But the absence of a trial meant that her family, and the wider public, never got to hear the evidence the detectives had gathered. Around her death, and around the person of her killer, an essential mystery would persist.

«

As painful as this was for the Gargans, the situation for the Dunne family was intolerable. It was as though, as far as the justice system was concerned, Donal's murder had simply not counted. Though Macarthur had confessed to shooting him dead, there were no witnesses to the killing, and Macarthur's claim that there had been a struggle could have complicated a conviction of murder, in that it might have suggested manslaughter; the potential difficulty to the state meant that he was never charged. They already had him on the first murder. He was going to prison for life anyway, and to their minds this was what mattered.

The Dunne family, for their part, were never told in advance about the state's decision not to proceed with a charge for the murder of Donal. They learned about it when the judge announced it in court. They were given no account of why this had happened, and learned about it only through details that emerged in the media. The family gathered a hundred thousand signatures demanding an explanation for why the charge was not proceeded with, and urging the director of public prosecutions to try Macarthur for Donal's murder, but nothing came of their efforts. They were told, via the media, that the DPP did not explain such decisions.

In 2002, twenty years after Donal's murder, a television current affairs show discussed the possibility of Macarthur's being released on probation. The following day, Christopher Dunne, Donal's brother, released a short statement to the press on behalf of the family. "It is difficult," he wrote, "to describe the pain and anguish felt by families in coping with the aftermath of crime. In our case we received no support whatsoever from the State." He was of the view, he said, "that a plea bargain was agreed on the nurse Gargan charge. This allowed the State the facility not to proceed with Donal's case and obviously stopped what would have been an embarrassing case for the government of the day."

«

One of the more unsettling effects of spending as much time as I did in Macarthur's company was that, although the murders were nearly always, either directly or indirectly, the focus of our conversations, it was often difficult to consciously bear in mind the reality of what this man did, and what it meant that he did it. There was a particular kind of cognitive dissonance at play, in the awkwardness of reconciling this spruce elderly person sitting in front of me, or walking beside me—this almost stately figure, speaking with authoritative composure about a matter of scientific or historic interest—with the knowledge that he had committed these extraordinarily brutal murders.

Sometimes it took an act of conscious remembering on my part, a deliberate effort not just to recall to my mind the abstract fact that he did what he did, but to try to imagine the terror and pain of his victims as he ended their lives in the most barbaric of ways for the most stupid and wicked of reasons. It was hard to conceive of what that might have meant for their families, and to imagine the endless expanses of their loss, which even the most comprehensively mapped narrative could not chart. Although I attempted to make contact with the Gargans and the Dunnes, I received no response. Even if I had been able to speak to them, I'm not sure it would have made it any easier to conceive of their suffering. It was decades since Macarthur had done these things, but I can imagine how little that might have meant to the people who lived every day with the consequences of his having done them.

Sometimes, I will think about Macarthur in the precise moments at which I am happiest. I will be in the garden with my daughter, watching her play in her sandpit, or kissing my son good night at the end of the day, smoothing my hand over his soft hair, and I will experience my love for them as an abrupt pang of tenderness that is not entirely distinct from fear, because to love a person that much is to feel, viscerally and insolubly, their vulnerability in this life, which is also one's own. And at such moments, I will remember Macarthur, and think of him as an emissary of the world's corruption and treachery, as an avatar of the forces that threaten this happiness and love. I will see him, at such moments, for what he is: the very worst thing that could possibly happen to me and to the people I hold close.

In that press statement, Christopher Dunne briefly recounts the apparent rationale behind Macarthur's actions, stating that he beat Bridie Gargan to death with a hammer in order to take her car, which he planned to use to get to Edenderry to get a gun, which he would use to commit a robbery. Then he writes: "He shot my brother at very close range, blowing his face away."

Although I have, over many years, read endless accounts of these murders, it is this sentence, in its shocking brevity, that feels to me most viscerally and painfully real. The reality of what Malcolm Macarthur did to Donal Dunne, and to those who loved him, is almost obscenely alive in his brother's words. I have to force myself to imagine what it would be like to say such things about a person I love.

And then I try to imagine what it would be like to read, in a newspaper (or in a book like this one), the account of the murder given by Macarthur himself in his statement to the Gardaí, in which he confesses to killing Donal Dunne with a single blast to the head and to noticing, as he dragged his body into the bushes, "that his head was in a mess." I try to imagine that this is somebody I love that he is referring to, my brother or my sister or my daughter or my son. But even in the abstract, the thought is too painful to be borne. Their faces, their bodies, are too tender, too alive, and too real. I can't do it.

PART FIVE

MONSTERED

———————

TWENTY-ONE

Almost forty years after his conviction, Macarthur was still capable of becoming irritated by the commotion surrounding his case. It was as though he thought of it as less a consequence of the murders he had committed, and of the extraordinary circumstances of his arrest, than a shameful manifestation of the unsavory press and the public's appetite for its product. He understood himself to be the villain of the story, of course, but that didn't preclude him from judging the puerility and sensationalism of people's interest in it.

This media coverage caused a good deal of what he called "collateral damage" to the lives of those closest to him, even if he himself was not much affected by it, for the simple reason that he was "otherwise occupied" at the time. Members of Brenda Little's family had to leave their houses. Wigs had to be worn to evade photographers and reporters. Paddy Connolly was forced to move out of his apartment and stay with a friend.

"The whole thing," he said, "was a bit of a frenzy, really. An extraordinary outburst of irrationality and emotional incontinence."

In the years that followed his conviction, imprisoned and with plenty of time on his hands to consider it, Macarthur came to feel that he had failed to give a proper public account of himself. He was not the person they imagined him to be, those people outside the courthouse, bearing furious witness to his iniquity—spitting, grasping, demanding to be shown his ghastly face. He was "monstered," as he put it, by the public, and in particular by the press. He understood that he had no one to blame but himself, and yet it felt like an injustice all the same.

He regarded himself as a realistic person: a man who accepted the obvious, who looked reality in the face and greeted it with stoic forbearance. But his situation, in the days and weeks after his arrest, was so disastrous that he was paralyzed by a sense of futility, such that doing anything to mitigate the circumstances in which he found himself was entirely beyond him, indeed scarcely occurred to him.

He simply accepted his fate and went along with it. And so he failed to assert himself, he said, did not bother to correct things people said of him that he felt were not true— that he was a sociopath, a psychopath, and so on. (How he might have gone about correcting people's perceptions in this respect, he did not make clear.)

In prison, he encountered people to whom he felt such labels better applied, people who he felt were entirely lacking in empathy or conscience. And he felt sure that he was not like those people. He was not what you would call a *natural criminal*. And this, he felt, was precisely why his criminal venture had failed. He had an analytical mind, but not the instincts of a criminal.

He had committed terrible crimes, it was true, but he was a man of inherent morality and decency, whose dire circumstances—partly material, partly psychological—had caused him to act in a manner utterly out of character. One could not extrapolate the meaning of a story in its entirety from the events of a single episode, however central that episode might be.

And because his actions had emerged not from some deep wellspring of violence within him, but from the intensity of the circumstances in which he found himself, it therefore followed that he was not in his nature a murderer.

«

There was, it seemed to me, a paradox at the heart of Macarthur's narrative of his life. When we spoke about the murders, he always wished to make it clear that he had acted in a logical manner. ("It was all," as he put it, "in the cerebral cortex.") The crimes took the form of a remorseless syllogism. He needed money: therefore the solution was to rob a bank: therefore he needed, by whatever means necessary, to get a car and a gun.

But the preservation of his own self-conception demanded that an act of such heartless rationalism be explained in a way that did not risk defining him as a person. And so it had also to be seen, in some fundamental sense, as an act of madness, one that had no obvious relationship to the larger narrative of his life. It had to be seen as an *episode*.

I told him once that I found it remarkable, given his extraordinary infamy as a murderer, how much value he seemed to place on his reputation—how frequently he made reference to his "good behavior," his essential decency, his love and respect for his fellow human beings.

"Well, it confirms my knowledge of myself," he said. "I think of myself as a normal person. People who know me well regard me as a very likable person. I have a *high likability factor*, I'm told. And I like people. I am very good with people. I am sympathetic and empathetic, and all those things."

As absurd as this may have sounded, it was not entirely wrong. He was a very polite man. He did sometimes invoke with an edge of bitterness people he had known in the past, but he spoke at all times with a fine decorousness and control. In all the afternoons I spent with him, he never once uttered even a mild swear word. A thing he could not abide, he said, was crude language, particularly when it was directed against women.

"I have always deplored," he said, "language or behavior that is sexist or misogynistic, that is disrespectful, or objectifying, or crude. I don't think I've ever been unmannerly in my life. I don't think I've ever been discourteous in any way whatsoever."

I started to point out that there were some obvious objections to that claim, when he cut across me.

"Apart from the criminal episode itself, yes, those were crimes," he clarified, as though the murders were somehow the exception that proved the rule of his otherwise unimpeachable good manners.

It was not that Macarthur tended to downplay the terrible immensity of what he had done. The plain fact was that he had ended the lives of two perfect strangers. There was no getting around it. He had murdered, yes, but he would rather not have done so, and he regretted it greatly. The whole affair had been a huge catastrophe, and had caused deep and abiding suffering to many people. But he saw himself, and seemed to want me to see him, as a murderer of a particular class: a murderer not by disposition, but by circumstance. It was not as though he had killed for the enjoyment of it.

The oddity of this self-justification was intensified, rather than mitigated, by its accompanying rationalism. I was reminded, again, of a line in Patricia Highsmith's *Ripley's Game:* "Tom detested murder unless it was absolutely necessary." Macarthur had, in the end, no great deal in common with the ingenious psychopath Tom Ripley, but there was something nonetheless Ripleyesque about this fastidious parsing of moral niceties.

«

As the months went on, my conversations with Macarthur came to circle closer and closer around the topic of remorse. There was, in his manner of speaking about his own contrition, something essentially abstract. I felt at times as though he were describing to me a wing of an old house that had been closed off to the public, and to which I could regrettably not be permitted access. I wanted something from him, something real and spontaneous. I wanted to see that he had suffered—not because of the consequences of what he had done to those two people, but because he had done it at all. Because he had killed them.

When I pressed him on this question, he said that, yes, he did feel remorse, a great and terrible remorse, but that he had never allowed it to overwhelm him, to become the defining fact of his life. Because what good would that have done, for himself or anyone else? People sometimes said to him that he must have been permanently damaged, ruined even, by the fact of what he had done. But he didn't think that this was the case.

Although I knew Macarthur to be a profoundly unreliable narrator of his own life, there were times, like this, when I was taken aback by his unwieldy honesty. It would have placed no great burden on him to exaggerate the extent of his contrition; presumably it would only have benefited him to do so. I wondered, in this sense, whether it was a manifestation of a kind of perverse integrity: that he was constitutionally incapable of claiming to feel an emotion he did not feel.

«

The longer I spent with Macarthur, the more remarkable I found his manner of speaking about his crimes. He had at his disposal an array of linguistic strategies with which to distance himself from the emotional reality of the murders. He would not say, for instance, "I did it"; he would say "It has been done." He would not say "I am responsible"; he would say "The responsibility is there." And, most strikingly of all, he would often forgo entirely the use of the first person singular, speaking not of an "I" but of a detached and generalized "you." "You cannot allow yourself to get into an emotional state," he put it to me, "so you compartmentalize."

This grammar of displacement was likely entirely unconscious, but it also revealed something important about Macarthur's relationship to the intractable horror of his own actions. None of this, I felt, could be attributed to anything so straightforward as dishonesty. Whether it was out of delusion or some self-inflicted psychic wound, he was incapable of narrating this story entirely in the first person. It was his life, but he could not tell it.

He was by no means in denial about what he had done. The murders were after all the central facts of his life; the only things, in the end, that could be said to be true. But his commitment to what he called stoicism was, to my mind, mostly a commitment to evading the emotional force of that truth.

One afternoon, in the living room of his little apartment, I raised again the topic of remorse. I was at my usual seat at the kitchen table, and he was sitting in his armchair, arms behind his head in an attitude of rigid repose. I asked him what it felt like, in the days after his arrest, to know that he would always have to live with the consequences of what he had done.

"I don't think I can recall," he said, rearranging himself in his seat, speaking tentatively and softly. "I can't retrieve it fully now. It's a combination of things, I suppose. It's not just guilt, although I did feel guilty. I knew that I had killed people. But it's everything. You feel sorry for yourself as well, because of what has happened to you. The consequences of what you have done. You're sorry for the effect the deaths have on the bereaved. The effect on the bereaved, in fact, is more immediate, because dead people are dead people. It's an awful thing to say, but that's the reality. They are past all of this—all of this *concern*. And the effect on my own family, of them coming to visit me in prison. The effect on Mr. Connolly's career, too. It's the whole experience, combined with knowing that you have done wrong. And ever since that time, I have envied people who have not done wrong. Instinctively, I have envied them. I would love to be able to say 'I didn't do that.' Not because of the consequences I faced, but simply not to have done it. That's a feeling I still have. Less so nowadays, I suppose, because you just have to get on with life. It goes into the background to some extent, but that feeling is still there. I don't want to overstate it. I'm philosophical about things I cannot change. One has to be stoic. It comes to the fore of the mind in certain circumstances, but it's always there. You dwell on it, you think about it. But I do envy people who haven't broken the law, and that will always be the case. My life is not ruined. But it is damaged."

«

I had often enough heard it said of Macarthur that he never demonstrated anything like repentance for what he did, neither in the immediate aftermath of his arrest nor in the decades since. This was true, at least in a technical sense. During questioning by the Gardaí, the only moment when he seems to have demonstrated any kind of emotion was the strange episode related to me by Tony Hickey—the eyes rolling back in their sockets, the heightened and scarcely coherent talk of regression. He had otherwise been coolly detached. In court, he had displayed no regret for his crimes, for the simple reason that he had not spoken, there being barely a trial at all. And neither, of course, had he spoken publicly of the crimes in the years since his release, despite a great many interview requests from print and broadcast journalists, from podcasters and documentary filmmakers.

When I mentioned to him this perception of his remorselessness, he said that he had read such things himself. He insisted, however, that he did have feelings, and that they were very powerful and profound.

"It is," he said, "a matter of *style*. There may be an element in this of where I was brought up, and how I was brought up, in that excessive emotionality was seen as fundamentally bad manners. There is an element of self-control, and of what you might call decorum. But it isn't that I have no strong feelings. Oh, I do, I do."

I asked him then whether there might be some connection between what he described as his *stylistic* approach to emotion and the fact that he committed these murders in the first place—whether it was perhaps his capacity for emotional distancing that had enabled him to do such terrible things. He sighed lengthily, not so much out of irritation, it seemed, as resignation.

"Yes, well," he said, "that could be. That could well be."

There were times, he said, when he would make himself remember certain aspects of the murders.

"When I think about the details," he said, "it is genuinely painful. But I do think about the details, because I feel it is in a sense good for me to be realistic, and to remember what I did. I don't do it very often, but I do it from time to time."

I asked him then whether this had something to do with feeling a need for atonement, and he shook his head. The term was perhaps too religiously inflected for his liking. No, he said: he made himself remember it simply because it had happened. And it would be wrong, factually wrong, to make oneself believe that it had not. It was not a spiritual or an existential question, in other words, so much as an empirical one.

I asked him what it was like to force himself to remember the murders. The first one, he said—meaning the murder of Bridie Gargan—was especially painful to remember. When I asked him why that was, he was silent for a long time—so long, in fact, that I wondered whether he might not answer at all—and then he spoke quietly, and haltingly.

"To shoot somebody," he said. "That is different from hitting somebody. Can't you see the point?"

"Do you mean that it's less intimate?"

"Intimate? Perhaps. I'm not sure. The experience is— I can't find the word. It's less intense on one's actual nervous system. I'm not doing very well at describing this."

He broke off again, and once more I had a sense of the closing off of something real and painful, though I was unsure whether it was me or him to whom access was being denied.

I wonder now whether, when he forced himself to think about the details of the murder, it was the murder as it actually happened that he remembered, or a milder version of it, like the one he had advanced to me, in which the hammer blows were intended only to subdue Bridie Gargan, and in which, when he left her in the back seat of her car and fled, she was exhibiting no distress.

"The outcome in any case," said Macarthur, "is that both lives were lost, so there is no difference in that sense. Two people lost their lives, and that's it. And I am the cause. I've never objected to the newspapers calling me *a double M*."

"By 'double M,'" I said, "I presume you mean double murderer."

"Yes," he said. "I accept that. I have no quibble about it.

That's just the reality. But yes, it's truly a stylistic thing, or a matter of personal privacy, how one expresses one's feelings. My style is to do it privately. But people who knew me very well would not agree that there was no remorse."

I told him that I myself tended to believe him when he said he felt remorse, but that a certain degree of openness, even emotionality, might be required for people in general to believe it.

"That's it, you see," he said, recovering now the energy and intellectual loftiness that had earlier deserted him. "There's a certain formula with these things. And that's why I regard the Irish as a slightly *unctuous* culture. As one of the world capitals of unctuousness, in fact. I don't object to it, but I do like a more restrained approach. You could even call it a more *dignified* approach, though I don't want to make too big an issue of that. That's just my outlook."

That afternoon, as I was preparing to leave, packing away my notebook and pen and taking my jacket from the back of the kitchen chair, he began to talk about his time in prison. (He was always doing this; I would say that I had to go—to pick up my son from school, to do some other work, to meet a person somewhere—and he would commence a disquisition on some or other aspect of his life or opinions. In the end, I learned to announce my departure well in advance of its actually being necessary.) He spoke of how various staff members of various correctional institutions had remarked on his apparent total normality. And then he caught himself.

"I'm in danger," he said, "of seeming to reduce the seriousness of what happened. Lives were lost. That's the fact."

He stared at the floor a moment, then gazed around the room. He tapped the sole of his shoe against the floor, as he so often did when he was pensive or uncomfortable.

"Lives were *taken,* I should say. That would be more accurate. I have never tried to evade that truth. I have never tried to minimize it in the slightest. I've never used the passive voice in speaking about it."

"Actually," I said, "you did just now say *lives were taken,* which would be a strong example of the use of passive voice."

"Well, yes," he said. "Okay. I took lives."

He didn't seem irritated by my pointing this out, but neither did he seem particularly surprised by, or reflective about, the forcefulness with which he had just contradicted himself.

«

For the most part, I was willing to grant Macarthur whatever argument allowed him to avoid seeing himself as a damned soul. I saw little point in taking an adversarial approach with him, because I felt that to do so might have led to his closing himself off against me, and would in the end have proven counterproductive.

But there were times when my frustration with his evasions was more than I could bear, and this gave rise, on occasion, to absurd exchanges. I remarked to him once, after we had been talking for the better part of a year, that he seemed to me a highly conflicted person. He took issue with the characterization, telling me that he was not conflicted at all, that he fully acknowledged the gravity of what he had done, and that he was now at peace with himself and knew who and what he was: a decent and moral human being who had acted, many years ago now, in a way that went strongly against his essential nature.

Perhaps a better word, I said, was *contradictory,* or even paradoxical, because the central fact of his life was that he had committed brutal murders, for which he took responsibility, and yet he fundamentally did not think of himself as a murderer.

"I have committed the act of murder," he conceded. "I

am somebody who has unlawfully killed. That's an action that took place, at one point, in my life of seventy-five years."

He might not want to be defined by these things he did forty years ago, I said, but the act of murder was nonetheless completely irreversible. Once you had committed murder, you are, irreversibly, a murderer.

"Well, let's not dwell on the obvious," he said.

I wonder now whether there was something strange, perhaps even cruel, about my repeated attempts to get him to admit not just to having committed murders, but to *being a murderer.* The distinction I sought was less a linguistic than a moral one: I wanted him to say not that merely he had sinned, but that he was, in the depths of himself, a sinner. I wanted to penetrate the carapace of self-possession and stoic composure, and to arrive at something painful and meaningful and true. Yet the more time I spent with Macarthur, and the more I heard of his story, the less I was able to believe in the existence of some ultimate truth of his life, or in the possibility, at any rate, of my ever locating it.

TWENTY-TWO

In 1992, almost a decade after her son went to prison, a tabloid reporter doorstepped Irene Macarthur at the small bungalow where she was living in Mullingar. The reporter asked her if she was looking forward to Malcolm's being released from prison, and she said that if it was time for him to come out, then it was time for him to come out. (It would be a further twenty years before he was actually released, and she would not live to see it.)

She then mentioned something that had long been a source of speculation: "He has written the book, of course. Did you know that?"

There had been reports in the press over the years that Macarthur was devoting his time in prison to the writing of some kind of memoir. The day after the verdict, the *Irish Independent* ran a story with the headline "Plans for a Fortune—from a Book about the Killings."

"Convicted killer Malcolm Macarthur," read the story, "may have plans to write a book about his own feelings and thoughts, before, during, and after the brutal murder which shocked the nation. He is reported to have told his girlfriend, Brenda Little, the woman with whom he had lived for years and who is the mother of his son, that he would make her a wealthy woman through the proceeds of the book."

I asked him once, over the phone, whether it was true that he had written such a book. He hesitated for a moment. He said that he had written something—a "document," he called it—containing an account of his life, the "criminal episode," and his time in prison. He had written it for his family, he said—not, as the press had reported, in the sense that it would benefit them financially, because it would never be published, but in the sense that it would give them some understanding of what he had done, and the life he had lived.

I told him that I would be very curious to see this document, but he said that he could not allow it. For a while, I became preoccupied with the idea of this written account, and of what it might reveal. I brought it up on a few further occasions but in the end relinquished the idea of ever getting a look at it, and eventually came to feel that whatever it contained probably didn't differ all that much from the things he had said to me.

When I thought about this document, with its unknowable contents, I was invariably reminded of the bookcase in Macarthur's apartment, and its covering of black plastic bin liners. The document, if indeed it existed, almost certainly lay obscured within, just feet from where I sat all those afternoons in his living room.

That black plastic covering came to symbolize for me the challenge I faced in writing about Macarthur: a kind of giant redaction mark, blacking out the sensitive information of his inner life, along with so much else I knew I could not know.

«

Prison was not, truth be told, the worst place in the world for a man who liked to give his time over to reading and thinking. Throughout the three decades of his incarceration, Macarthur was able to continue his intellectual life more or less unhindered. While other prisoners were smuggling in heroin, he was getting deliveries of a variety of periodicals, scientific and otherwise. He was, for some years, the only inmate of Mountjoy Prison to have a subscription to the *Times Literary Supplement*. (John Banville spoke in an interview once about an acquaintance of his who was, back in the 1980s, in a newsagent's near the prison and saw a copy of the *TLS*. When he told the woman behind the counter that he'd take it, she told him that unfortunately it wasn't for sale, that it was to go up to Mr. Macarthur in the prison.)

Because of the intense publicity surrounding his crimes, the authorities worried at first that he might present a target for gratuitous thuggery, and so he was held for a time in the training unit, down in the basement of Mountjoy. But eventually he was introduced into the mainstream of the prison population. A former prison guard told me that he was always in great demand, among the less literate prisoners, as a writer of letters and a dispenser of advice, legal and otherwise, and that he was well liked, too, among the guards themselves.

He had never once received so much as a verbal warning on any disciplinary matter—no small achievement for a man who had served thirty years in prison. There were places he would much rather have been, of course, but he had done what he had done, and there was no changing it, and there were worse ways in which a man might languish in his middle years. The murders had, in a sense, originated in his refusal to relinquish a life of leisurely learning and reading; the irony was not lost on him that, in incarceration, he had found something strangely like this freedom.

No, it was not the experience of prison itself that was a cause of pain to him, but the opportunity cost associ-

ated with imprisonment. There were things he would have
liked to have done. Were it not for his criminal episode and
his subsequent long incarceration, he and Brenda would
almost certainly have had another child. She was a beautiful
woman, and it made him very melancholy to think of all that
he would miss. Not that she had abandoned him through
the years of his incarceration—both she and their son, as
unnamed sources in the tabloid press often pointed out, were
regular visitors in the various facilities.

He tried, in those early years, to be as much of a father
as he could. The homeschooling had ended with his conviction, of course, but by the time Colin got to transition year,
at age fifteen, he began to lose interest in his education and
was considering dropping out of school entirely. Macarthur,
who was then in Arbour Hill Prison, decided that he would
try to once more take an active role in his son's education.
When Colin came in to visit him, he would assign him some
reading—mostly history, though occasionally English literature and other topics—and set him an essay question. When
he came back for his next visit, he would bring the written
essay with him, and Macarthur would sit down with it, giving his comments and a final grade.

«

His mother visited him, too, though less often. In the
early years of his sentence, she came two or three times
annually. They never discussed the murders; she never asked
him why he had done what he did. They talked about other
things: old family friends, former servants. Who was getting
married, who had died.

In the first days, when he was on remand, there were
arguments. After she had learned that her son had been
arrested for the murders, Irene had sent Mass cards to the

Dunne and Gargan families, expressing her sympathies and certifying that their children would be prayed for in church. This may have been in questionable taste, but for Macarthur it was the legal implication that was at issue: he had not yet been tried for the crimes, and his mother's expression of condolences with the families of the bereaved may not have helped his case.

Macarthur was also irritated by his mother's willingness to be interviewed. She appeared in the media on a number of occasions in the days after his arrest, at a time when he felt she should have been keeping her own counsel. Some of her comments in these interviews were, at best, ambiguous, and at worst outright damaging.

When David Hanley interviewed Irene on RTE radio, for instance, he asked her whether she believed in capital punishment.

"I'm afraid I do," she replied, "and have always done so."

"When a murder is committed," said Hanley, "you feel that whoever committed it should be hanged?"

"I've got the old-fashioned belief," she said, "of a life for a life. I think that comes into the Bible, doesn't it?"

"So you feel," he said, "that your own son should be hanged?"

"It's very difficult for me to say that now," she said airily. "But I know that my first reaction, when I heard that there had been this murder in the park, was that I wouldn't even waste money on a trial."

Later, Hanley asked her whether she was going to stand by her son.

"Well," she said, "by standing by him, I mean I wouldn't dream of judging anyone. In other words, I will continue on as I did, being friendly."

«

Although neither of Macarthur's parents ever worked, his mother did train and qualify as a nurse, and if his father had to name a profession on an official form, he would have said that he was a farmer. Does it mean anything that the people he murdered were a nurse and a farmer? Surely not. Their professions had no bearing on his reasons for killing them. It's an unsettling coincidence, no more and no less.

«

In 2003, twenty years after Macarthur was first sent to prison, he got word that he was to be transferred from Arbour Hill to Shelton Abbey, a minimum security prison in County Wicklow. Shortly after he learned of this, he spoke to his mother on the phone and informed her of this pleasing change of circumstances.

"I'm changing address again, Mother," he said. "Shelton Abbey, down in Wicklow."

"You've been there before, of course," she said.

"Have I?" he said.

"Yes," she said, "although you were probably too young to remember."

Before it was sold to the state and converted into a minimum security prison, Shelton Abbey, a vast gothic manor, had been the ancestral seat of the Earls of Wicklow. Macarthur's parents were on social terms with William Howard, the eighth and last Earl of Wicklow ("Billy Wicklow," to those who knew him well), and they had once or twice motored down there with their son for a Sunday visit. Neither Macarthur nor his mother, in that phone call, dwelled on the vertiginous irony of the fact she'd just revealed to him: that in the years since he visited this stately home as a child, the house had become a prison, and he himself a murderer about to be sent there.

After he moved to Shelton, Irene stopped coming to see him. The trip down to Wicklow was a little far, and her health was not what it had once been. For the last eight years of her life, she was not among his visitors.

When Irene Macarthur died in 2008, Macarthur was let out on day release to attend the funeral. He took a bus from Wicklow to Meath, and he laid a bunch of red roses on her grave. He returned to Shelton later that evening.

«

Prisoners serving life sentences for murder can go before the Parole Board after twelve years in custody, and are often granted early release in return for good behavior. The average custodial sentence for murder is about seventeen and a half years. Although Macarthur's disciplinary record was pristine, and although he was recommended for release by the Parole Board, he was repeatedly denied by successive ministers for justice. There are a number of reasons why this might have been the case. His sheer notoriety, and the political scandal attached to his case, certainly counted against him, as did the likely impact of his release on the families of his victims.

In 1993, as Macarthur approached the twelve-year mark, Donal Dunne's brother Christopher made a public appeal not to allow the killer to be released on parole. "You don't forget these things," he said. "I would like to see him serve his full life sentence. If it is feasible that some guy who killed for no reason whatsoever could be released early, somebody should be asking questions."

The responsibility for his release would rest with the

minister for justice. Twelve years into his sentence, the serving minister was Máire Geoghegan-Quinn, the woman who had stood beside Macarthur in the car park after the hurling match that day in 1982. She declined his appeal.

Years later, the minister was Michael McDowell, who as a young barrister had served on Macarthur's legal team, and who was thus obliged to recuse himself from any matters relating to the case. The responsibility was passed down to Willie O'Dea, a junior minister in the justice department, who was unsympathetic to the case put forward by Macarthur's lawyers for early release.

After Irene's death, O'Dea told the press that his decision had been informed, at least in part, by his understanding that Irene Macarthur was terrified of Malcolm's getting out of prison. "She believed that it was not safe to release him, and I was told that she feared for her own safety. I took that into account when I had to decide on his release."

After her death, Macarthur was allowed more regular day releases, as part of a structured program of reintegration. He would get on a bus and spend the day in Dublin or Dún Laoghaire. He would go to art galleries and museums, and walk around the city for an afternoon, before getting on a bus back to Wicklow and returning to prison before nightfall. Soon enough, the press got wind of these releases, and his brief trips to the city were attended by tabloid articles about the "Gentleman Killer," or the "GUBU murderer," who had been permitted once again to walk among us. One day, an older woman recognized him on the street and stood in his path, scolding him for having the nerve to show his face in public. "Life should mean life, Malcolm," she said.

On another occasion, he was walking toward the National History Museum on Kildare Street when he was spotted by press photographers standing outside Leinster House (the seat of parliament) next door. He turned immediately and walked in the other direction, but one of the photographers followed him up Molesworth Street and onto Nassau Street. A bus happened to be coming to a stop, and Macarthur got on. Later that same day, under the headline "Murderer Macarthur Enjoys Another Day Out," the *Evening Herald* ran a photo of him walking upstairs to the top deck of the bus, bound for nowhere in particular.

A few months later, after eighteen years of rejection, the justice minister, Alan Shatter, granted Macarthur temporary release. He was to be released on license, which meant that were he to breach certain terms, he could be taken back in without any sort of hearing. Life, in that sense, did mean life. It was freedom of a tentative and circumscribed sort, but it was freedom nonetheless.

It had been decades since Macarthur had known such liberty, and he expected the outside world to seem incomprehensibly vast and open. But no. Dublin felt smaller somehow. Bartley Dunne's was gone, replaced by an ugly faux-Georgian redbrick hotel, on the ground floor of which was a bar and diner called Bartley's, whose lurid art-deco-style decor was an insult to the memory of the original. In the days and months after his release, he would sit on a bus or a tram and look around, and see people gazing down intently at the screens of their phones. This was entirely new, and strange. People dressed differently, too. Only rarely did you see a well-dressed man now, or an elegant woman. It was all jeans and anoraks, tracksuits and trainers. Even the money had changed, the euro having been introduced more than a decade previously.

«

When Macarthur was released, Christopher Gargan was contacted by a reporter, whom he told that he would not accept an apology from his sister's murderer. Christopher was fourteen when Macarthur murdered Bridie, and the pain and sadness of her loss had defined his life since then. He and his siblings still thought about her almost every day, he said. His parents had died in the early 2000s. He said that "things got very tight" in the house after the murder, and that he felt it "knocked years off them."

He did not think that Macarthur should be released, he said, because after all, "who knows what he is capable of? In this country they don't serve life for a life. He should serve for the rest of his life."

When the reporter asked Gargan if he had any words for Macarthur, he said, "I have nothing to say to him."

In a 1995 television interview, Bridie Gargan's sisters Ann and Frances spoke about their own experience of pain and loss. It was not just a sister who had been taken from them, Frances said, but their best friend. "She was a very considerate and kind girl," she said. "She always had time for everybody. She was always the one to organize the nights out, and we'd go out, maybe dancing, maybe for a drink, whatever. It took us a long time to rebuild our lives, and to adjust without Bridie."

"Everybody took it very, very hard," said Ann. "And everybody still misses her, so they do. We do have family get-togethers, for birthdays and different things, and we do have a meal at home. And just before the meal, there's always that two minutes, where you know that everyone is thinking the same thing. And we usually say a prayer for her, and then have our meal. But they don't really be the same."

«

I sometimes thought that the reason Macarthur more readily and fluently expressed remorse for what he did to

Patrick Connolly and to Brenda and their son than he did for his victims' families was simply that it was easier for him to conceive and speak of. Brenda Little's life, as a mother and as a person, has no doubt been defined by what happened in 1982, as, just as surely, has her son's. (This seems a safe assumption, but it is only that, because it was a condition of Macarthur's agreeing to speak to me in the first place that I would never approach them. This struck me as no great concession, because from the small amount I did know of Brenda and Colin Little, the prospect of their ever consenting to speak to me seemed vanishingly small.)

The course of Connolly's career was radically altered by Macarthur, though it was by no means sunk. After his resignation as attorney general, he returned to practice law. His colleagues believed that, had it not been for the GUBU business, he would have been a likely candidate for the Supreme Court. But people generally understood that his involvement in the affair was no fault of his own, and he went on to have a long and successful career at the bar. When Connolly died a bachelor in 2016, he left €100,000 to Brenda Little, along with his share of an apartment in one of the better neighborhoods of Dublin's Southside. To Colin, he left a sum of €75,000, as well as his collection of vintage cigarette cards.

Macarthur did real and profound damage to the lives of his family and friends, in other words, but it was not impossible to fathom the depths of this damage. The harm that he did to Bridie Gargan and to Donal Dunne and to their families, on the other hand, was so vast and absolute that for him to think about it, to truly reckon with it, would be to risk a kind of moral self-annihilation.

I could not imagine what such an undertaking would involve. But the more I found myself treading and retreading the same conversational ground with Macarthur, the more I came to realize that it was precisely this kind of reckoning that I had been seeking from the start. I wanted to know that he had truly suffered for what he'd done. After the better part of a year of such conversations, I began to wonder whether such a moment would ever come.

«

After his release, Macarthur had all the free time he could ever have wanted. He had, in fact, nothing but free time. He had to live off a small state pension, it was true, but he had no obligations. His rent was covered by housing assistance payments. Colin was in his mid-forties now, with a partner and a child of his own. Macarthur didn't see much of his son or his grandson, though this had as much to do with their being in the UK as it did with the life he himself had lived. Travel was more or less out of the question, given the nature of Macarthur's license release. He was alone, and, for what it was worth, he was free.

He had his walks. He went along to events in Trinity, and to the occasional book launch, the occasional talk. He went to the cinema pretty frequently.

One evening in the autumn of 2012, only a week or so after his release, he had gone to see a foreign film at the Irish Film Institute. He went alone, as he would do most things. When the film ended, he emerged from the theater into the echoing atrium of the building, and went to the café to buy a pot of tea. As he returned to the table with his tea, he noticed a man staring at him. He did not recognize the man, but, as was often the case in those days, the man clearly recognized him. Because of the news of his release, his face had been in the papers all that week. The man broke away then from the small group of people he was with and approached Macarthur's table.

"I know who you are," he said. He said this not in a threatening manner, but as a statement of fact.

"Oh, do you?" said Macarthur.

He said he was a close friend of the parents of Bridie Gargan, the young woman he had brutally murdered thirty years previously.

"You know what you did," he said. He backed off a little as he said these words, as though he were wary of getting physically too close to the man who had killed his friends' child.

"Of course," said Macarthur. "Of course I know."

"You know what you have done," he repeated.

"I do," he said. "I do know."

Macarthur asked the man to sit with him, but he said no. And then he walked away, and disappeared back into the crowd.

In the years that followed, Macarthur thought of this man often, and of their brief exchange. He wished that he could have sat and talked with him for a little while, he said. Under the terms of his release, he was barred from reaching out to the families of his victims—to "the bereaved," as he called them. Had he been able to do so, he sometimes felt that he would like to contact them, privately. But he often thought, too, that this would be the last thing he should ever attempt, that it would be the last thing they would ever want.

He wished he had been able to speak further with this man, at the café at the Film Institute, because he might have been a kind of proxy for the family of Bridie Gargan, perhaps even a kind of confessor. He would have liked to have told him some things that he could not have said to Bridie's parents, even while they were alive. He would have said that he was sorry for what he had done, for what he had taken from them. He would have spoken of his deep regret, for taking their daughter's life, and for the impact of that loss upon their own lives.

But the man left, and so he said none of this. Instead he sat alone until he had finished his pot of tea, and then he put on his coat and left to catch his bus.

TWENTY-THREE

One warm afternoon in late autumn, nearly a year after I first came to know him, I arranged to meet Macarthur outside his apartment. We ambled the streets of the south inner city for two or perhaps three hours. At one point he stopped to give money to a homeless man sitting with his back against a wall and a paper cup in his hands, greeting him briefly but politely. As we continued walking, he told me that the man had been a former inmate in Mountjoy while he had been there.

"I always acknowledge a fellow alumnus," he joked.

A couple of weeks previously, he told me, he had been strolling past Stephen's Green, along this very street, when a horse and carriage had passed coming in the opposite direction. The driver greeted him, and he recognized him, too, as a fellow former prisoner. Later that afternoon, he had gone into the Shelbourne Hotel to use the toilets, and as he was walking out again through the lobby, he heard a voice calling him by his first name. He turned and saw a man whom he did not recognize, somewhat younger than himself.

The man introduced himself, saying that he had been the passenger in the carriage earlier, and that as they had passed the driver had explained to him who Macarthur was. The man was a dentist in town for a conference, and he wanted to know if Macarthur would join him for dinner. He accepted the invitation, and they passed a very pleasant evening together at the Ivy on Molesworth Street, not far from the Shelbourne.

I could tell that Macarthur relished the memory of the experience. Although this man, this dentist, had perhaps been motivated by a ghoulish curiosity, the plain fact was that he had invited him to dinner, and that they had enjoyed one another's company and conversation. It had been the sort of evening, I supposed, that Macarthur had often had in his previous life. It must have been exhilarating to have experienced, even briefly, what it was like not to live in abjection and shame, to be served fine wine and expensive food, and to enjoy the company of an educated and convivial dining partner.

«

I knew that Macarthur was lonely, and I had no doubt that his loneliness was a major reason for his having agreed to speak with me in the first place. He told me one day that, before the pandemic, he had been planning to start getting out and about more—to "power up," as he put it, his social engagement. He would like to be known, he said, for something other than the fact that he had committed two murders—at least among a select group of people. It was his conviction that, socially speaking, he had a considerable amount to offer.

"I know that I have done the worst possible thing," he said. "But my instincts for kindliness and consideration and generosity are strong. Every day I perform little gestures of kindness. I usually give something to the mendicants. I give

over perhaps ten or fifteen euros a week to them. I rarely
pass one without giving something. And I insist upon opening doors for people. Or if I find a five-euro note in the
supermarket, as happened recently, I hand it in. I have these
instincts for decency and compassion. I have a very strong
instinct for the human species, affectively."

I believed all this absolutely. I could well imagine him
finding five euros in the frozen food aisle and heading
straight to customer inquiries to hand it in with a somewhat
stiff and formal flourish. I had seen him with my own eyes,
on a number of occasions, open his pocketbook and give
sums of money to homeless people, to "mendicants," as he
called them—and not just to those who were fellow alumni.
It would have been absurd to call him a good man, but I
could see that he was capable of behaving with decency and
kindness.

On the rare occasions when he made new acquaintances,
he didn't try to hide what he had done, but neither did he go
out of his way to make it known. Sometimes he would introduce himself by name, and he would ask whether the name
rang a bell, especially if the person was of an age where they
would be likely to remember him. He liked to meet people,
he said, and to be himself, and to let them deal with the con-
trast between their expectations and the reality with which
they were met.

Before the pandemic, for instance, he had been a frequent attendee of public talks at Trinity College: literature,
history, and so on—those same appearances that had provoked my interest years before I met him. His fellow "habi-
tués," as he put it, tended to be older people, and therefore
much likelier to recognize him. There was a social element to
such events; after the talks, there would be glasses of red and
white wine, little bowls of crisps, mushroom vol-au-vents.

People would get talking to him, and by some or other conversational means his identity would become apparent. For the most part in these situations, people, including himself, tried to affect normality.

He told me about one particular fellow habitué, an American. On his strolls through the Trinity campus, Macarthur would often see this man sitting alone on a bench beside the cricket grounds. He knew he had seen him at talks, and he was curious about him; he wondered whether he might be a lecturer of some sort, or perhaps a mature student.

He attended an open night once at the 1937 Reading Room, a small library on the campus that was rarely open to the public, and on his way out, he had said hello to this man. He had taken note of his American accent and asked him where in the States he was from. The man had told him Massachusetts, and they had taken it from there. Macarthur spoke of his time at university in California. The American told him he had lived for most of his life in Boston but had come to Dublin in his retirement. He owned several properties around Massachusetts, and he lived off the rental income.

At one point, as they were talking on the steps of the building, a third habitué, an Irish woman, had come out through the door and interrupted them. Excuse me, she said, but aren't you Malcolm Macarthur? The very same, said Macarthur.

She didn't linger long, and as she walked away across the cobbles of Fellows' Square, Macarthur turned back to his new American friend and asked him whether that name happened to ring a bell.

"Phoenix Park?" said the American.

Macarthur nodded, and told him to please not be concerned. And he did not seem, in fact, to be concerned. He didn't back away, at any rate. Nor did he ask him any questions about all that. He seemed to receive it as a piece of interesting, but not vital, information. He never brought it up again, said Macarthur, although he did once or twice ask him about Irish politics, as though he considered him to be a kind of insider, which, in a strange sort of way, he was.

The American was an interesting person, Macarthur said. A collector of clocks. A fellow atheist and Darwinian. He was a very liberal-minded person, he said, and they agreed with each other on most topics of social significance. And if ever he wanted to meet up with him but didn't know where he was, all he had to do was walk into Trinity and sit on a bench at or near the sports grounds, and invariably the American would walk through the campus on his way to pick up some groceries at Marks & Spencer, or on his way back home from having done so, and Macarthur would greet him as he passed, and they would stroll together for a time.

The American seemed to appreciate Macarthur's erudition, and as they walked together through the city their talk would range through history and science and philosophy. If the American happened to be walking home, Macarthur was always careful to break off in another direction well before they got to his street, because he did not wish to give him the impression that he was expecting an invitation. He had no desire to make things awkward, or to press himself upon this man.

He had not seen this American fellow, he said, since all this dreadful business with the virus had started. The man was about his own age, in his mid-to-late seventies, and not exactly at the peak of health. He hoped that he was still around. As he talked about this wealthy retiree, Macarthur had about him an air of hesitant wistfulness. I understood then that he held this man in something like real affection.

«

I have said that what I wanted from Macarthur was evidence of real remorse, real suffering. I wanted him to be tormented by what he had done, to see him tremble in terror and awe at the moral magnitude of his iniquity. I wanted to witness the breaking down of his ego defenses, the revelation of some terrible emotional truth within. I wanted him to be Raskolnikov in the final pages of *Crime and Punishment*, confessing his guilt, falling to his knees and weeping before God.

I am asking myself now why I would want this. And I think that it has less to do with a desire for some kind of justice than with a need for the sense of resolution such an emotional catharsis would provide. In failing to confront the awful enormity of his sins—in failing to be annihilated by it—Macarthur had failed me as a character. He had denied me the satisfaction of an ending.

«

One afternoon, early in the new year, Macarthur called me on the phone. He was worried—to the point, I felt, of paranoia—about a podcast the BBC was making about his crimes. I'd heard about it the previous week, and learned that its release was imminent, and I'd told him about it. He'd since become concerned that the BBC might be secretly recording him, even perhaps accessing CCTV footage, via the Gardaí. I told him this was highly unlikely, that from both a legal and an ethical perspective, this sort of thing was basically unfeasible. I had to explain that CCTV recordings, even if they were accessible, wouldn't be of much use for a podcast, which I explained was an audio form, much like a radio program. (Despite his interest in science, Macarthur knew next to nothing about computers or the internet.)

I'd learned about the BBC project from John O'Mahony,

who had mentioned in passing that he and Tony Hickey had been interviewed for it. For my own part, I was dismayed to find that, after eighteen months or so of working on this story, of coming to think of it as my own, I was no longer the only person with a claim to it. I knew that they had not been able to get access to Macarthur—that they had not, in fact, even been able to find him. And so I felt I had to strike a balance between reassuring him—that the BBC was neither secretly recording him nor colluding with the Gardaí—and making him wary enough not to speak to them. He was, after all, my character.

"I presume," I said, "that you won't be talking to them."

"No," he said. "Perhaps I could speak to them off the record, but not for the podcast."

"Listen," I said, with a forcefulness that surprised even myself. "Saying something is off the record is not some kind of magical incantation. It's not binding. It's a gentleman's agreement, is all, which a journalist may not honor with someone like you."

It was not clear to what extent he understood this as me simply protecting my own unique asset in what had suddenly become a more crowded market. He seemed to think I was purely protecting him from potentially unscrupulous actors, and he was grateful.

"You know," he said, "I've been genning up."

"What does that mean, genning up?"

"Genning up? You don't know this expression?"

"I don't think I've ever heard it."

"Well, it mustn't be a thing people say anymore."

"Certainly not anyone I know."

"It means studying up. I've been studying up, *genning up*, about my own case. And why I might have done what I did," he said, employing as always the vague language with which he spoke of his crimes.

"Money?" I said.

"Well, yes, money. But I mean why it was that I used the particular technique I used."

"Murder, you mean."

"Well, the adoption of criminal means."

"Say more," I said.

"Well, I won't say anything over the phone."

The Gardaí, I thought. The BBC.

I told him I would call around the following afternoon.

I was skeptical of this apparent epiphany. I had—after close to a year of our labyrinthine conversations, of immersing myself in the press clippings, documents, and stories that formed a kind of composite portrait of his life—resigned myself to Macarthur and his crimes never being more than partially knowable, like an underexposed photograph whose subject is visible only as a darkness. But as the evening went on, my skepticism gave way to curiosity, and my curiosity, in turn, to hope.

I speculated on what it was he had unearthed, in his "genning up." I remembered what he had said, several months back, about how I might never fully understand what his crimes had all been about. I had a sense at the time that he was alluding to some large and crucial piece of information, either biographical or psychological, that he had resolved—for the time being, perhaps forever—to withhold, and that once revealed would make everything clear. I thought of the black plastic covering his bookcase, of the "document" he had spoken of.

As the evening wore on, I became preoccupied with the idea that an unknown truth, one that had hovered for so long just beyond my reach, was about to be placed into my hands. Perhaps this truth would take the form of the document itself? I could not help but hope, against what I knew

to be my better judgment, that some final illumination was
at hand.

«

The following day, the government announced the lifting of almost all Covid restrictions. It had been far too long
in coming, and yet it felt abrupt, and somehow unexpected.
There was a sense that the pandemic was, if not at an end,
then no longer the framing device of reality itself—that it
had been relegated, at last, to a subplot. Already there were
more people on the streets, more movement, more life.
The day was bright and clear and cold. All of this seemed
to me almost uncannily appropriate, as though the end of
the restrictions and brightening of the weather amounted to
some compound pathetic fallacy reflecting my own sense of
impending illumination.

When Macarthur came to meet me at the door of his
building, I was a little surprised to see that he was still wearing a mask. I remembered then what he had said when we
first met, that masks allowed him a measure of anonymity,
and that he intended to keep wearing them as long as he
possibly could. In the lift on the way up to his floor (we rode
together now), he said he'd been out of the apartment for a
stretch over Christmas, and that the dust had gotten out of
hand. It was a real problem, he said, the problem of dust. He
couldn't figure out where the stuff was coming from.

If the apartment was any dustier than usual, it was not
obvious to me; it looked much as it had always looked. A
couple of towels were drying on a rack between the couch
and the radiator. Though we were by then well into the new
year, there were some Christmas cards on the frosted glass
table, from people whose names I didn't recognize. There

was, too, a DVD case lying on the table: *Brideshead Revisited*. I asked him whether it was the one with Jeremy Irons in it.

"Oh yes," he said. "The 1981 ITV serial. That one they did recently was a travesty."

He mentioned some distant connection, via his mother's side of the family, to the real-life family on which Waugh had based the Marchmains of Brideshead. He'd told me about this before, but I had been unable to keep the lineage straight in my mind.

Then, standing in the middle of the room, he cleared his throat lightly and tugged smartly on the lapels of his light brown jacket, as if to announce that his presentation would be beginning. He started by specifying that what he was about to say was what he called an "ex post facto rationalization"—a deduction, from the vantage of the present, of what he might have been thinking at the time of the murders.

"I've been trying to dredge my memory on this question," he said, "and I have retrieved something that seems to me to be symptomatic of the disorder of thinking I was undergoing at the time of my episode. And I recall thinking, in the time before I embarked on the criminal venture, that if—and the word 'if' is very important here—*if* I were to apply myself to some important project, and *if* I were to achieve something of significance, something that might be worth writing about, the inclusion, in the narrative, of an account of the mundane activity of having to make a living by earning money would, aesthetically speaking, constitute a *blemish*, or an imperfection, on that narrative. Therefore the solution was criminality. And I don't mean *aesthetically*, in what I would regard as the superficial Wildean sense of the word, but in the deeper, philosophical sense. This aesthetic sense of my life as a narrative, and that the narrative had to be untainted by earning money. Because that was, in my mind, an inferior activity. Time not given to the higher pursuits, the intellectual pursuits, would have seemed to me to be *degraded* time."

I was scrawling his words in my notebook, trying to get it all down. I underlined the term "degraded time," and then circled it with my pen. I felt it must mean something, although I couldn't yet say what.

Macarthur gestured toward my notebook. "Now the crucial thing, again, is that the sentence begins with '*if*,'" he said. "*If* I were to achieve something important. Had that sentence begun with '*when*,' then we would be in the realm of personality disorder. Of grandiosity, megalomania, and so on. And there was none of that. It was a disorder not of personality, but of thinking. I believe it was a form of temporary insanity, quite frankly."

I asked him then whether his belief that the murders were a result of a "thinking disorder," a temporary insanity, allowed him to separate himself from the fact of what he had done, to believe in some sense that it hadn't really been he who had done it.

"Morally, yes, of course it does," he said. "That's why every day, in prison, I knew that I was not the type of person to have done that."

"But the reality," I said, "is that you did do it. And so by definition, you are exactly the type of person to have done it."

"Quite so," he said, with conviction. "But I didn't do it through acting *immorally*, because I was being compelled, or impelled, by a disorder of thinking. My ethical side was overwhelmed. Disconnected, if you like. It wasn't functioning. Because if it had been functioning, I wouldn't have done it."

He spoke then for a time about what he called his "ironic" view of life. I found it difficult to parse exactly what he meant by this, and he himself was unsatisfied with how he was expressing it. It had to do, as far as I could tell, with the tension between the great cosmic significance of humanity as a whole, and the perfect meaninglessness of individual human lives. This, he said, was the central human problem, the ironic tension between these two facts.

I said that I could view this belief of his, this essentially abstract conviction that the individual was of no consequence, only in the light of the fact that he himself had murdered two such individuals almost forty years ago. He replied that an individual was meaningless only in the larger scheme of things, when one took the cosmic view. Taken in isolation, he said, the individual was unimportant. But there was, in reality, no taking an individual in isolation, because we did not function in isolation.

I was irresistibly drawn to this idea that it was in "aestheticizing" his life—in conceiving of it as a story composed of plotlines, setting, characters—that he had come to commit his crimes. After all, since meeting Macarthur and beginning to write about those crimes, I myself had been preoccupied with a similar problem: How does one turn a life, or a death, into a story? How does one shape disparate events into something that is not only cohesive but ultimately satisfying? Was it possible that Macarthur grappled with a version of this problem?

Was it possible that, had he not viewed his life in such terms, Bridie Gargan and Donal Dunne might still be alive?

It was an extraordinary idea, and yet it seemed to me too neatly satisfying to be anything but anticlimactic. It was, in the end, repellant for precisely the same reasons it was seductive.

For a time as Macarthur continued to speak, I strove to make sense of such arguments, but after a certain point I stopped trying. Philosophical abstraction was, in the end, no help in understanding Macarthur's reasons for committing murder. Perhaps philosophical abstraction was itself the reason.

It was late in the afternoon by now, and the living room, which got little natural light at the best of times, was growing dimmer by steady degrees. I began to wonder whether I should ask him to switch on the light, but I did not. As the room got darker, Macarthur himself, in his beige jacket and beige trousers, seemed to fade into the lighter beige of the walls, so that at times I had a strange sense of his dematerializing completely, becoming a disembodied voice in the room, an unbroken stream of endless assertion, that no matter how closely or how long I followed it would never take me anywhere near to the truth. I had a strange intimation, in that moment, that this voice would never make sense, and that it would never leave me.

Eventually, it was time for me to go, and as I took my leave I flicked the light switch on the wall by the kitchenette. Nothing happened; the room remained dim. Perhaps he had failed to pay his electricity bill; more likely the bulb just needed to be changed. Neither of us made any comment either way.

Macarthur walked behind me out of the living room, and as I fumbled for a moment with the lock on the front door of the apartment, he said his usual curt goodbye and slipped into the bedroom. Before I stepped out into the hallway, I turned and looked back. The door to the bedroom was open a crack, but there was no light within. He had withdrawn into its shadows, and I could see nothing, or almost nothing, but darkness.

ACKNOWLEDGMENTS

This book lived with me for many years before I began to write it, and a number of people, and conversations, brought me to a point where I was able to begin to work on it. Without the encouragement and enthusiasm of my wife, Amy Smith, I would not have begun the project, and her insights were crucial in all sorts of ways throughout the writing process. She helped me to see things in new and clearer ways. For this, and for so much more, I am grateful to her. Ed Caesar was, from almost as early in the life of the book, an invaluable and reliable source of advice and support. Ed also read an early draft, which helped me a great deal. In late 2019, I had a conversation with my US agent, Molly Atlas, which finally convinced me that this was a story that needed to be told, and that I was the person to tell it. It was Molly's enthusiasm that marked this book's transition from long-standing preoccupation to living project. I remain, too, extremely fortunate to have Karolina Sutton in my corner as my UK agent. The presence of both Molly and Karolina, throughout the writing of this book and throughout my career, has been a great reassurance; I could not hope for two more supportive and attentive agents.

As I wrote the book, I was fortunate to be able to process my experiences, and my thinking about them, through conversations with Sally Rooney; Sally's early reading of the manuscript was an important moment in its development. Rosa Lyster, over at the London office, was also a source of endless insight. I am also very grateful to Alice Gregory for reading an early draft, and for the conversations we had about writing and structure. Her discernment was invaluable. Adam Kelly and Dan Kois read later drafts, and their input was hugely helpful. I was also very fortunate to be able to draw on the deep wisdom of David Kenny, at various strategic points throughout the process.

Yaniv Soha, at Doubleday in New York, has been my editor since my first book, and my work with him has amounted to what I think of as an ongoing collaboration. I am deeply grateful for Yaniv's instinctive understanding of what I wanted this book to be, and his sensitive and insightful approach to my writing. Anne Meadows, in her time at Granta Books in London, played a similarly crucial role in shaping and improving this book. Her enthusiasm, and her editorial curiosity and intelligence, meant a great deal to me, and still do. Laura Barber, also at Granta, saw this book (and its author) through a particularly difficult period, and I am deeply grateful for her coming along when she did. I would have been lucky to have one good editor for this book; the fact that it has had three great ones seems, frankly, a bit much.

I'd also like to give my thanks to Katie Raissian, Sam Bungey, Trevor White, Ian Cobain, and Pamela Cassidy, all of whose advice and assistance shaped this book in various ways.

My gratitude is also due to the people, named and unnamed, who took the time to speak to me for this book. John O'Mahony and Tony Hickey, in particular, spent many hours telling me their stories, and answering my questions. Lastly, this book would not exist in its present form had

Malcolm Macarthur not agreed to speak with me about his life, and the crimes he committed in 1982. He took a risk in doing so, and the experience was often an uncomfortable and difficult one for him. I am grateful for his time, and for his willingness to answer my questions.

Finally, I wish to thank the Arts Council for their support of this work in its earliest phase.

NOTES

The story told in these pages is, in its basic outline, well known in Ireland. The murders committed by Malcolm Macarthur in 1982, and the political fallout that resulted, were the subject of a great deal of reporting at the time of the events. In writing this book, I have drawn heavily from the work of the countless Irish journalists who covered the investigation, arrest, and conviction and who reported on Macarthur's family background and early life.

This is not, however, primarily a work of archival research. Its content, and to some extent its form, is determined by a series of conversations I had with Macarthur, in 2021 and 2022. These conversations ran to dozens of hours. Most took place in person, at his home, but there were also many hours of phone calls. Where I have quoted Macarthur's words directly, these quotations have been drawn mainly from audio recordings, and occasionally handwritten notes. Macarthur's version of the events of his life, and of the crimes he committed, frequently differs from that recorded in the newspapers at the time, and at times from the statement he provided to detectives, and so the questions of truth and reliability are frequently to the fore, and often irresolvable. There are times at which I have left it to the reader to decide for themselves, but also times at which I felt it necessary to say when I found Macarthur's version of events unconvincing.

The account of the investigation in Part Four of the book, along with a range of secondary sources, draws in large part from a series of conversations with two retired detectives, Tony Hickey and John

O'Mahony, who investigated the murders of Bridie Gargan and Donal Dunne and were instrumental in the arrest of Macarthur.

ONE

The paragraph that begins "It wasn't until years later . . ." contains a reference to a young Malcolm Macarthur sitting in a bar and reading *Le Monde*. This detail, which may or may not be reliable, came from a conversation I had with a man who drank in the same bars as Macarthur in the 1970s, and who wished to remain anonymous.

TWO

The newspaper article about Macarthur's brief encounter with the economist David McWilliams is by Ken Foy, and appeared in the *Evening Herald* on November 14, 2011. The account of Macarthur's appearance at the literary event in the Long Room Hub is drawn from two sources: John Spain's *Irish Independent* article "As Banville Spoke, He Spotted a Familiar Face in the Crowd . . ." (December 15, 2012), and from John Burns's brief description of the event in his *Sunday Times* "Aticus" column (December 9, 2012). Trevor White's experience of the event is drawn from his own journal, a copy of which he generously provided me with. The account of Macarthur's presence at the launch of former justice minister Alan Shatter's memoir is taken from an article by Liam Collins in the *Irish Independent* (September 20, 2017).

In this chapter, and throughout the book, I quote liberally from the lengthy statement Macarthur provided to detectives after his arrest. My source is the reproduction of the statement in an article in the *Sunday World*, entitled "Macarthur in Cold Blood" (April 18, 2004). The book *It Was Murder*, by John Courtney, the former chief superintendent who led the investigation into the murders, also contains lengthy sections of the text of the statement.

THREE

The article in which Macarthur is quoted speaking about lockdown regulations is by Padraig O'Reilly and appeared in *The Irish Sun* on March 25, 2021.

FOUR

The account in this chapter of my first meeting with Macarthur is drawn from written notes I took immediately following the encounter. Subsequent conversations were recorded at the time.

FIVE

I refer in this chapter to the handwritten notes that detectives found in Macarthur's room in Patrick Connolly's apartment. My source here, and throughout the book, is a facsimile reproduction of these notes in an appendix to Stephen Rae's book *Killers: Murders in Ireland*.

SIX

The story about Macarthur's grandfather Daniel Macarthur, and the haunting at Breemount, is drawn from an article entitled "Malcolm Was 'Too Bright Altogether' Says Farm Worker" that appeared in *The Irish Press* on January 13, 1983. The story of Macarthur's accident as a child comes from a farmhand's account of the incident in the same article, and from his mother's account in the *Evening Herald* article entitled "A Squeamish Boy Who Grew Up to Be Killer" (January 12, 1983). I draw heavily here, and elsewhere in the book, on a long interview Irene Macarthur gave to the journalist David Hanley, for the RTE radio show *This Week*, on January 16, 1983, a copy of which I was provided with by RTE's archives service. Irene also gave a number of other print interviews around this time, which I have also drawn on here and elsewhere. The article containing recollections of Macarthur as a young man, entitled "No One Guessed the Boy in the Cravat Would Go On to Kill," is by David Reilly and appeared in the *Sunday Independent* on June 6, 2010.

One of the more contentious issues, throughout my conversations with Macarthur, was that of his parents' marriage. I have relied heavily, in my writing on Macarthur's early life, on his mother's account of her relationship with her husband. This account was often at odds with Macarthur's own version of his childhood and his parents' marriage.

SEVEN

Macarthur's time as a student in the United States was covered only in very broad terms in the reporting in 1982 and 1983. The account of that experience here is drawn entirely from my own conversations with Macarthur.

EIGHT

The quotes from Irene Macarthur about her son leaving his mark "on Western Europe" come from the *Evening Herald* article "A Squeamish Boy Who Grew Up to Be Killer" (January 12, 1983). The account of her first encounter with her grandchild draws from the same article. The article exploring the suspicion that Macarthur may have murdered his father is entitled "Chilling handwritten notes that show twisted mind of Malcolm Macarthur" and appeared in the *Sunday Independent* on July 18, 2004. The account of Daniel Macarthur's illness and death that follows is drawn from my conversations with Macarthur.

The descriptions of Bartley Dunne's are drawn from Macarthur's own recollections, from a long and detailed article about the bar on comeheretome.com, a website devoted to Dublin life and culture, and from the *Irish Times* obituary of the proprietor, Barry Dunne (September 24, 2016). I also draw on *A Kick Against the Pricks,* the autobiography of the politician and gay rights campaigner David Norris. The quotes from acquaintances about the perception of Macarthur as an academic ("he was a nuclear and an astrophysicist") are taken from an *Irish Times* article called "Quiet Academic with an Eccentric Air" (January 13, 1983). Details about Brenda Little's life before meeting Macarthur, and about the early days of their relationship, come from various journalistic sources, including "How Brenda Met Malcolm," in *The Irish Press* (January 13, 1983), and Joe Joyce and Peter Murtagh's book *The Boss.* Joyce and Murtagh's book about the political career of Charles Haughey contains a superb chapter on Macarthur and the GUBU scandal; this, along with Murtagh's excellent reporting for *The Irish Times* at the time of the trial, was an invaluable source for my book.

The interview in which Patrick Connolly refers to Macarthur

as "the sort of man you would be happy to have at a dinner party" appeared in an episode of the television series *Thou Shalt Not Kill*, which was broadcast on RTE in 1995.

NINE

My main source on the period of Macarthur's life directly preceding his return to Ireland from Tenerife before the murders was my own conversations with Macarthur. As I make clear in these pages, the difficulty of distinguishing truth and falsehood, and the question of the reliability of memory, are always to the fore in my thinking about this story, and never more so than here. The statement Macarthur provided to detectives after his arrest is also a frequent source in these pages, along with Joyce and Murtagh's book *The Boss*. I also draw on a number of newspaper articles on the background to the case, including "Secret of House in Glasnevin" and "Playboy Lifestyle Led to the Murderous Plot" (*The Irish Press*, January 13, 1983).

TEN

The account, in this chapter, of the days immediately preceding the murders is again drawn largely from my conversations with Macarthur, and from the statement he gave to detectives after his arrest. It is also informed by Joyce and Murtagh's reporting in *The Boss*, and to a lesser extent by a chapter on Macarthur in a book by Stephen Rea called *Killers*. (The details about the books on the philosophy of mind and forensic medicine come from Rea's book.) There are also numerous details taken from an array of newspaper articles that appeared at the time of Macarthur's conviction. The 1995 episode of RTE's *Thou Shalt Not Kill* on the crimes was also a useful source of information, particularly on Macarthur's visits to gun clubs.

ELEVEN

My account of the murder of Bridie Gargan in the Phoenix Park in this chapter, and of the events immediately preceding it, is again informed by a combination of Macarthur's statement and my own conversations with him. I also draw on a series of interviews with Tony Hickey and John O'Mahony, who were involved as detectives in the investigation of the murders. Paddy Byrne's perspective of the assault comes from a 2011 article in the *Irish Examiner* ("Witness Breaks 30-Year Silence as Killer Is Released"), and from an interview in *The Daily Mail* from around the same time ("Bridie Stood and He Lunged at Her: Only Witness Who Saw Slaughter of Nurse Gargan Tells of the Nightmare Event," November 20, 2011). The reporting on the case in *The Irish Press* by Tom Brady, Gregg Ryan, and Michael Keane at the time of Macarthur's conviction was also a very useful source. The quotes from Vincent Gargan, Bridie's father, are taken from the *Irish Press* article "Grief of Gargan Family Goes On" (January 13, 1983) and from Alan O'Keefe and Ces Cassidy's article "Bridie: Gold Medal Girl They All Miss" in the *Irish Independent* (January 13, 1983).

TWELVE

As in the previous chapter, my sources in telling the story of the murder of Donal Dunne are Macarthur's statement and my conversations with Tony Hickey and John O'Mahoney. Although my conversations with Macarthur did touch on both murders, he was reluctant to speak at length on the topic, out of what he claimed was a concern with further upsetting the families of his victims. (He did not, as he put it, want them learning anything new from my book about the moments of their loved ones' deaths, a prospect which he felt would be intolerable.) He did speak at more length, however, about the hours preceding his murder of Donal Dunne. The collected descriptions of Macarthur provided to Gardaí that I quote are included in an appendix to Joyce and Murtagh's book *The Boss*. Along with numerous newspaper reports from the time of the conviction, I also draw in these pages on the accounts of the crime in Stephen Rea's book *Killers* and in John Courtney's *It Was Murder*.

THIRTEEN

Along with my conversations with Macarthur, Joyce and Murtagh's *The Boss* was once again an invaluable source in my reconstruction of the days between the murders and Macarthur's arrest. My interviews with Tony Hickey and John O'Mahony were also very useful in reconstructing Macarthur's activities in this period. The story of Macarthur's encounter with his former neighbors on Fitzwilliam Square is drawn from my conversations with Macarthur, and from various archival newspaper sources; the version of these events in *The Irish Times* on January 13, 1983 ("Robbery Planned After Wasting Inheritance," by Willy Clingan and Dermot Kelly), was especially helpful. Much of the coverage of the murders and the investigation in *The Irish Times* was by Peter Murtagh, the paper's security correspondent at the time. Many of these articles—about the discovery of the sweater, the linking of the two murders—were read by Macarthur as the investigation was unfolding, and as he was attempting to evade the Gardaí.

FOURTEEN

The account of the attempted robbery at Harry Bieling's house was constructed from a number of sources: Macarthur's statement to the detectives, the account of the events provided to me by Tony Hickey and John O'Mahony, the excellent and detailed reporting in *The Boss,* and Macarthur's own recollection. The chapter on Macarthur in Stephen Rae's *Killers* contains crucial details of the incident. I also drew on an *Irish Times* article from December 15, 1983, entitled "A Visit from Malcolm Macarthur."

FIFTEEN

My main source of information on the investigation into the murders of Bridie Gargan and Donal Dunne was the series of conversations I had with Tony Hickey and John O'Mahony over several months in 2021. Their memories of the events were, on the whole, extraordinarily detailed. I also drew on the chapters on Macarthur in Joyce and Murtagh's *The Boss,* in Stephen Rae's *Killers,* and in *It Was Murder,* by John Courtney. An interview with Courtney published in *The Irish Times* on January 15, 1983 ("Macarthur Phoned Gardai Before Arrest"), was a useful source of information for these pages. An article by Sean Flynn in the *Sunday Press* on January 16, 1983, "Dragnet for a Killer," was also a helpful source of information on the investigation.

SIXTEEN

Aside from the sources listed above, and the material drawn from my conversations with Macarthur, the period of the investigation outlined in this chapter is constructed from my conversations with Tony Hickey and John O'Mahony.

SEVENTEEN

As with the previous chapter, the account of Macarthur's arrest and interrogation in these pages comes primarily from my conversations with Hickey and O'Mahony. Because he was involved in not just the arrest but also the subsequent interviewing of Macarthur, Hickey's recollections were of particular value here.

EIGHTEEN

The interview with Patrick Connolly I write about in this chapter is from the 1995 RTE television series *Thou Shalt Not Kill*. The account of Connolly's experience of the arrest and of its immediate aftermath is drawn from this interview, along with numerous other sources—including Courtney's *It Was Murder* and Joyce and Murtagh's *The Boss*. The text of Macarthur's extraordinary note to Charles Haughey is included in Courtney's book. I also drew on Connolly's statement to the Gardaí, a version of which was published on the front page of *The Irish Press* after his resignation ("Connolly Resigns," August 17, 1982). The coverage of the events in the August 31, 1982, issue of the political periodical *Magill* was also a useful source of information.

NINETEEN

As with elsewhere in the book, my account of the political scandal that resulted from Macarthur's arrest draws on the excellent reporting in Joyce and Murtagh's *The Boss*. *Magill* magazine's coverage of the events in their July 1983 issue was also a rich resource. I also quote from an account of Haughey's "GUBU" press conference in Frank Dunlop's book *Yes, Taoiseach*. The coverage of the affair in the Irish newspapers, in particular *The Irish Press* and *The Irish Times*, was also an invaluable archival source in my writing about the scandal and the events around Connolly's resignation. Gary Murphy's 2021 biography *Haughey* was also a useful source of details about Haughey's life and career.

TWENTY

Much of my account of the hearings and Macarthur's conviction comes from contemporary reporting in *The Irish Times* and *The Irish Press*, published in mid-January 1983. The account of the legal machinations that led to the state's decision not to prosecute Macarthur for the killing of Donal Dunne draws heavily on *Magill*'s coverage—in particular "Justice Behind Closed Doors—the Malcolm Macarthur Case," published in the July 31, 1983, issue of the magazine.

The striking description of the sound of the crowd outside the courthouse is from Mary Kotsonouris's memoir *'Tis All Lies, Your Worship*. An account of the scenes outside the Dublin District Court is outlined in an article in *The Irish Press*, "Angry Mob Jeer Man at Court Appearance" (August 16, 1982). A front-page article in the *Evening Press* outlines a similar incident ("Macarthur Attacked Near Court," August 19, 1982). I also draw on the *Irish Independent*'s coverage of these scenes ("Macarthur Hit as an Angry Crowd Surrounds Court," August 20, 1982).

The statement from Christopher Dunne quoted in this chapter appeared in *The Irish Times* on August 30, 2002, under the heading "McArthur Poses 'Threat to Society and Our Family.'"

TWENTY-ONE

As with most of the final section of the book, this chapter is based on my conversations with Macarthur.

TWENTY-TWO

The interview with Irene Macarthur I quote from here appeared in the article "Macarthur to Tell All in New Book," by Kevin Farrell, published in the *Sunday World* on August 30, 1992. The public appeal by Christopher Dunne against Macarthur's parole in 1993 was quoted in an article in the *Evening Press* on November 16, 1993 ("Do Not Parole This Killer: Victim's Brother in Plea to Authorities"). The quotes from former justice minister Willie O'Dea about Irene Macarthur's fear of her son's release are taken from an article that appeared in the *Meath Chronicle* on September 6, 2008 ("Death of Irene Macarthur, Mother of 'GUBU' killer"). The interview with Bridie Gargan's younger brother Christopher, in which he responds to the prospect of Macarthur's release, was published in an article by Luke Byrne in the *Irish Independent* on November 15, 2011 ("'Who Knows What He's Capable Of?'"). The television interview with the Gargan sisters is from the episode of the 1995 RTE series *Thou Shalt Not Kill* on Macarthur's crimes.

TWENTY-THREE

The material in this chapter is drawn entirely from my conversations with Macarthur.

ALSO BY

MARK O'CONNELL

NOTES FROM AN APOCALYPSE
A Personal Journey to the End of the World and Back

We're alive in a time of worst-case scenarios: The weather has gone uncanny. A pandemic draws our global community to a halt. Everywhere you look there's an omen, a joke whose punch line is the end of the world. How is a person supposed to live in the shadow of such a grim future? What might it be like to live through the worst? And what on earth is anybody doing about it? Dublin-based writer Mark O'Connell is consumed by these questions—and, as the father of two young children, he finds them increasingly urgent. In *Notes from an Apocalypse*, he crosses the globe in pursuit of answers. He tours survival bunkers in South Dakota. He ventures to New Zealand, a favored retreat of billionaires banking on civilization's collapse. He engages with would-be Mars colonists, preppers, right-wing conspiracists. And he bears witness to places, like Chernobyl, that the future has already visited—real-life portraits of the end of the world as we know it. What emerges is an absorbing, funny, and deeply felt book about our anxious present tense—and coming to grips with what's ahead.

Science

ALSO AVAILABLE
To Be a Machine

VINTAGE BOOKS
Available wherever books are sold.
vintagebooks.com